The Community of
Women and Men
in the Church

A Report of the World Council of Churches' Conference
Sheffield, England, 1981

The Community of
Women and Men
in the Church

Edited by
CONSTANCE F. PARVEY

FORTRESS PRESS

Philadelphia

Biblical quotations, unless otherwise noted, are from the Revised Standard Version of the Bible, copyright 1946, 1952, © 1971, 1973 by the Division of Christian Education of the National Council of the Churches of Christ in the U.S.A. and are used by permission.

Copyright © 1983 by World Council of Churches, Geneva

First Fortress Press Edition 1983

Library of Congress Cataloging in Publication Data
Main entry under title:
The Community of Women and Men in the Church.
Bibliography: p.
1. Man (Christian theology)—Congresses. I. Parvey, Constance F. II. World Council of Churches.
BT701.2.C59 1983   262'.7   82-71831
ISBN 0-8006-1644-8

9591G82 Printed in the United States of America 1-1644

Contents

CONTENTS

CONTENTS

Preface

"Adam and Eve, where are you?" This variation of an ancient question was the main emphasis in an ecumenical study program "The Community of Women and Men in the Church," located in the Commission on Faith and Order and carried out in cooperation with the Sub-Unit on Women in Church and Society.

Under the direction of Constance F. Parvey from 1978–1982, the program enjoyed the most extensive grassroots participation of any such project in the history of the World Council of Churches. Persons who participated in it discovered that some of their burning problems were touched by the direct questions posed in the study book. For the first time, many people began to share their understandings and views of their roles as women and men in the church, as well as in private and public life. These questions dealt with the real ground of human existence.

As proposed at the WCC Fifth Assembly (Nairobi, 1975) and authorized by the Central Committee (1976), the program's mandate called for continuing theological study with reflection at various levels of church life, leading to change in three specific areas: 1. *Theology.* "A thorough examination needs to be made of the biblical and theological assumptions concerning the community of women and men in church and society." 2. *Participation.* "In order to be truly free, all people must participate in working toward their own liberation. This can be seen in all struggles for human rights and to overcome oppression." 3. *Relationship.* "A third area of urgent concern is the inter-relationship of women and men who frequently exploit one another. This exploitation often takes the form of misuse of power over each other which is linked with the lack of understanding of mutual identity."

This report traces the four-year development of the community program from its beginnings in hundreds of local study/sharing groups in different parts of the world, through its clarification and maturation in a number of regional and specialized consultations which explored key issues at greater depth, and finally in reaching its culmination at an international consultation in Sheffield,

England, to consolidate the initial findings and to formulate recommendations for critical follow-up activities in the common witness of the World Council of Churches and the churches themselves.

Whether in the communal exploration of theology, participation, or relationships, many women and men testified that they were inspired and guided in this exciting venture by the liberating message of the word of God.

The Old Testament declares that the first Adam (humankind) consists of male and female persons who are created equally in God's image for life in community. The New Testament proclaims that the church consists of male and female persons who are baptized equally into Jesus Christ, confessed to be the true image of God as the last Adam, and thereby as renewed persons reunited together for life in community. Moreover, it is a basic affirmation of the entire Bible that such community life in the Spirit of God is distinguished by peace and justice, freedom and fullness, joy and love, unity in diversity.

Now, the community study has also taught us much about contemporary community life. Above all, one thing has become clear: in a world of great social, political, and economic change, the forms of community and partnership in family and life styles are deeply affected. Whether we like it or not, many familiar roles of living together have to prove their worth in totally new circumstances. The question today is whether these time-honored roles are still protecting, helpful, and life-enabling for the individual and for the community. How do churches participate responsibly in these dramatic changes in our world, and how can they help women and men both within and outside the churches to develop possibilities of living and working together in community? Struggling with the issue of new identity, of a new sharing of responsibility and participation in the life of the church, of new and old forms of life together as women and men, can lead us to deeper community and help the individual and the churches to express more human authenticity.

This report invites the reader to participate in the ongoing community study process. It enables you to follow and to become part of the experiences of others in the venture of building a worldwide ecumenical community. Respect for each other and for the different traditions and backgrounds from which we come is of the utmost importance in reading and discussing these materials. Only by acknowledging the genuine differences of all the interdependent members in the body of Christ can we build a new community in which Jesus Christ is the cornerstone.

WILLIAM H. LAZARETH
Commission on Faith and Order

BÄRBEL VON WARTENBERG
Women in Church and Society

Acknowledgments and Thanks

At each critical point in "The Community of Women and Men in the Church" study, people with the talents and capacities required seemed to come on board.

The vision of the community study is an impetus for change, for evolution within and toward an improved common life. It does not propose new organizations or buildings. It suggests a profound process: as women and men we must see through cultural stereotypes that inhibit us from living the gospel together in our time and for the future.

These are the words of Midge Meinertz Beguin, written in October 1979, when she did a project review of the community study. Perhaps the most valuable part of the study has been the friendships and new models of working together at every level that the program has generated. More than anything else, it has been a *community* process, where thanks and appreciation are required at every point.

When I arrived in January 1978, Lukas Vischer and Brigalia Bam were directors, respectively of the Sub-Units on Faith and Order and Women in Church and Society. Their initial guidance in the long-term planning over the uncharted waters was enormously helpful. The WCC Central Committee appointed an Advisory Committee to oversee the work: Mary Tanner (England) and Juan Stam (Costa Rica) from the Commission on Faith and Order and Margaret Sonnenday (USA) and Martti Lindqvist (Finland) from the Working Group on Women in Church and Society. Their counsel and encouragement steered the study's course under the diligent and able moderatorship of Mary Tanner.

In the spring and summer of 1978 when we needed help in developing the study book, Jean Scott (Canada) came to help organize the content, layout, and design, and a Lutheran World Federation seminar organized by the Women's Desk tested our questions for local use. Karen Foget (USA) designed and contributed our now familiar logo. In 1979, as the group reports began coming in, in so many languages, many volunteers helped in their reading and interpretation. Isolde Boehm (FRG), an intern at the Bossey Graduate School that year, was of special assistance.

As the regional and specialized consultations were gaining momentum in 1980, Melanie May (USA), a Bossey graduate student, did valuable research in preparation for the Niederaltaich and Amsterdam consultations. Julia Campos (Mexico) worked as part of our staff to develop the community study in Latin America. Denise Peeters (Belgium) volunteered her time to help with the French reports and the European regional meetings.

Houda Zacca, Orthodox, of the Women's Desk of the Middle East Council of Churches, organized a consultation in Beirut on the study and Isabella Johnston of the All-Africa Conference of Churches, in cooperation with Daisy Obi and Mercy Oduyoye (Nigeria), organized the African regional meeting. Ilsa Tamez and Irene Foulkes (Costa Rica) organized the Latin American meeting in cooperation with Julia Campos. Russell Chandron and Christi John of Bangalore, India, organized the first consultation in Asia, and Jeanne Audrey Powers and Jerry Boney of the Commission on Faith and Order of the National Council of Churches, USA, organized the last of these six regional meetings.

As we were preparing for the Sheffield international consultation, Janet Crawford (New Zealand) joined our team as conference organizer. With the administrative skills needed to make an international consultation happen smoothly and with grace, she worked in cooperation with the Sheffield committee under the leadership of Jean Mayland.

From the beginning my colleagues in Faith and Order were a source of daily encouragement and joy: C. S. Song (Taiwan), Geiko Müller-Fahrenholz (FRG), Stephen Cranford (USA), Renate Sbeghen (Switzerland), Anne Williamson (Scotland), and later Hans-Georg Link (FRG) and Michael Kinnamon (USA). The picture would not be complete without mentioning the role of the community study task force that helped out creatively during our 1979 financial crisis and in 1980 gave itself wholeheartedly to the planning of the Sheffield meeting. Here, Aharon Sapsezian (Brazil), Jean Masamba (Zaire), Gwen Cashmore (UK), Wesley Ariarajah (Sri Lanka), Pricilla Padolina (Philippines), Marie Asaad (Egypt), and Tudor Sabev (Bulgaria) must be singled out.

To carry this program, costing more than one million Swiss francs plus all the locally and regionally borne costs, a special thanks must go to Luis Carlos Weil, who died in 1979 before he could see the funding to realize this plan. The person who carried out his vision and advocated the program and its financial support was Midge Meinertz Beguin. Without her eyes that could see the "power released" by the study, this small ecumenical boat might have sunk.

More than fifty churches and donor agencies provided the financial support for the study. We are particularly indebted to the dozen or so donors who were with us from the beginning and who have stayed with us to the end of this formal part of the process. We are equally grateful to the many who contributed sums, large and small, as they were needed. Each donation served as a sign of the commitment that motivated it. Of deep personal satisfaction were the over thirty individual donors, women and men, who contributed sums from twenty dollars to one thousand dollars. Contributions came from Canada, Denmark, the Federal Republic of Germany, Finland, France, India, the Netherlands, Sweden, Switzerland, Taiwan, the United Kingdom, and the USA. In addition, regional meetings received local financial support from churches and agencies, and each of the specialized consultations was cosponsored with a local partner who contributed substantially to the budget. It must also be noted that of the thirteen or more translations of the study book, only two were done in Geneva. Special acknowledgment must go to those people who accomplished this work around the world for their skill and ingenuity in doing the translations and funding the printing of the study book and of their reports, some of which were quite elaborate. Words of appreciation must also go to Caroline Ruever who organized and carried out a statistical analysis of the local group reports and to some ten people around the world who helped shape our bibliography in four languages.

This adds up to saying a big "Thank You" to many people. Those of you who have contributed will recognize yourselves as part of this large, worldwide community.

No words of appreciation would be complete without mentioning the many people on the WCC Central Committee who took seriously the Fifth Assembly mandate and who kept themselves informed and involved in the community study in many ways. A personal word must also go to Doreen Potter for the spiritual/musical contribution she gave so creatively to the process and to Philip Potter who recognized the long-term importance of this work in the movement toward the unity and wholeness of the church.

Finally, my thanks to my two colleagues, present directors of the Sub-Unit on Women in Church and Society and the Commission on Faith and Order, Bärbel von Wartenberg and William H. Lazareth, who each brought special gifts to mark Sheffield as a turning point on the ecumenical route map.

I end with thanks for the cheerfulness of Lee Weingarten who typed this manuscript and deepest appreciation to Isa Schmidkunz and Yvonne Itin who were faithfully on board almost every day over these years making sure that all the steps were taken to keep this small vessel of the larger ecumenical ship in communication and on course.

To those above and to the many not mentioned, my deepest appreciation for this shared voyage.

CONSTANCE F. PARVEY

PART ONE

ABOUT THIS BOOK

1

The Church—Women and Men in Community

Sheffield—A Summary of Major Presentations

A banner of rainbow colors overlooked the assembly, as three hundred participants and guests from churches the world over rose to sing "All People That on Earth Do Dwell." The World Council of Churches international consultation "The Community of Women and Men in the Church" had begun. On the platform were the local hosts, representatives from the Sheffield churches and the British Council of Churches, as well as the queen's representative and the mayor of Sheffield, a woman. The delegates had come to seek in common assembly a new vision of the community of women and men in the church: a vision that would encourage women to explore and affirm their full contribution and would encourage men to take seriously and self-critically a new relationship of the partnership between women and men. The consultation's subtheme, "A Chance to Change," signaled the need to reexamine sources in Scripture and church teaching and practice and to stretch forward with concrete recommendations so that a renewed vision of women and men in the church might become manifest. This first chapter outlines the consultation's process—its opening days, dynamics, and sharp differences as it moved toward genuine listening and dialogue in seeking a common voice. The full texts of the plenary addresses and other consultation documents are found in successive chapters of the book. The inserts throughout this first chapter are responses to issues of women and men in the church received from local and regional groups who have participated in the community study process.

At the opening of the consultation a host recited some milestone memories of local church history:

You have come to stay in Yorkshire . . .
York is the home of the Northern Primate of the Church of England
. . . Christianity came to York many centuries ago
through the influence of a women.
Ethelberga, the daughter of King Ethelbert of Kent,
came North to marry Edwin, king of Northumbria.
With her was Paulinus, a priest, her spiritual counselor.
Their influence for good bore fruit.
On Easter Day in the year 627 the King was baptized at York
in the Church of St. Peter the Apostle.

With the lady mayor beside him and Ethelberga being called forward from the past, Robert Runcie, archbishop of Canterbury and president of the British Council of Churches, began his opening remarks. Though the larger context of the meeting was the renewed partnership of women and men, the archbishop concentrated his attention on the ordination of women and women's ministries. "There is real danger," he stated, "that an overconcentration on the issues involved in the ordination of women may reinforce a clericalist view of the church: the only ministry worth exercising is an ordained one." He listed some of the valuable work that women do and have done in the church, noting mystical theologians such as Julian of Norwich and, closer to our time, Evelyn Underhill. He confessed that the church is "lamentably behind in giving women a voice."

In discussing the situation of women ministers in Japanese churches, our study group felt that a mixture of misunderstanding of the Bible and Confucian ethics rooted deep in our society were the causes for the strong tendency to lower the position of women and women ministers in the church. In order to overcome this, systematic Bible study must be encouraged and continued, and good leaders must be trained.

—JAPAN

The remarks of Philip Potter, General Secretary of the WCC, followed immediately. Potter based his comments on his knowledge and experience with the study, including reading local reports. He stressed how reading the reports had affected his rethinking of questions of authority and interpretation of Scripture, of the nature of the church, of the need to rewrite church history as a history of women and men, of the need to deepen our theological understanding of what it means to be human. He challenged our attitudes toward sexuality and underlined the tremendous burden that poverty puts on women's lives.

After morning tea, the consultation reconvened to hear two theologians from the Evangelical Church of the Federal Republic of Germany, Elisabeth Moltmann-Wendel and Jürgen Moltmann. Their dialogue presentation, "Becoming Human in New Community," inaugurated the first of four plenary sessions.

Elisabeth opened the dialogue. Church history begins, she said, "when a few women set out to pay their last respects to their dead friend Jesus. . . . This story as told by Matthew is generally known as the Easter appearance of the women, but never as the beginning of church history." She commented on the male church and masculine theological terminology. Jürgen followed, explaining that "patriarchy is a very ancient and widespread system of male domination," that it was not introduced by Christianity but that Christianity proved "incapable" of successfully opposing it. Elisabeth spoke about the new courage of Christian women to become themselves and how this comes into "collision" with the church and its patriarchal style. Jürgen replied that it was hard for men to follow women in this new way; it called for deep rethinking of themselves and for overcoming the male attitude of "concealed domination" that lay beneath the Christian virtue of "service *for* others." Elisabeth, referring to her opening remarks, asked: "How are we to explain the fact that almost two thousand years ago a viable community of women and men failed to materialize?"

Woman wavers between Eve and Mary, passing on her way by some of the faces of the Old Testament women. She could resemble Delilah in her deception and betrayal; the three daughters of Lot in their cunning and trickery; Tamor in her persistent single-mindedness to secure an offspring; Rahab in her slyness; Bathsheba in her sinfulness; and Ruth in her perseverance and tranquility. It is noteworthy that the Savior descended from four of these women whom the evangelist Matthew deliberately listed in his lineage.

—MIDDLE EAST REGIONAL

Many questions followed: about the relationship of the "heavenly Father" to the "Abba, Father" that Jesus used, whether Christian tradition is hopelessly patriarchal, and if individual autonomy should really be a goal for Christians.

The formal opening on Saturday was European in style and context: the barren British moors just over the hill were reminders of the long dark winters, while the lighted summer nights made our stay more pleasant. With the exception of the address by Philip Potter, it was Europeans who presented their perspectives on the issues for which we had assembled.

"Poor Folks Don't Have Such a Luxury"

Sunday morning was spent in local churches. In the late afternoon we gathered once more to hear two non-European theologians, Father Tissa Balasuriya, O.M.I., Roman Catholic priest from Sri Lanka, and The Rev. Jacquelyn Grant, African Methodist Episcopal Church from the United States. Balasuriya's paper, "Women and Men in New Community—Insights from Liberation Struggles," pointed out the dominating role that men play in every aspect of power and authority. A man's personality, he said, is given priority in education, training, and development, and "a woman's personality is made to seek fulfillment in relation to a man." He underlined the importance of class analysis—the linking of racism, classism, and sexism. He proposed that sexism was not quite the same, that "questions concerning the sexes are first personal and only secondly externalized in social relations . . ."

Grant, a black woman theologian, took issue with the distinction made between racism and sexism. Conventional white male theology, she said, has kept both women and Blacks "passive and docile." She acknowledged that it is hard for Third World women to align themselves with women in dominant cultures, yet she felt that their coming together is necessary. She contended that classism, racism, and sexism are all ingrained and inextricably linked. "The majority of Blacks are poor because they are black." She disagreed that sexism is personal and private, saying that "the personal is political and structural." Sexism, she warned, could not be separated from other struggles for justice and human dignity.

Heated responses followed these reflections. A voice from Asia confirmed the Balasuriya thesis, saying, "Baptism in our country gives the dominants a sense of being 'the people of God' . . . It is identified with the colonizing power." Someone from the Caribbean asked, "Where is education on your list which also in our context contributes to oppression?" A voice from Africa declared, "You say that revolutions need to be humanized; revolutions are explosive!" Another added, "Do you know what poverty does to the mind

The society in which we live has perpetuated and institutionalized the subjugation of women in all fields of life—social, political, economic and religious. . . . Some among us feel very strongly that it would be impossible to deal with this question on the level of the church because the church is very much conditioned by the life in the society. The liberation of women can only be effected with the liberation of all other forms of subjugation.

—ASIA REGIONAL

of the oppressed? . . . If I go home and raise peoples' consciousness, what will happen? Our prisons are overflowing! Christ used a whip to drive out corruption; today it will be with AK47s.'' A voice from Europe commented, ''Where are the old people? What about the children? I'm unhappy with the language you are using; it puts feminist things in a masculine way. It makes them loveless.''

At the end both Balasuriya and Grant responded. Balasuriya said, ''It is difficult to be human and to try to humanize, yet we cannot believe that humans are incapable of change. . . . It is the task of those who believe in transcendent values to bring change to bear in one's life. . . . It is difficult to struggle.'' Grant asked, ''How do we raise the consciousness of people who have no power? They're suffering now. It is better that they be aware of the problem so that they can be a bit prepared. . . . As for children—I had children in mind. They are both male and female. . . . There is always a danger when one attempts to intellectualize about concrete situations. Poor folks don't have such a luxury.''

On Monday the presentation by Jean Baker Miller, a psychiatrist from the United States, raised a major question already in the air: ''What happens to people when they exist in unequal relationships with each other?'' Miller acknowledged that her reflections came from within one cultural context, that we are all conditioned by what our societies think we should be. She stated, ''Those parts of life which a culture needs but doesn't value highly tend to be relegated to other people, and these people are usually considered less important or inferior.'' This is often the fate of women and women's work.

Houda Zacca, an Orthodox participant from Lebanon, responded. ''We cannot discuss roles of women and men without mentioning the church. For us, psychological terms are impossible. Holiness is what really matters. Total giving and devotion of one to another is the goal. . . . Only in the church, the body of Christ, can the person become unique. . . . In our society, both men and women are oppressed. . . . Our goal is to create a religious society; women and men participating equally in God's creation. If we live in subjection to Christ, the differences in the sexes will be abolished.''

In the discussion that followed an Orthodox woman expressed appreciation that a ''horizontal rather than a vertical view of church hierarchy'' had been expressed. She felt that Miller's paper implied that women who do traditional work feel devalued. She questioned this and asked, ''Are the terms 'masculinity' and 'femininity' a big cosmic joke, or do the differences in the sexes really exist?'' A man from Europe asked, ''Have we a tendency to overemphasize the dichotomy between women and men? What about a new identity for men?'' A woman from Africa posed the question, ''I am told that

---

The church cannot afford to continue preaching the equality of all human beings and races in Christ and yet allow its practices to be a living contradiction to this truth.

—NIGERIA

---

racism or classism should be important to me because I'm from the Third World, and I am told that sexism is only personal and that it is really an importation from the United States. Yet, I am also told by my African students that I am their first woman professor. Do I need a psychiatrist? Do I fight all three oppressions or just one?''

The Energizing of Tradition

The plenaries established a strong case for the need for change, yet raised a related question: is tradition only an obstacle or are there resources within it that can be foundational for the renewal of the church and the human community?

Elisabeth Behr-Sigel, theologian of the Orthodox Church of France, and Rose Zoé-Obianga of the Presbyterian Church of the Cameroon addressed this question, speaking both to church and cultural tradition.

Behr-Sigel maintained that it is only within the dynamics of the authentic tradition that we can find the radical newness of the church which is the basis of real liberation. In line with the energizing force of tradition, she affirmed that we are called ''to invent new styles of communal life, new styles of family

7

life in our society and church.'' Living the Trinitarian life, she declared, is both the foundation of genuine community in the church and its goal. She criticized Western theology for its neglect of this vision of the church and the Orthodox tradition.

Zoé-Obianga called the traditional models of organizing Christian community life "fetters of freedom," underlining how they subordinate women. She emphasized how important it is for the church in Africa, in searching for alternative models, to look into its own traditional identity and to "draw upon elements that are capable of responding adequately" to contemporary needs. She stressed the value of participation and cohesion in African community life over against individualistic competition but also acknowledged the limitations of some African traditions, calling on the Christian community itself to go beyond them. Our witness as Christians, she declared, must be in solidarity with the poor and oppressed. "The vision of the gospel in Africa must assume humanity's 'African face'.''

The common opinion today is that the woman is the husband's property, and this is reinforced both by men and by the ignorance of women. Many women have no rights, or they don't know that they have them or how to exercise them. In several polygamous societies, the first wife has an important status. She has authority both in relation to her husband and to the other wives.

—AFRICA REGIONAL

Both of these presentations took as their starting point the fundamental importance of Christian and cultural tradition, both recognized their possible limitations, both were propelled forward by a vision of God with God's people on earth where the "human face" of God is and can be present.

We Are Because We Participate

"We are because we participate" was a phrase lifted up by Rose Zoé-Obianga. This phrase caught on at Sheffield and marked the transition in the consultation itself.

Early in the meeting delegates from the Third World issued a statement urging that efforts toward new worldwide community must be seen not only in relation to the church, in a narrow sense, but against the larger societal background of the "desperate struggles against exploitation and poverty, hopelessness and despair." As with other struggles against injustice, those who suffer most are the ones provoked to speak. Meeting in the First World placed the burden of interpretation on those who live and feel these experiences most. For participants coming from the Third World, ecumenical sharing was not enough; the injustices of partnership in the "old economic order" loomed too large. Third World participants wanted to make sure that women's issues, though keenly felt, were not dealt with in isolation from the global "web of oppression" with its particularly enfeebling effects on the poorest of the poor.

The Europeans responded to the Third World statement. They took the challenge seriously by outlining their own divisions, power conflicts, and Third World within. One Third World participant, writing after Sheffield, said: "Despite all of the distance between us—'class', 'race', and 'culture'— we felt intuitively that at Sheffield there at least began to surface a spirit of understanding and embryonic solidarity. Increased consciousness began to bridge the great differences among us—men and women—in all the 'worlds'."

Seeking a Common Base

While the plenaries formed the beginning of the common dialogue, the heart of the meeting's production came from the section work. There were seven major subject areas with about thirty people, representing a wide range of cultures and churches, working in each. Each subject focused on women and men in community—in description, analysis, and next steps. The hard issues were hammered out in these smaller working groups. Evident in the work of these groups were the global dimensions of daily value choices and deliberations. Preceding the section reports, the Third World Statement—European Response points out both the misunderstandings and the need for listening between the section work could begin.

Taken altogether, the work done in these section groups forms part of the "fruitful agony of travail," referred to in the Sheffield letter (page 93), a travail we can anticipate when we confess together the Christ who lives though

---

Women and men irrespective of nationality have been brought up within a particular pattern. . . . Women often seem as not having been made in the image of God, but in the wishful thinking of men!
—FEDERAL REPUBLIC OF GERMANY

---

crucified. The section work reveals a deep commitment to the church, its tradition and its divine calling to be "the people of God." It suggests a renewal of the church from within, quickened by an inversion of some of its priorities and values. The work challenges major issues that hinder making manifest the church as a true community of women and men and, finally, it proposes new directions.

Bible Study

Daily Bible studies provided continuity to the consultation and a common reference point to the variety of perspectives on new community debated and discussed. Phyllis Trible, professor of Old Testament at Union Theological Seminary in New York, gave four presentations. She began with the Genesis 2 creation story, moved to the Fall in Genesis 3 and then to the poetic expression of divine/human fulfillment in the dialogue of lover and beloved in the Song of Songs, and ended with the model of radical faithfulness in the story of Ruth. Based on a thorough knowledge of the ancient texts, she opened up fresh ways of viewing Scripture and challenged the assumptions of male-biased interpretations. In her style and content she put forth the case that Scripture must be understood in the context of the whole community, inclusive of both women and men.

Worship

The picture would not be complete without attention to the life of worship. The flute and the classical guitar were the musical instruments for daily worship. Prayer, preaching, and poetry appeared in many forms.

What is not written are the many prayers and petitions printed on the hearts of participants: prayers for the safe return home of a woman from the Sahara, who would spend one month traveling back to her village; prayers for "missing persons," disappeared from the parishes of some of those present from Latin America; prayers for the families of the dead and those suffering the violent night bombings on the city of Beirut, renewed during the days of our meeting; prayers for the Christian community in Poland; prayers for wives, husbands, children, and loved ones, for the churches, their unity, and their renewal as an authentic community of women and men, across barriers of race and class.

"Woman, Why Are You Weeping?" (chap. 5) is one portion of the consultation's worship, the sermon in the Sheffield Cathedral preached by Pauline Webb of the Methodist Church in Great Britain.

Post-Sheffield

"The Voices of Sheffield" (chap. 6) contains the recommendations transmitted to the WCC Central Committee, its units and sub-units, and through these channels to the member churches and to partners in ecumenical sharing. The introduction by Mercy Oduyoye of Nigeria is the statement she made to the August 1981 Dresden Central Committee as she transmitted the Sheffield recommendations to the WCC's highest governing body for their deliberation and action.

The "Letter from Sheffield to the Churches" describes what participants learned, received, recognized, and rejoiced in. Going through several drafts before it was approved, it invites the churches to pray "that you will join us in giving reality to the vision which we have seen." The introduction by Jean Mayland of Sheffield was made as she carried the Letter, on behalf of the consultation, to the Central Committee, asking that it be transmitted to the churches.

"The Community of Women and Men in the Ecumenical Movement: Held Together in Hope and Sustained by God's Promise" (chap. 9) is a personal reflection based on my own experience with the study as I have listened and learned during these four years. It is influenced by engagement with the local and regional groups, as well as by the three specialized consultations and the events of Sheffield and Dresden.

The Appendixes contain a list of participants, a survey of the documentation on the program to date, and a bibliography, useful for the many levels of ongoing grassroots work which was the expressed desire of Sheffield and its motivation.

Sheffield marks the culmination of a long preparatory process. The future of the conference starts with those who will use this book.

The Roots—How Sheffield Came to Be

The impulse for the study on the Community of Women and Men in the Church was the June 1974 Berlin consultation, "Sexism in the 70s," organized by the WCC Sub-Unit on Women in Church and Society. At that meeting a new initiative was launched to ask the churches to examine the roles of women and the implications for the churches of the new levels of women's participation in theology, ministry, and mission. It was evident that to do this work, the churches needed to be involved at the point where issues of the nature of the church and its striving toward unity were being assessed in light of changes in the human community. A recommendation came from Berlin that such a study be undertaken. It was directed to the Commission on Faith and Order which met in August that same year in Accra, Ghana.

Jesus healed, taught, and kept company with women and had a group of female disciples. The fact that there are many pericopes about healed women and parables with female symbols in the gospel tradition—such as the yeast, the lost silver piece—implies that there were many female teachers and disciples in the early church. The Acts confirms this. Jesus' teachings on divorce must have meant a radical deviation from the Jewish law and custom relating to the value and importance of women.

—SWEDEN

At Accra the specific profile and recommendation for the community study were shaped. Aware of disunity, yet taking careful steps toward mutual recognition in baptism, Eucharist, and ministry; aware of gaping human division and injustices, yet taking steps toward reconciliation—it was in this setting that the community study found its first theological expression:

> Baptized into his death and resurrection, we Christians died to our sinful selves and received power to live in loving community through the newness of his life. We are to discern and foster the gifts of the Spirit in one another. Yet the severed and distorted relationship between men and women continues to reveal both the presence of the suffering Christ in the world and the need of reconciliation. Injustice appears in different forms. Whether one considers the professions, churches, government, remuneration, possibilities of advancement, or decision-making power, women receive the lesser share. Called as men and women together to become signs of the promised kingdom, we hope for a true and complete community in Christ.

The following February, a small group of representatives from Berlin and Accra met in Geneva to prepare a working paper on the community study for consideration at the Fifth Assembly of the WCC in Nairobi, Kenya, during November 1975. The resulting booklet was a major concern for two sections of the Nairobi Assembly, the section which dealt with questions of church unity and the other with questions of justice and human liberation. ''The Community of Women and Men in the Church'' encompassed both concerns and was adopted as a priority program emphasis by both sections.

This double-adoption gave rise to important questions debated the following year by the 1976 WCC Central Committee: Where should this new study be located? Was it primarily a women's issue, one of justice for women, or was it primarily an issue of unity, having to do with one baptism into the body of Christ and a common confession of Jesus Christ as Lord? It was finally acknowledged that these two dimensions had to be held in tandem and in tension and that the community study must be a joint effort between the Sub-Unit on Women in Church and Society and the Commission on Faith and Order. It was further decided that the program should be lodged in the Commission on Faith and Order, that its fundamental character was to be that of an ecclesiological study, an issue of inclusive community, more than of a ''justice'' or a ''women's issue'' per se.

This was a painful decision and gave the program its basic challenge: Can unity and justice live together? Can women enter into a true dialogue with men toward new community without being absorbed into ''men's community?'' What capacity do our male structures have to change? Are we, as women and men in the churches, prepared for the creative and difficult theological re-searching that this new dialogue implies? Can a process be found that builds common ground for unity and, at the same time, respects real differences, provisional or long-term as they may be?

The next question was how such a study should be carried out. At a meeting held in the summer of 1977, several basic principles were set out regarding the study method:

1. It should not begin with what people *should* think but invite them to a dialogue.
2. It should develop a method of theological reflection that begins at the level of experience, trying to learn firsthand what is the reality of full partnership, or lack of it, between women and men in the church's life and teachings.
3. It should promote sharing among churches and Christian groups on the basis of experience and ecumenical dialogue in concrete local places.
4. It should encourage discussion about the problems of women and men, with women playing a formative role in stating how they identify and see the problems relative to the broadly changing roles and expectations of women and men in marriage, family, work, society, and church.

5. It should encourage theological reflection and identify main points for future theological studies, and reflection, in light of the changing relationships of women and men, regarding fundamental issues of faith such as the interpretation of Scripture, theological education and church teachings, the shape of the church itself, and the character (the distinctive marks) of its witness and mission.

The study was projected for three interlinking levels: One would be a broadly based study, an invitation for churches to participate in such a way that it could be useful on local congregational levels. The second level would be primarily for people who specialize in theology in order to begin some theological reflection on certain specific questions related to faith and order. The third level would be an international consultation on this topic, involving a broad spectrum of participation from member churches.

The Study Book

The study book was designed during 1978 and submitted to the Commission on Faith and Order for comment and approval at its Bangalore, India, meeting in August of that same year. An official invitation for the member churches to participate in the study, along with the study book, was sent to the approximately three hundred member churches in October 1978. The first editions were in English, German, and French. The letter stated:

> It is hoped that through exploring from a biblical and theological perspective the origin and nature of our roles as women and men over the centuries and today, we may come to new levels of appreciation, cooperation, and mutual respect in Christian life and thought. . . . We invite your careful attention to the study guide in order that, during the year 1979, the special contributions of your church may begin to find their way into the study process.

The issues to be addressed in specialized consultations were: women and the ordained ministry, authority of Scripture, and theological anthropology, taking into consideration the role of Mary. In addition, local findings were to be balanced by regional meetings in the various areas of the world in order to ensure regional balance in the responses and to give the regions a chance to reflect on their diversity and their own common points before the international consultation. The intention was to enable the main themes to emerge from within the various churches and local cultural/political contexts.

The study would work in four stages: broadly based local groups in member churches and Christian organizations; regional meetings in the major continental and oceanic areas; specialized consultations on three topics at the center of discussions on Christian unity; and an international consultation that would gather these findings, reflect, and recommend guidelines to the WCC and its member churches for the future.

When the study book first went out, it raised many doubts. From Western Europe some groups said, "It is for the Third World, not for us." From Africa people said, "It is not adapted to our way of work." From Asia and Latin America some said, "These are not our problems." From the United States some said, "We have already dealt with these issues, why impose another program on us?" From Eastern Europe people said, "We don't want a 'women's study', our concern is how to live in partnership, when in fact partnership in work is the reality of our life." From a number of places men said, "Why should I attend a group to discuss these issues? I don't see the problem." Some women said that the program was "too smooth. . . . You are jumping to community without facing the deep division and breakdown of communication between women and men in our culture."

Along with criticisms came more orders for the study book. From the initial printing of nine thousand, the circulation grew to an estimated sixty-five thousand copies, in numerous translations done at local levels. Some translations were recast to suit local contexts and church situations. What seemed appealing about the study book was its format of questions, its suggestive empty spaces, and a few pictures. Groups did not have to answer the particular questions in detail, but they did find ways to use the questions as a method of work suitable and adaptable to their situations. Groups found the questions stimulating, allowing them a new style of doing theology, starting not with the answers but with daily, concrete questions. The questions covered a broad range of topics: identity, changing roles, marriage and family, Scripture, church teachings, worship, ministry, Christian unity, issues of justice such as race and class. Behind these specific questions were some basic ones: What is the present situation in your church? Why are things the way they are? What is your vision of the community of women and men in your church? How can you move from where the church is now to your vision of community?

The method for study was open; it required critical analysis; it was positive. The focus was not on what is wrong with the church, but on how women and men can participate creatively in the life, thought, and shaping of the church itself. The emphasis was not upon the church as an "object," but upon the church as a reality in which we are identified and about which we have a commitment in faith, as both laity and clergy.

Seeking Foundations

Two decisions had a particular affect on the study and its future. First, the community study was made a joint venture of two sub-units, cooperating through an advisory committee composed of two people from the Commission on Faith and Order and two from the Working Group on Women. Second, the 1976 Central Committee had determined that the study could not be supported by, or draw on, existing WCC funds. This meant that the program was outside the ongoing budget and that churches contributing to the central treasuring of the WCC were not contributing to this new endeavor. One hundred percent of the funding had to come from sources outside normal giving to the WCC.

These decisions led to another unique aspect of the community study: who should fund it? Some thought that the women of the world should and would fund it, particularly some of the powerful women's organizations in the churches of Europe and North America. But some of these groups said, "This is not a women's study. It is primarily a Faith and Order study, a 'church study' in which we are cooperating." Some constituencies behind Faith and Order said, "This is a women's study; the women will have to fund it." So, in a sense, the community study was born without parents, without a tradition of institutional support behind it.

Nevertheless, enough funds were raised in 1977 so that a Study Desk could be established and a staff person invited to begin the work in January 1978. That is where I came in. The financing proved to be difficult; the study did not fit guidelines familiar to established supporting agencies. Luckily, the program had some early friends; donations from churches and church women's organizations kept it going into 1979. But by the autumn of 1979 the program was in a crisis. It had gained a broad constituency of interest. Expectations had been raised about this new effort. Yet the program was running out of money. For the WCC at large, there were still funds to raise for the consultation on the Program to Combat Racism to take place in the summer of 1980. Many asked: How could another financial effort be launched to support the community study too?

Two critical things happened at this juncture that kept the study going. First, various other programs of the WCC, realizing that the community study was alive and that the issues it addressed touched needs in the common work, chipped in small amounts. This "rescue operation" saved the program from going under in the fall of 1979. Second, in February 1980 the WCC Executive Committee decided to: "reaffirm its decision to authorize the continuation of the study for another year until 1981 in view of the fact that the financial conditions set in September 1979 have been met."

These events turned the balance sheet. In terms of program, the first of the regional meetings of the study had already taken place in Asia (1978) and the Middle East (1979), and African and Latin American meetings were projected. The first of the specialized consultations had been held on the "Ordination of Women in Ecumenical Perspective." Plans were in progress for two other meetings to be done jointly with local partners: "Toward a Theology of Human Wholeness" with the Ecumenical Institute at the Abbey of Niederaltaich, a Benedictine abbey in the Federal Republic of Germany, and "The Authority of Scripture in Light of the New Experiences of Women" in partnership with a local working group in Amsterdam. The "rescue operation" of September 1979 and the green light of the February 1980 Executive Committee enabled the program to begin to prepare for Sheffield.

Choosing the Site

How is a site for an international meeting chosen? Where should it be? Is there a global middle point or crossroads? England was selected as a location for a very practical reason: the most expensive item of a large international meeting is transportation, and London was the cheapest place to fly from and to. London itself did not seem like the right place to meet. Because the study had grown out of local communities around the world, a city more internal to the country seemed more appropriate. Martin Conway of the British Council of Churches suggested Sheffield. The University of Sheffield could provide fine facilities with its many small meeting rooms stacked high in the glass and steel Arts Tower, its spacious dormitory living units at Earnshaw, its university refectory, and Firth Hall, its Victorian ceremonial assembly room, where dark walls were lined with portraits of distinguished founders and university "fathers." Firth as a setting for plenaries was a good reminder of the past, and the brilliant rainbow banner of the consultation plus the light coming through the hundreds of small leaded window panes indicated a bright future.

When Sheffield was chosen, it was not known that the mayor to be elected would be a woman, Mrs. Enid Anne Hattersley. She honored us by opening our meeting and by receiving us in gracious English style for a festive dinner in the Sheffield City Hall. On the latter occasion, she voiced her concerns about racism and her doubts about feminism. Her own experience had convinced her that women have a chance but that black people in South Africa do not. Philip Potter responded to her challenging reflections, pointing out

17

how racism and sexism are both basic theological concerns, linked yet distinct. He stated that both must be overcome for world community to become truly human.

As the public leaders of the city welcomed us, so did the churches and many Christian families. On Sunday the entire conference visited in local congregations. All had luncheon invitations with families who shared their problems openly—the rising unemployment, the racial tensions in neighboring cities, the effects of inflation, the role that the church plays or ought to play to help renew the daily life. For participants coming from fifty-five churches the world over, it was important to hear that problems in a "rich country" are similar to problems in poor countries, even though there are great differences in the magnitude and impact of these world dynamics. Many hosts and guests were struck in a personal way with the connection between industrial plants being closed down in northern England and new plants opening up with newer equipment and cheaper labor in the countries of the Southern Hemisphere. Some reflected on what this can mean for the economic life of women and men.

The People Gathered

Of the two hundred forty people registered for the Sheffield consultation, First and Third World participation was about equally balanced. In terms of women and men, women were in the majority. One hundred forty people were official voting participants, representing ninety churches. The other hundred were observers, consultants, stewards, press, and staff. Twelve Roman Catholics participated. The Roman Catholic Church is not a WCC member church, but it has official membership on the Commission on Faith and Order, cooperating in this and other specific aspects of the Council's work. At local levels as well, many Roman Catholic groups participated in the study through local ecumenical agencies and networks.

Some Basic Questions

These introductory comments point to some basic questions of the community study: In a divided world, what should be the character of the one church we seek? Are women's issues a "separatist" question? How do the new questions women are raising relate to other kinds of questions facing the church, for example, poverty, maldistribution of resources, racism, violence, and war?

In the chapters to follow the voices of Sheffield speak for themselves. Their echo will be heard for a long time as we struggle with the questions they raised.

PART TWO

FROM THE PODIUM:
PLENARY PRESENTATIONS

2

1354 Years from that
Easter Day

The Community of
Women and Men
in the Church

ROBERT RUNCIE, Archbishop of Canterbury

I am invited to speak about my hope for unity and this consultation: unity in the Community of Women and Men in the Church.

On a subject with a number of mine fields to negotiate, I will also try to avoid what Rosemary Ruether has called a high-minded neutrality which hides a commitment to the status quo.

I will begin with the observation that the church's ministry *to* women, at least in my own tradition, is often exercised badly and insensitively. This is, I think, because the ministry of the church to women, and in the church by women, has had a very odd history. After the sixteenth century, the Protestants, and especially the Quakers, in their commitment to the priesthood of all believers, were committed to the view that the Spirit moved all, but the Quakers found that women had to be restrained from being moved for they were unduly garrulous. Yet their predecessors, the Lutherans, the Calvinists, and, to a degree, the Anglicans, not only took the legitimate areas of ministry *from* women—notably the baptism of the newly born in which Calvin asserted that the midwife who had been responsible for baptism par excellence "may not usurp the functions of men, let alone priests, by baptizing"—but also saw the area of activity of women solely in terms of seducing or, if virtuous, child rearing. Luther too came to much the same conclusion. He noted that "men have broad shoulders and narrow hips, and accordingly they possess intelligence. Women have narrow shoulders and broad hips. Women ought to stay at home; the way they were created indicates this, for they have broad hips

20

and a wide fundament to sit upon, keep house, bear, and raise children.'' The results of these insights have been many. In the first place ministry has become a masculine professional status occupation. It has become largely a matter of priesthood. Yet the contemplative nun, the nurse, the teacher, and social worker, are all ''ministers,'' and some of them by definition female ministers. It is indeed significant that within the Anglican communion more contemplative religious are female, and women in 1975 were studying more in the field of education, where they accounted for seventy-one percent of all students, than any other single profession.

It is therefore an imperative for the churches to regain a wide concept of ministry which is not narrowed by the jurisdictional inhibitions of those who cannot recognize a ministry unless it is institutionalized by the formal authorization of a bishop, a presbytery, or a congregation. Indeed, there is a real danger that an overconcentration on the issues involved in the ordination of women may reinforce a clericalist view of the church: the only ministry worth exercising is an *ordained* one. Yet in my own communion, and in the history of Western Christendom, Dame Julian of Norwich, Evelyn Underhill, and a whole host of persons who act as such divers things as marriage guidance counselors and spiritual advisers, without that being entered positively on their passports (though it would show in their diaries), in reality are ministers. It is a reality because, as the Roman Catholics and Free Churches have recognized (more perhaps than the Anglicans), women, who are not necessarily feminists nor would necessarily offer themselves for the priesthood, do not see their contribution to the church solely in terms of altar flowers, inspiring as these creations may be. They have encountered, as a matter of historical fact, the enormous needs which they and they alone can fulfill. Dame Josephine Barnes has recognized this in medicine, and in her stand for one hospital for women has tried to state the need for certain problems to be dealt with in certain ways. These problems are not merely medical. Women of maturity can often help other women, particularly the battered or hardpressed, with their problems of pain or prayer simply because the problem hardly needs stating, and female ministry goes beyond to those who see that precisely because women have been undervalued for so long they may instinctively identify with others—for instance, prisoners as with Elizabeth Fry, or prostitutes as with Josephine Butler, to say nothing of homosexuals who are similarly placed.

Women do not simply need to be trained for ordination for these roles. Indeed, some of the more imaginative courses for them are those which train them in spirituality—two month courses by the Roman Catholics, for instance—or in the recognition of their own selves, body, mind, and spirit, wombs and wit, which all churches are beginning to undertake. But much is still to be done.

This gives me the opportunity of stressing the importance of this World Council of Churches consultation as the forum for the ecumenical discussion of this whole subject in which all the Christian traditions can offer the richness of their varieties of ministry. Anything less than the wide spectrum of traditions represented here runs the risk of being interpreted as partisan. The "ecumenical argument" on the ministry of women can be a two-edged sword, and I am convinced we must patiently listen to all the churches.

But the consultation is not simply about the ministry of women in the church, it is a sign of the reflection that all the churches are giving to the phenomenon called "feminism." The women's movement today is no longer simply feminist. It is not a united movement, and it is all the better for that. It divides between those who want to burn their bras, refuse to marry, and insist on doing all that men do—even to playing games which are anatomically painful— and those who ask for something more difficult to articulate. That something is the freedom to be women. It consists in *not* being constrained by male attitudes to ministry, to work, to the family, or above all to God. But to be heard in the very depths of their being: in their love which has to extend to troublesome children and in that extension learns to reach out beyond conventional boundaries and which has often to accept a measure of physical weakness. This may breed not militancy but a very real humility. It takes many forms: women need and have to accept their need—for maternity leave, for retraining, for care facilities sometimes for their children—but above all they need to accept from others an understanding that they just may not be simple shoulders and hips as Luther would have had them but more complex beings, perhaps even more complex than men, and for that reason they may be a source of fear.

I hope in the rhetoric of the feminist movement the churches will not lose the real message of a Christian feminist movement which is about complementarity in ministry and the unity of sexes in the Godhead. "Differences do not argue superiority or inferiority," so R. H. Hutton told Emily Davies, the great pioneer of feminine education in the nineteenth century. But differences can argue, or be made to argue, superiority or inferiority. Let us see that this does not happen and that we dignify through the insight of our various traditions the legitimacy of difference and the legitimacy of the variations of the ministry which men and women can bring to the unity of the church.

I believe that the consultation by sharing its insights on the ministry of women and men in the community of the church can play a very important role in the visible unity of the church for which we seek and pray.

A Chance to Change

PHILIP POTTER, General Secretary,
World Council of Churches

This is the second time that I have been involved in a conference in Sheffield. In 1949, as secretary for the Student Christian Movement, I organized a conference here on Britain and Africa, with British and African students. At that conference there was for the first time in the postwar period a real confrontation between the African and British students and between the students and the authorities, because we had here the secretary of state for the colonies and two former colonial governors. I can well remember the ways in which they were made to tremble and fumble by the radical questioning from both the African and British students who raised the issues of power, of domination and oppression, and of racism.

That was in 1949, and the struggle continues today. Indeed the struggle has become clearer as the issues have had to be taken up not just by students but by the churches themselves. In many cases extraordinary things have happened in the course of these thirty-two years, helping to prepare the ground for the meeting in Sheffield.

What then is our agenda here? It is to consider the issues of liberation from sexism, the systematic, historical, and present subordination of women by men, and their liberation for a truly human life as a community of women and men in church and society.

How have we come here? To understand how we need to go back to the First Conference on Faith and Order on the issues of unity in 1927 at Lausanne. There were, believe it or not, as many as six women present there among hundreds of men. And they were not only present, but they presented a statement in which they asserted, ''That the right place of women in the church is a question of grave moment and should be in the hearts and minds of all.'' That of course was the polite language of the time. They reminded the church fathers also that if the churches were seeking deeper unity they would have to reexamine the question between the relationship of women and men. Ready as usual, the churches repeated these phrases for several years until we met together for the inauguration of the World Council of Churches in 1948. At

23

that first assembly we declared that "the church as the body of Christ consists of men and women created as responsible persons to glorify God and to do his will." And the statement immediately went on to say, "This truth, accepted in theory, is too often ignored in practice."

For years the World Council of Churches went no further in speaking about the cooperation of women and men in the church, family, and society. But between 1974 and 1975 there was a conference in Berlin, and there was also an assembly where two things happened. One was in the section entitled "What Unity Requires" which spoke of the community of women and men and the wholeness of the body of Christ. The section saw that "the unity of the church requires that women be free to live out the lives which God has given to them and to respond to their calling to share fully in the life and witness of the church." Incidentally, the same section that dealt with the issues of a fully committed conciliar fellowship in each place and in all places, reminded the churches of the call to convergence on the issues of baptism, Eucharist, and ministry. As I understand it, what the 1975 Assembly was trying to say was that all these issues were at stake and had to be considered together. It was in that sense that we set out on our work.

And how did we go about it? Certainly not from above. It was not possible at all for Geneva to do anything from above on this issue. In fact the history of the ecumenical movement is the history of the things that have happened because they happened from below. And much of the work that brought us to the Nairobi Assembly was done through women's groups from below. Indeed, before the World Council of Churches was formed in 1948, there was a worldwide study done from local situations all over the world, and it was out of that study that the Assembly took the action it did. But it also asked a very able and committed woman, Kathleen Bliss, to write a book on the subject of the service and witness of women in the church coming out of this study. Because of the work from below people like Kathleen Bliss and Madeleine Barot, who for so many years guided that work, were able to carry out their task. Indeed, Madeleine Barot did not come from above. She had been the founder of CIMADE during the war—that most pioneering and creative enterprise from which women and men were together rescued even from the jaws of death and enabled to live. So, it was on account of that embodied work which Madeleine carried out among women all over the world that we have come to this point today. And Madeleine Barot is only the symbol of so many others whom I could mention here.

The other impulse came from the Assembly section on "Structures of Injustice and Struggles for Liberation.'' It concluded its analysis of the injustice of sexism by asserting: ''The freedom and unity of Jesus Christ includes both halves of the human community; therefore it is imperative to the unity of the church and society that the full participation of women be given urgent consideration and immediate implementation.''

I would like to share with you what I have learned from just reading the reports which have come out of these three years of study on the Community of Women and Men in the Church. Three years which the archbishop has so rightly characterized as a most imaginative piece of work guided by Constance Parvey. I have read these reports, but I have also read between the lines, because as an old ecumenic I know that reports are only a sort of algebraic sign of a very great depth of well-buried meaning. What I have learned from this decoding exercise is that, compared, for example with the anger and frustration of the 1974 Berlin conference on sexism, I felt here through this enormous study which has gone on in so many parts of the world, the incredible pain and agony of it all—and with it the extraordinary love and patient endurance and perserverance which lie behind it.

I perceived also the tremendous insights and wisdom—which have been lying there wasted for so many years and which are still emerging, thank God, for our enrichment—which have come out of this common effort largely by women. I have been aware, reading these reports, of the impotence of our male-dominated churches to see, hear, feel, decide, and act. And incensed with this impotence, I wait for the potency which God's Spirit can bring to us. For me, this study is a veritable test of our faith and of the ecumenical movement which is concerned about the unity of the whole people of God, as a sign and sacrament of the unity of all the peoples of the world.

Now, what are some of the issues which have arisen from this process and which are urgent and inevitable for our attention as churches and as Christians? First of all, throughout this study, what has emerged most powerfully for me is the need to rethink the whole question of authority and interpretation of Scripture. The more I meditate on it, the more I realize that even more than the issues of racism and social injustice, the way in which the relations of men and women have been dealt with in the Scriptures themselves and the way in which we have interpreted what the Scriptures have said have brought seriously into question how we understand the total revelation of God in Christ expressed in the whole canon of the Scriptures. We have systematically left aside as our criterion of judgment the central nature of God's revelation and have clung to all the things that strengthen and confirm our attitudes of domination and of hierarchical oppression. It seems to me that this discovery challenges the way in which we deal with the Scriptures, and we shall have to do some hard thinking about this.

Secondly, we have to come to terms with our ecclesiology, our understanding of the church, the "laos," the laity, the whole people of God. What *do* we mean when we speak of the church as "the whole people of God," as we have been saying in the ecumenical movement for the past nearly forty years? What does it mean for the way that the church functions? What do we mean when we say loftily in our ecumenical documents that the unity we seek is a unity in which there is a conciliar fellowship in each place and in all places? If there is a fellowship, a real sharing of life with life in which we are all in council together, then it means both women and men are in council together, that decisions are made together, and that decisions are made by those who have the gifts required without regard to sex or culture. Then our whole conception of ministry has to change. We have used the word "ministry" which means being the servants, but "ministry" has been turned into "hierarchy," into "patriarchy." We know that the servant is the one who empties himself or herself, not seeking to have power and domination. We talk about the servant church but, in the whole length and breadth of the life of the church, we have set up all kinds of individual and corporate forms of hierarchy which enshrine power attitudes and structures. And may I say, women and men both have acquiesced in it. This provides one of the challenges to which this meeting will speak.

And then there is our whole understanding of tradition and traditions. We have made a great sacred cow of our different traditions, but what I find, as a student of history, is an urgent need to rewrite church history as the history of women and men in mission and service. Our existing church history is largely a history of men. For example, when our new World Council of Churches' president, the patriarch of the Church of Georgia in the USSR, came to Geneva on an official visit two years ago, it was only by chance that I went to the library and found out that the first missionary to his church was St. Nina, back in the fourth century. It is only by chance that a lot of us are now beginning to pick up a few things about the role of women in the first centuries. It was Queen Bertha who gave land to St. Augustine and his followers on which Canterbury Cathedral was built. Again, at the close of the seventh century there were many mixed religious houses, and the five of them in Kent were governed by women. One of the things this conference ought to do is to send us all back to do our homework so that we can begin to discover the real tradition in the life of the churches and why the churches became so male-oriented in the way that they did.

Furthermore, it will be interesting for us to see what the role of women was in the renewal movements of the church. My impression is that wherever there were renewal movements women were often in the lead. Consider the women prophets in the early centuries, then the vast number of women mystics and the books they wrote, and combined with that mysticism their active service in the community in the Middle Ages. Then after the Reformation in this country there were the Quakers, of whom we have heard so much, where there was equality between men and women, as also among the Moravians and even the Methodists. The Methodist movement in the eighteenth century owed a tremendous debt to women all up and down these islands, and indeed in other parts of the world. Today, all around the world, wherever there are renewal movements, base communities of people who are developing their consciousness and going out and daring the oppressive authorities, there are women in the vanguard.

In the same way, women played a distinctive role in the missionary movement both at home and abroad from the very earliest centuries. This fact needs much more historical research as does the role of women in the ecumenical movement, starting with the YWCA and the Student Christian Movement in which so many of us men learned how to live with women as equals, without knowing how to carry it on from there.

What I have further observed in these writings gathered by the community study is a deepening of our theological understanding of what it means to be human—and in quite new ways. First of all, our whole understanding of sexuality is challenged. We are called to take it more seriously, especially in our theology. Secondly, we're challenged to see that being human means dealing with the issue of dualism. The whole division between flesh and spirit, often putting flesh as woman and assuming spirit implicitly in terms of man, has been a heresy, even worse than a heresy in the life of the church; or again the dualism of private and public—women being private and men public— keeping men with the mentality in which the ordinary human virtues were private while in public it was the survival of the fittest which reigned. This dualism is also challenged by our new understanding of what it is to be human. And the third dualism which is being challenged is that of meekness over against power—that meekness belongs to women and power to man. Because of the inability to relate these two things, our humanity has been brutalized, and we are in this pursuit of death by rearmament and war.

Another thing I have seen in this study is the central relationship between identity and community. The heart of God's revelation of humanity was male and female. In that he indicated to us that there is no homogeneous, uniform way by which God wills that we should live, but rather in full recognition of our diversities and through those diversities we find our unity and community.

And lastly, what I have learned from these studies has been a fresh impetus for our call to justice and peace. We have been talking a great deal about development as self-reliance. But we haven't noticed that in most of the world, especially the poor world, it's the women who have been carrying the tremendous burden of poverty and development. And it is they who have been showing what self-reliance can mean. Just to take one simple example, we talk in our development work about appropriate technology, when technology itself originated in ancient cultures largely due to the efforts and ingenuity of women. The struggle for peace in a war-obsessed world is only possible when women are deeply and decisively engaged politically.

Some years ago I had to prepare for a women's conference, a study on the first chapters of Luke and especially the Magnificat, and I read a commentary by Lagrange, the great Roman Catholic Semitic scholar. In that study he brought out, and I later pursued, the origins of the word "Mary," that other person who has been used and abused by the churches concerning the role of woman. Now, Mary comes from a verb *mara* which has two roots. One root means to be fat, and to be fat in Semitic terms in those days meant to be beautiful. Of course, I dare say this was a very acceptable thing, as we can see in the whole iconography of Mary. In fact Lagrange decided that this was the better root of the word. But he was honest enough to say that there is another meaning of the word *mara* and that is to revolt—to lead a revolution. That is clear if you read the Magnificat where the mighty are brought down from their seats, including ecclesiastics, and the humble and meek are exalted. Now that in itself is an indication of our problem. Even in terms of our scientific and biblical work on the meaning of the word *mara*, we men deliberately chose it to mean just to be fat and beautiful but not to revolt, to work for change. And yet what Mary as the Theotokos, God bearer, came to teach us was the beauty of holiness, the total commitment to God and to God's purpose, but also the power of healing and renewing love for a chance to change men and women toward one family in justice and peace.

Becoming Human in New Community

ELISABETH MOLTMANN-WENDEL
and JÜRGEN MOLTMANN

I

Elisabeth:

Church history begins when a few women set out to pay their last respects to their dead friend Jesus. It begins when, contrary to all reason and all hope, a few women identify themselves with a national traitor and do what they consider to be right, what in their eyes equals quality of life, namely, loving one who has sacrificed his life, never abandoning him as dead. Church history begins when Jesus comes to them, greets them, lets them touch him just as he had touched and restored them in their lives. Church history begins when the women are told to share with the men this experience, this life they now comprehend, this life their hands have touched.

This story as told by Matthew is generally known as the Easter appearance of the women but never as the beginning of church history. Officially, church history begins with the mission of the men apostles and, officially, no women are present on that occasion. Right up to the present time many churches have traced their origin back to this apostolic succession. Almost all the leaders of these churches are male and depend mostly on males for their order and their ideas. The idea of God is conceived mainly in masculine terms: male leadership roles are used to describe what God does—God reigns, judges, governs; what God is corresponds to what men would like to be—judge, king, ruler, army commander. In the process women's experiences of Jesus have been forgotten—Jesus as a friend who shares their life and is ever near them, a friend who offers them warmth and tenderness in their loneliness and powerlessness. The feminist movement in the Western world has given many women the courage to discover themselves, to express again their own religious experiences, to read the Bible with fresh eyes and to rediscover their original and distinctive role in the gospel. For these women feminism is not a white, Western, bourgeois movement but one deeply rooted in the gospel.

In the social upheavals and cultural crises of the last fifteen years many other groups have made the painful discovery that God is on the side of patriarchy. Above all, God has become a stranger to many women in the Western world. It is no longer possible for them to reconcile God with their conceptions of life and with their identity. Certainly, patriarchy is not to be blamed on the men. Men should not feel or be held personally responsible for it. Patriarchy is a cultural form dating back thousands of years, and many cultural and economic achievements of our world would have been inconceivable without it. But, essentially in the last two centuries, disastrous associations with colonialism and racism, capitalism and sexism, have arisen out of patriarchy, leading us to start seeking the fundamental causes of these evils. In the process it has become alarmingly clear that colonialism, capitalism, racism, and sexism have been supported, justified, and even religiously glorified by a patriarchal Christianity. "Gott mit uns" ("God with us") were the words inscribed on every German soldier's belt buckle in the First World War. In the name of a triumphal, social-reforming God, people were enslaved, workers exploited, and women taught to hold their peace. And only minority groups of Christians protested against all this.

Today women are once again setting out to discover life, to enliven all that has become dead, to know Jesus as the one he once was for them. They are seeking to liberate themselves from the patriarchal domination in which their thinking was done for them as well as for others who were not considered fully adult. They want to free themselves from being treated like children, to be free from the tutelage which denies them any say at all, or allows them only a limited say, in society. They no longer want to accept the values imparted by the patriarchal world system—either for themselves or for their children or for society as a whole.

What do women want? I would like to take a little time to consider this question, for many people even in the church are afraid of women. Men are afraid that women hate them; women are afraid of women who could cause their traditional roles to become insecure. There is a fear of any kind of radicalism which supposedly is not in harmony with the love of Christ. What women want is a new community in which those with power begin to listen to those without power. A community where there are opportunities for the powerless to express themselves and get organized. A community in which power is redistributed and those in power learn to give up their power—for the sake of justice. Women want a community which is not obsessed with profit and economic growth but concerned with the basic needs of all human beings. They are able to stand up for all this passionately and credibly because they have firsthand experience of what it is like to be treated like children, to be in tutelage, without rights, to live a life secondhand (the husband's or the man's), to give life but to be allowed to fashion it only within a limited domestic circle and not in society as a whole.

What women want is a whole life, one which embraces body, soul, and spirit, no longer compartmentalized into private and public spheres; a life, moreover, which fills us with a trust and hope transcending biological death. This seems a huge and impossible utopian program. In the last analysis, however, it is simply taking seriously what can be read in the prophet Isaiah's visions of peace and in a part of what the apostle Paul once recognized in a flash of inspiration—namely, that in Christ there is neither Jew nor Greek, neither slave nor free, neither male nor female. It is also the old vision of the women which we find in the song of Miriam, one of the oldest passages in the Bible: trust in the God who has thrown horse and rider—today we can say sex and domination—into the sea. This feminine tradition, which is found in many women's songs—of Hannah, of Deborah, Judith, and Mary's Magnificat—and which has always been with us, makes us keenly aware of what is happening in the world and what is going on within ourselves, in our bodies, in our souls, and in our spirit.

Women on the way to discover life.

Women in a church which is firmly in masculine hands.

In which direction lies the way?

Certainly away from a patriarchy in which women have been oppressed, silenced, and are unable to speak for themselves. Away too from the church and its patriarchal structures? Away too from God who, as Kate Millett said, was always tied to patriarchy or, perhaps to be more precise, was always occupied with patriarchy? For many women, even among us, this decision still has to be made.

Jürgen:

You have been asking: is God on the side of patriarchy? Let me attempt to answer that by being self-critical and asking which God this is.

It was not Christianity which introduced patriarchy into the world. Patriarchy is a very ancient and widespread system of male domination. Christianity proved incapable of successfully opposing this system. Indeed, quite early on, Christianity was already taken over by men and made to serve patriarchy. This had a crippling effect on its liberating potential, as has been perceived by theologians of hope, liberation theologians, and political theologians in other contexts when they criticized the "Constantinian captivity" of the church. The liberation of women and then of man from patriarchy goes hand in hand, therefore, with a rediscovery of the freedom of Jesus and of the energies of the Holy Spirit. Leaving the monotheistic God of rulers and males behind us, we shall discover from the sources of Christianity the God who is in relationship, the God who can suffer, the uniting God, the God of fellowship and community. This is the living God, the God of life, who was distorted through a patriarchal system with its idols of power and domination. In this living God the male too will experience deliverance from the distortions which he himself has suffered and still suffers under patriarchy.

Oppression obviously has two sides: on the one side, there is the tyrant, on the other, the slave; here the dominating man and there the serving woman. Oppression destroys humanity on both sides: the oppressed person is robbed of humanity and the oppressor becomes an inhuman monster. Both suffer from their true nature, with the difference, of course, that one of them suffers in consequence, whereas the other appears to feel fine. On both sides, however, liberation from oppression is needed. But how is this possible for men, whose ideas and feelings are deeply influenced by patriarchy and who seem to enjoy their privileges?

The starting point for us men, just as it is for you women, is to become aware of the real situation and to realize the extent to which patriarchy cheats us out of the blessings of true life. Each man can achieve this anamnesis for himself by asking how he was trained as a child to ''become a man,'' what feelings he was expected to suppress, what instincts he had to control, what roles he was taught to adopt. He was trained to be a worker, a soldier, a father, a breadwinner, a conqueror, and a ruler. The first lessons he learned therefore were self-control and self-possession. He was terrified of becoming a ''nothing,'' a ''nobody,'' and was ruled by the desire to ''make something of himself.''

Patriarchy cut the male in half. It split him into a subject, consisting of reason and will, and an object, consisting of heart, feelings, and physical needs. He had to identify himself with the former and keep his distance from the latter. This isolated the male and brought about a certain self-hatred. This division in the male is reflected and takes an aggressive form in the male subjugation and domination of supposedly ''frail,'' ''emotional,'' and ''physical'' women. It is also reflected in the other reality that every ruler not only needs people at his command but also a throne to sit on. As can be seen from such symbols as Isis and Horus, Mary and the child Jesus, the throne on which the male ruler is seated is the mother. This division of the woman into mother and wife

32

is a product of patriarchy. Unresolved mother-fixations and "machismo" vis-à-vis other women go together. There must be an end to both mothering and domination if the man is to become both free and mature.

The distress of the divided and isolated male is reflected in the majesty of the God of patriarchy. He is the Almighty, the Lord, the Absolute. He determines everything; nothing influences him. He is incapable of suffering. According to Aristotle, he loves only himself and causes everything to accord with his self-love. If he is assigned human traits, they are male traits. Knowledge of him ascends from the family patriarch (*pater familias*) to the national patriarch (*pater patriae*), from the national patriarch to the patriarch of the church, and finally reaches the greatest patriarch, the Father of all in heaven (*omnipater*). And in the legitimation of authorities, one then descends from the heavenly Father of all. Between this heavenly Father of all and the mystery of Jesus' "Abba, Father" there is no connection. On the contrary, this God of Patriarchy arises from the first division of the world into heaven and earth: heavenly father-mother earth.

The God of patriarchy is often portrayed through Christian forms in terms of the head and the body. The man is the head of the woman, Christ is the head of the man, God is the head of Christ (1 Cor. 2). Only under the man as head is the woman in God's image but not for herself alone (Augustine, Thomas Aquinas). He is the leader, she the led (Karl Barth).

The distress of the male Ruler-God lies in his lack of a name and his loneliness. He is defined only by his function as ruler and proprietor of the world. Who he himself is remains unknown. Thus patriarchy divides, separates, and isolates God. A God who is no more than "the Almighty" is not a God but a monster. Any man who emulates this God becomes a hapless beast; he is no more than an expression of the will to power. Since the modern, white male became afflicted with this "God complex" (H. E. Richter), patriarchy has ceased to be a source of order and protection and has instead become a source of destruction and fear.

You said that women today are on the way to discover life, a life which is whole and one of community. Men who wish to discover life for themselves and then in community with women must shake off the pressure of patriarchy, as they would some nightmare, and eliminate these suppressions of true life so as to become full human beings. What happens to us here is rather like what happened to the disciples who hear the women's Easter message and then, half-believing, half-disbelieving, go off to find for themselves the living Lord whom they had forsaken shortly before his crucifixion. In this common "resurrection-movement" we men could discover "the new community of women and men" which delivers us from patriarchal distorations and opens up to us the wholeness of human life.

Elisabeth:

Both men and women are crippled, but in different ways and with different consequences. You still cling to the throne of Isis even though we no longer want to be the mothers who carry Horus.

Women today, therefore, should lead the way to new community of women and men. They should do so not so much in order to make good the discrimination they have suffered and the injustice which has been inflicted on them. This precedence of women need not be humiliating for men. They should see it more as an opportunity to leave women room to discover and point out the obstacles along the way. For only in this way can a sustainable community grow.

Since we began to discover what *our* life is—our life as women, our life in solidarity with all the women in the world who suffer discrimination, our spiritual life, our life as Christian women, a life which we want to take hold of, feel, endure, change—we have constantly come into collision with the barriers of our Christian tradition: our faith is the faith of the "fathers." Our religious testimonies are derived from a Bible edited by the patriarchs, obviously to the exclusion of any female participation in the process. Christian life is celebrated in our hymns in a paternalistic style. In our theology the man "leads" and the women is "led" (Karl Barth). And when we inspect it in greater detail, we find that the tradition from which we are supposed to live is full to the brim of hostility toward women. In any case, the life assigned to us as women is not a whole life. According to one biblical passage, we women are to be saved by childbearing, you men by faith. We are the first to sin. But even if we turn a blind eye to these biblical blunders, the life assigned to women is a secondhand life, life as supplementing that of the man, life from the Spirit and the Word but not life in the unity of body, soul, and spirit. In the distorted, patriarchal view our bodies have for far too long been considered embarrassing, unclean, repulsive. In short, it is not life in its wholeness but a halved life.

Can the Christian tradition offer us any help to extricate ourselves from this halved life? Where do the sources and motivations exist for this in respect of our identity? What Christian traditions can accompany and support us on the way to wholeness? What Christian traditions can also help the man to be "whole" and give him an identity other than that of a patriarch?

Jürgen:

It is very true that the biblical, Christian, and church traditions were mainly written and edited by dominating men. At first sight, therefore, they provide little help for the liberation of women. History, it has been said, is always written by the victors. The oppressed have even been deprived of the conscious memorial of their own history of defeat and suffering. But these traditions "from above" can also be read, contrary to their intention, "from below." When we do this we discover in the histories of tyrants the suppressed histories also of the rebels against tyranny. In this sense, in and underlying the male history of the church there is also a history of Christian women, a female history of the church. To some extent, you yourself have rediscovered this history and found within it symbols and motifs which can lead women out of a divided life and into a whole life. Let me mention only three examples of these here:

1. For centuries, Christians have learned the story of the Fall as it is told extremely graphically in the second account of creation (J). This account also includes the first male disclaimer of guilt: "The woman whom thou gavest to be with me, she gave me fruit of the tree . . ." (Gen. 3:12, *RSV*). Unfortunately, we find this in the New Testament as well: "For Adam was created first, and Eve afterwards; and it was not Adam who was deceived; it was the woman who, yielding to deception, fell into sin" (1 Tim. 2:13–14, *NEB*). This was used to prove woman's inferiority.

The story of the Fall as told in the first account of creation in the Priestly tradition (P) was more or less forgotten. This tradition makes no mention of the apple, the woman, and the serpent, or of Adam—innocent if not very bright—but speaks of something quite different: "Now the earth was corrupt in God's sight, and the earth was filled with violence" (Gen. 6:11, *RSV*). Of what did the corruption and sin consist? It consisted in the spread of "violence" among humans and animals. God therefore decided on the destruction of both in the flood. Evil and sin here are at their origin nothing other than violence, brutality, and "rape." Redemption means, therefore, a "nonviolent life" as commanded and promised by Jesus in the Sermon on the Mount. If we had paid heed to this account of creation, the myth of women's inferiority would not have arisen.

2. Women today ask sharply: 'Is God a man?'' In fact, the Christian doc-

trine of God is spoken of chiefly in male terms: Father, Son, and Holy Spirit. Is this really true, though? There is an ancient but suppressed tradition of the maternal office of the Holy Spirit, the divine motherhood. The Christian communities which were subsequently driven out of the mainline men's church found it natural to speak of the Spirit as the mother of Jesus. In Ethiopian pictures of the Trinity the Spirit is depicted as a mother. The nuclear family—Adam, Eve, and Seth—was often used by the Greek church fathers too as an image of the Triune God on earth, which certainly presupposes that the Holy Spirit is female and an archetype of the mother. Nor was it mere chance that Count Zinzendorf rediscovered the maternal office—the motherhood—of the Holy Spirit when founding the Pennsylvania community of brothers and sisters in 1741: "This is the divine family upon earth, for the Father of our Lord Jesus Christ is our true Father, the Spirit of our Lord Jesus Christ is our true Mother, because the Son of the living God is our true brother."

Personally I find this idea helpful not only because it discovers the female principle in the Godhead but also because it picks up an element of the truth in pantheism. If the Spirit is our mother, then I am able to feel that I am not only "under God," but also "in God." This idea delivers me from one-sided monotheistic father images of God and helps me to experience the whole God with my whole being. It helps me to find the community-God in our own community.

3. Finally, it seems to me that the undoubtedly difficult and abstract development of the doctrine of the Trinity in the Christian concept of God was nevertheless already paving the way for victory over the masculine ruler-God. It is true, of course, that "Trinity" sounds just like something out of the abstract male theology "from above." What I mean by it, however, is the mysterious whole by which our whole life is embraced.

There is always a mutual interaction between knowledge of God and our self-knowledge. The theology of the Western church located the divine image of humanity in our "reasonable soul" which governs the body. By its control over itself and over the earth, humanity—that is, the male—corresponds to the ruler-God. Individualism in view of humanity and monotheism in view of God are twinborn.

Since we know today that humanity constitutes a unity of body, soul, and spirit and finds its salvation in experiencing the wholeness of life, it cannot be only the human soul which is the divine image on earth. Humanity itself in its bodily nature, humanity itself in the community of women and men, corresponds to God. To which God? There can be only one answer: to the

God in relationship, the unifying God, the God of community, that is, the Triune God. The rule of this God is not "divide and conquer" (*divide et impera*); the Triune God is present, rather, in the uniting of the divided and in the healing of what is separated and torn into pieces. The mighty man may be an imitation of the Almighty but only a human community in which human beings have all things in common and share all things, irrespective of individual characteristics, can be an image of the Triune God. This thought helps me personally to seek God not only in heaven above, not only in the inward depths of the soul, but also and above all between us in our community.

You asked: What can help us to liberate ourselves from our divided life? What Christian traditions can help us along the way to wholeness? Our traditions are always a collection of past hopes and past experiences. These have their value, but it is only a limited value. No tradition can settle the future. At best, traditions can prepare the way into the future. What the Spirit itself creates is always something new and always full of surprises. The Spirit is not tied to the traditions but takes from them that which points the way to the future. Christianity is more than a tradition, it is a hope.

Elisabeth:

Many women will still find it difficult to rediscover themselves in the female correlations of male conceptions of God. What they are really asking is whether we women should rediscover our identity in male symbols—supplemented by feminine ideals.

Women will put more trust in their own imaginations than in the tradition. They are already developing their own language: God is the baker's woman. Jesus can be their sister. They can pray: "Our Father-Mother in heaven . . ." Feminist theology—its very name sends cold shivers up the spine of many theologians!—is for many women the only possible way they can speak freely and discover themselves to be daughters of God. Women have a culture of their own. It is still very different in the different countries of Asia and Africa. It is a more concrete and pictorial culture than the corresponding male culture in each case, though it is often buried underground. For us, therefore, theo-fantasy takes its place alongside theo-logy and frequently reexcavates the buried sources.

For theology, largely commandeered by men, what matters most is that it should take seriously not only past experiences and traditions but also contemporary and coming experiences and traditions—theo-fantasy. Life, including Christian life, is much more diverse and colorful than any written tradition. What will be important here is that men learn to listen and sit at the feet of women, as Mary sat at the feet of Jesus.

II

Elisabeth:

A new community can only mature and bear fruit if women remain autonomous human beings. The contribution they can make to community will not be a vital and lively one unless they retain their singularity, specificity, distinctiveness as women. The life women have been looking for and have now rediscovered will only become everyone's common concern if they continue to make it their cause.

Many find that statement difficult and paradoxical, women as well as men. We are used to thinking of the church as a great big loving family in which everyone is self-effacing for the sake of others, forgetful of self in the interests of a great cause. Everyone and everything should be united in one great first person plural—one great "we."

If women and men are to come together in a new community, they must say goodbye to such wishful thinking. They must each separately accept the pain of division and even the possible deprivation of love. They can discover themselves, in their wholeness with all its unexplored possibilities.

Many women in the church may find this particularly hard to accept, for they have got used to sacrificing themselves readily, taking a back seat; it has become almost second nature to accept that this is their Christian life style. Men find it hard because they have got used to working with women who are always eager to help and because, in virtue of their official rank in the churches and the power that goes with it, the men have turned the cause of Jesus into a patriarchy of love. We have to relearn what loving means; we must learn a love which makes others mature instead of smothering them or glorifying them, a love which creates an area in which there is no domination.

The responsibility which men have become accustomed to assume and the renunciation which women have become accustomed to practice are patterns of behavior which derived from a strict allocation of sex roles. The life of our churches is based on patriarchal patterns of behavior from which no new community can possibly grow today. Women have begun to free themselves from these roles. How are the men to be liberated from these roles?

Jürgen:

Before I come to the question of the church, I think you should try to develop one point a little further. It is the men who are mainly "disconcerted" by women who emancipate themselves from age-old subjection. Women should not cover up this fact out of love nor should we men deny it out of pride. We are becoming insecure in the masculine roles which have been instilled in us. We have to relearn everything, and every existential experience of relearning is painful. But the problem lies still deeper. The man also feels that his manly pride is violated. His sense of self-respect is shaken. His patriarchal identity disintegrates. He no longer knows who he really is. One reaction to this is aggression. But the most common reaction is depression.

Women are experiencing their new identity, their dignity, and their liberation into complete humanity. The reason men find it difficult to follow them in this way is because, to discover the starting point for their liberation into complete humanity, they have first of all to return deep inside themselves. They have to break through the hard crusts of their alienation in order to reach the core of their human nature. Moreover, man must abandon self-righteousness if he is to learn to trust his humanity. To put it simply, the ruling "lord" in man must die so that the brother can be born, ready for honest friendship.

For men this also means no longer identifying themselves with the male caste but instead breaking out of the male code. To do so may earn them contempt, and they may become lonely. In the education of the child to "manhood," the male caste has always played the leading part. It also brands its dissenters as "traitors."

Any man who is willing to abandon the masculine privileges conferred on him by the patriarchal society must also learn to abandon his male responsibility for the so-called weaker sex. The "noble," "knightly," and "gentlemanly" overtones of this morality make its abandonment particularly difficult for many of us. But men who welcome and respect the coming of age of women must also learn to limit and to give up this "responsibility"-feeling.

III

Elisabeth:

The churches sometimes seem to me just like men's associations. Can they possibly cope today when so many women who have been kept in tutelage are "coming of age"? Is the church prepared to take seriously these women who have rediscovered their subjectivity? And by "taking them seriously" I mean recognizing their rights and according them power. This subjectivity is potentially explosive; it could produce an explosion of previously pent-up creativity. It has implications for many church traditions. It calls into question religious images and forms of church life. Many women today are saying: "We are the church." Does their way lead to a new community of men and women?

Jürgen:
   The Christian church finds it particularly difficult to limit responsibility clearly. The reason for this is that, in the church, the supreme values are service, care, sacrifice for others, and, therefore, responsibility. This mild dictatorship of love, this "patriarchy of love," as you call it, is very difficult to escape. Are not Christians always on active service and do they not exist only "for others"? I also used to believe that, but not anymore. It now seems to me to be actually false and a concealed form of domination. Christians are in the first place simply "with others." Only as those who delight in life with others do they then, when need arises, also sacrifice themselves "for others." Their love comes up against its boundary in the autonomy of others. Not even Jesus came to fetter human beings to himself by his ministry, to make himself indispensable for them. "Your faith has saved you," he habitually says when people want to thank him for being healed. Your *own* faith! God exists "for us" only in our distress, for it is God's will to live "with us" in eternity. God wants us as "autonomous human beings," as you rightly said.
   As long as a church regards itself as a "servant church," as a "church for the nation, " or a "church for the world," or "a church for others, " it will always regard the subjectivity and adulthood of those it "cares for" as a threat to itself. Only when this "caring-from-above" church becomes a community of the people will it welcome the autonomous subjectivity of women, of workers, of disabled people, as energy of the Spirit. In the established churches there are few women pastors and no women bishops. But in many basic communities in Latin America, the leadership of women is a matter of course. Up to the present, only persecuted communities and basic communities have experienced the full range of charismata in the free community of men and women, a community without "above" and "below." Paradoxically enough, it will be from "below" that the Spirit will come into the established male churches. We should look for the Spirit where human beings become autonomous agents of their own lives and take the initiative for themselves.

IV

Elisabeth:
   The power which is renewing women today in opposition to partriarchal structures and their own insecurity and discouragement, the power which

liberates them and enables them to stand upright like the healed crippled woman, the power which enables them to discover their sisters, is the power of the Holy Spirit. For many women the Spirit has been for long enough something exceptional, miraculous. But many women are now finding in the power of the Spirit that self-identification that the male church, the male God, the man Jesus, was unable to give them. They speak of the Holy Spirit as female, the Holy Spirit who in the language of Jesus was also of the female gender. This is not something which is happening for the first time today. In the long history of the patriarchal church women were able again and again to breach the dominant structures in the power of the Holy Spirit. But the church constantly distrusted both the women and the Spirit, condemning their works as extremism, heresy, paganism. The Holy Spirit was chained to official ministries and robbed of the renewing power.

Today, on the way to a new community, is it possible for us to begin trusting the Holy Spirit once again—the Spirit of extremists, crackpots, outsiders, visionaries, the Spirit of those who saw and touched life as did the women on Easter morning and whose reports seemed to the disciples as no more than "idle tales"? Can we, contrary to all reason, venture together on a new start in the name of this Spirit? Can the age-old suspicion and distrust of women— except when they speak cautiously, rationally, in a male language—be dispelled?

Jürgen:

Many find it hard to accept the feminist appeal to the Holy Spirit because they are not sure whether it is really the Holy Spirit or some other spirit to whom they are appealing. There have always been many different charismatic and spiritistic communities, inspired by a variety of spirits, not only the divine. Fearing the chaos of spirits, therefore, the church quite early in its history tied the Holy Spirit to the successive holders of the episcopal office, especially in the old doctrine of the monarchical episcopate. In addition, the Western church also tied the Spirit to the chain of Christology by means of the *Filioque* clause in the Nicene Creed. The Spirit then becomes simply the internal subjective reality of Christ, of the Word and Sacraments of the church. No room is then left for the creatively new or for the surprises of the Holy Spirit, not even room to expect them.

If we are to be ready for the new and surprising work of the Holy Spirit, I suggest we differentiate more clearly between the *source of the Spirit* and the *criterion for discerning the spirits*.

The source of the Spirit is God, and what comes from this source is as colorful and diverse as creation itself. This is why, when Christians in the New Testament spoke of the Spirit, they always spoke in superlatives of the fullness, the richness, the inexhaustibility of the Spirit. This was how they themselves experienced the Spirit. Everyone had gifts of the Spirit in abundance. None suffered any lack.

But the criterion for differentiating between the different spirits was for them the remembrance of the crucified Christ. Anything that could stand in the presence of the crucified Christ was divine Spirit. Anything that contradicted the crucified Christ, because it was the spirit of power or vanity, was rejected.

To come back to the story we began with, how did the women actually recognize the risen and living Christ? They might also have taken him for a ghost or some other figure. They recognized the risen Jesus at once because they had remained faithful to him right up to his death on the cross. The women recognized him at once by the marks of the nails and from his way of dealing with them, familiar to them from experience. Nor is the life-giving Spirit to be recognized in any other way. The Spirit brings us into the liberating community of Jesus and brings Jesus into our midst in a uniting way.

Elisabeth:

One question I find inescapable: how did it happen that this experience of the women disappeared so soon without a trace? How are we to explain the fact that almost two thousand years ago a viable community of women and men failed to materialize? Was it the fault of the women, who showed more confidence in the social structures than they did in themselves, obeyed men more than they did God, retreated into their ancient female roles, and failed to trust in the renewing power of the resurrection? In our different countries and different churches we champion the cause of the women. Some of these women are struggling simply to survive; others are claiming their right to be pastors or priests. It is a question of money, influence, teaching posts, a better social order. We live in different societies and have different assumptions.

There is one thing, it seems to me, which is important and which we all share: all of us need to begin again to trust ourselves and the renewing power of our religious experience; to trust our capacity to communicate life by all our senses and energies; not to give up in the face of overwhelming structures and never to lapse back again into an illegitimate obedience; to become ourselves again, in body, soul, and spirit, so that this spark may spread to men, to brothers and fathers, to mothers and children.

3

Male Domination and Women's Identity

Women and Men in New Community: Insights from Liberation Struggles

TISSA BALASURIYA, O.M.I.

The story of humankind is a long history of different forms of oppression. The domination of women by men is one of these.

There is a great deal of similarity in the cause of women and of people who have been oppressed due to race or class. In a special way there is a similarity in the struggle of women and of the people of the Third World (for lack of a better term). The similarities in the modes of domination indicate that the paths of liberation may also have similarities, and hopefully linkages.

It is also useful to recall that we are to a considerable extent not responsible for what we are—our sex, our race, and in some ways even our class. This consideration may help us to face these issues calmly and frankly even though they affect us deeply as oppressors and oppressed. In fact within every one of us there is something of the oppressor and oppressed.

Sex, Race, and Class

Sex is by nature biological, not determined by us, not (easily) changeable. Race is also by birth and historical in origin. Class is changeable, dependent on incomes, wealth, and status. However it is not easy to "declass" oneself, especially from a position of privilege. Sex is of a person; race and class are of groups.

Sexism, racism, and classism are of human social making. We seek liberation from sexism and not from sex; from racism, not from race. Class, however, is in itself undesirable. Therefore we desire a classless society. We

43

must recognize the biological, historical, cultural, and functional differences, but these should not make for the inequality of persons or groups. In this the weak, the poor, and the dominated can raise the consciousness of others through their struggles for identity, dignity, and equality.

Some Common Characteristics of Sex, Race, and Class Dominations

A common feature in sexism, racism, and classism is the tendency to regard others not as free, responsible persons, but as objects, things to be used for one's pleasure, power, or profit.

The dominated are made to exist for and in the function of the dominant. Even psychologically the dominated are made to accept the values, goals, priorities, and social structures of the oppressor. The relationships and roles in society and the terms of trade in economy are determined by the more powerful. Power is used to maintain the privilege of the dominant.

The status quo of privilege for the powerful is given the sanction of law, morality, culture, civilization, peace, religion, and even of holiness. The dominated are deprived of power; if they oppose their subjection, there is repression that can be psychological or perhaps physical and violent. The powerful may give "aid" to the weaker who are regarded as handicapped and unfortunate. But the relationships of superiority and inferiority are maintained. These are buttressed by the ideology, myths, and even theology advanced by the dominant. Consequently there is an enormous thwarting of the human potential of the weaker sex, race, and class, as well as an impoverishment of the dominant themselves.

Sexism

In cultures around the world men tend to determine the purposes, roles, and value of women's lives. Personalities of men are given priority in a male-dominated society. Women come in more as helpmates. A woman's personality is made to seek fulfillment in relation to a man. The man is considered the chief breadwinner as it is the work of the male that is considered more productive. Child caring is considered so much a concomitant of childbearing that the father leaves almost the totality of it to the mother. Yet women's household work is not considered to be of economic value.

Educationally women have generally had fewer opportunities than males. Hence also in employment.

Politics is considered normal for men and abnormal for women, except where women have been born to high rank, such as queens. It is men who decide; and they decide according to their perceptions and interests. Public institutions and work relationships are thus organized to take into account men's needs. Since women have often been excluded from the decision-making processes, they are generally less aware of the ramifications and consequences of economic and social policies.

If decisions in the churches are made by the ordained clergy and power in the churches is in their hands, then excluding women from ordination is a form of discrimination that denies women the benefits of the use of power in the churches. This is also to keep them away from serious participation as responsible persons in the life of the churches. This means they are doomed to be permanently marginalized.

Racism

Racism is an attitude which considers one race superior in rights and dignity to another and leads, as a consequence, to the oppression of one race by another. Racism can at a rather universal level affect the color groups of humanity: black, white, yellow, brown. Or it can be at local levels in the interrelation of races like Sinhalese and Tamil in Sri Lanka, or English and Welsh in Britain. Racism within a nation is different from racism among races. Racism within a nation is more closely related to language, religion, and culture. The land base of the racial groups is important for racial identity. Minority groups have particular difficulties when they are dominated by the majority race because they are generally unable to change their minority status.

Race is a powerful bond among people. Marriages are generally within one race group. Nationalism and patriotism are closely linked to race. The passions of racial enmity are often aroused in times of war or even in democratic elections. The survival of a race is a major cause that evokes human loyalties and sacrifices.

A dominant race tends to build political, economic, and social institutions and cultural traditions to serve its own interests and maintain domination over subject, or marginalized, races. Religion is invoked to legitimize such a position of power. Christian teaching concerning the need of baptism for salvation has resulted in the missionary impulse of the white race, a consciousness of their being the ''people of God'' over and against all other peoples.

Politically, the world system has been built up by white expansion, colonization, and imperialism. We must admit that there is and has been a grave situation of white colonization linked to a view of white superiority. The whole world system of modern nation-states has been formed by the expansion of the white race. Minority, or marginalized, races have to struggle to maintain their identity, to affirm their rights, and even to survive. The indigenous peoples are often made to feel that their quality of being is determined by adopting the culture and value patterns of their dominators. Women and men in the dominated races often cooperate in the exploitation of the minority, or marginalized, races.

In issues of discrimination and liberation from racism the common interests of women and men, who benefit from such a process, generally outweigh the differences between women and men of the same racial group. In the interests of families, clans, tribes, and castes, racial injustices are perpetuated by both women and men. The family system has a way of creating an identity among its members which can often give subjective legitimacy to much wrong done to others.

Race, class, and sex, instead of being forces which militate against each other, can combine to further the discrimination against different groups of persons. The myths of racial superiority are fostered within the family and by the educational system. Women and men can be equally racist and classist.

In the interrelations of the races the women of a more powerful race may be as much for domesticating the women of the weaker race, as their men may be. In this, sisterhood may not be a more powerful bond than the female-male relationship of the dominant race.

On the other hand, race and sex can also combine in the process of liberation. The revolutionary cause is stronger when women and men combine for a common objective. Freedom fighters are often impelled to take risks to their own lives in order to make life better for their families and descendants. Participation of women in the struggles of liberation of peoples and classes can help in developing the strengths and rights of women—though it is often the case that women are subjected to traditional forms of oppression once the actual struggle is over.

A much more relevant trend would be established if women and men could relate across their racial frontiers to identify with their sisters and brothers of another race, especially an oppressed race. It may be relevant to ask how sisterhood, due to the common interests of women, is a more potent force for such liberative alliances? How could the evils of patriarchy be seen as a greater common enemy, or danger, that the togetherness of women and men on racial lines. This is a question women of the oppressed races should ask their sisters of the oppressor races.

Classism

A class is a group of persons having similar economic interests. Differences in classes are intensified by income and the consequent access to opportunities in education and employment. Influence and power in most societies depend very much on one's class position.

As in sex and race the dominant class tends to form the social institutions, mentalities, myths, customs, and traditions to suit its own needs and advancement. The affluent class generally controls the means for influencing opinion—namely, education, mass media, institutions for maintaining law and order, and so forth.

State power within a country is generally controlled by the powerful class and thus becomes a means of perpetuating the domination of the wealthy. The poor, because of their divisions, lack of organization, purpose, and consequent powerlessness, continue to be poor.

In economic activity the relationships among the classes are such that the poorest receive much less income for the work they contribute to the productive process. The terms of trade are unfavorable to the poorer classes, to Third World peoples, and in general to women—all of whom are assigned functions which are less remunerative. Or rather what these groups do is depreciated in value. The price mechanism is a means by which certain privileges are retained.

In addition, class consciousness is deeply ingrained in persons. It is manifested in one's mentality as well as in one's possessions and demeanor. Social intercourse is mostly among persons of the same class. The life styles, the location of houses, the system of transportation, the recreation clubs, all help to maintain class differences.

The class system also influences families. Often marriages take place among members of the same race and broad socioeconomic class. Social relations are influenced by income levels and ownership of capital. Educational opportunities in free-enterprise countries depend more on class than on personal abilities, or even on sex or race. Indeed, in church services the classes do not really commune with each other, even though they sing the same hymns and receive the same Lord in Communion.

We have reason to hold that within the nation-states it is class that is the main dividing line, the major contradiction in society. Sex and race differences are often less important than economic divisions, unless of course race itself implies an economic discrimination as between blacks and whites in South Africa.

The priorities of the women's movements are different according to the race, class, or nation to which the women belong. Women of the European and North American continents are mainly concerned with obtaining equal rights with the men within their society. They do not necessarily have objectives of transforming their own social structures or international relations.

On the other hand, for the women of Asia, Africa, and South and Central America their main problems concern the entire social system in which they are involved together with their men. The greater oppression of women in the "Third World" is recognized as related to the ongoing exploitation of the poor countries and races by the rich and powerful nations. These considerations induce the women from the poorer countries to press for a more radical approach to the women's movements. They want the women to give priority to overall social transformation within their countries and in international relations.

The women's movements have not yet expressed themselves strongly on the liberation of other women from the structures of economic or racial domination in other countries. Antisexism alone does not have this dynamic of liberation from class and race domination. The same is true of the other struggles. The emancipation of the workers or of an oppressed race does not necessarily mean a triumph against male domination.

We see from this that the importance of each of these struggles cannot be reduced, and it is necessary to maintain the autonomy of the struggles. It is not a question of merely asking which is more important or whether we suppress one for the sake of another. It is also necessary that these struggles not be isolated from one another. The forces of exploitation gain by dividing the victims. Sometimes the oppression is twofold or triple and overlapping. A poor black woman is oppressed in her class, her race, and her sexuality. Liberation, to be satisfying to all, has to be integral.

Dissimilarities of Domination in Sexism from Racism and Classism

The experience of persons as sexual beings is in each individual woman and man. Each person has close links of love with someone of the other sex: spouse, parent, brother or sister, children, relatives.

A race or a class is a moral or legal entity. It is not one physical person. The experiences and memory of races and classes are collective and historical; their aspirations are beyond the lives of given individuals. The questions concerning the sexes are first personal and only secondly externalized in social relations in work—incomes. The issues of race and class are first collective and structural and secondly personal and internalized. The sexes are attracted toward each other: there is generally a closeness and identification that races and classes as collectivities cannot achieve. The reciprocity of the sexes is much more intimate than the complementarity of the races or the collaboration of classes as partners in economic life. Classes compete; races coexist; the sexes cohabit.

Considerations of sex tend to personalize issues. When dealing with women and men we touch individual persons—bodies, minds, wills, emotions—a psychosomatic whole. In race and class we deal with a collective psyche. Race and class domination is a common or community reality shared by many. Sex domination has a personal character.

Sex has, all the same, a strong social, economic, political, and cultural character. The domination of sex can and is socialized and expressed in the relationships of women and men in society. Income differences, status, even mentalities are very much the result of social conditioning and forces. Cheap female labor and prostitution are significant modes of sex exploitation.

In race and class relations the basic demand is for justice and dignity. In relationships between women and men more is demanded—understanding, sharing, and love.

While the modes of domination have similar characteristics the nature of the basic relationships between female and male are fundamentally different from those between groups such as race, class, caste, tribe, or religion. Women and men, it would seem, are made for each other. The liberation and fulfillment of one is inextricably linked to the liberation and fulfillment of the other.

These dissimilarities make the domination and the movements of liberation concerning the sexes a different kind of complexity from those concerning race and class.

Processes of Liberation

Our goal should be integral human liberation so that the relationships of persons and societies can be fulfilling for all persons everywhere. This requires an acceptance of persons and races by one another and the elimination of a society based on the exploitation of one class by another. This is an ideal, a utopia, almost an impossible dream. Yet the better urges of the human spirit and the promises of God in the Scriptures are of such a nature. In interpersonal relations perhaps a much deeper approximation to the ideal is possible and is dependent on us, than in the relations of race and class.

The interrelations, similarities, and differences in the forms of domination in sex, race, and class have an impact on the processes of liberation. These processes can be spoken of in general, though each situation requires individual consideration. The processes of liberation may be set down logically as follows.

1. *Awareness.* Awareness, especially by the dominated, of the problem and its deeper causes is essential to combat sexism, racism, and classism. Awareness is more than mere information. It implies an evaluation of the situation in terms of good and bad, desirable and undesirable—in relation to one's rights and duties and the goals for social life. With such a judgment the motivation for change can be developed. The oppressed must motivate themselves to struggle fearlessly against domination and to pay the price for it. The oppressor too needs a self-purification in order not to benefit from the exploitation of the other, to get rid of one's prejudices, and to work toward the goal of a just community. The dominated can contribute much to consciousness-raising among the oppressors.

The formation of a group is an irreplaceable step in liberation. Alone one is powerless, easily discouraged, or pushed to senseless excesses. The women's movements have learned much about the need and potentialities of groups for awareness building, motivation, mutual support, liberative action, and ongoing evaluation.

Friendships, alliances, and networks can grow from the functioning of groups. A wide mobilization of the oppressed is essential for a successful struggle. This can counter the divisions among the dominated, a major obstacle to liberation. The oppressors are clever at fostering and maintaining divisions.

2. *Option.* Flowing from these friendships, alliances, and networks is the personal and group option to struggle for integral liberation. This implies a will to change the situation, to face the obstacles on the path. Awareness of the obstacles—both within us and in society—is part of the process of struggle. Our internal, mental, psychic obstacles are the more difficult to overcome. Our determination to struggle must be maintained by our conviction in the justice of our cause.

The option to struggle is sustained by the struggle itself. We must strengthen ourselves against giving up, being frustrated, retreating, copping out, choosing the easier path of subservience, or even seduction. The awareness may bring a certain anger in the process, and anger can have a creative role in helping us to channel our discontent into action.

3. *Nonviolent Forms of Struggle.* There is a basic difference between violent and nonviolent forms of struggle. In race and class, physical violence has long been a way of seeking liberation—however sad or gruesome it may be. Between the sexes too there is much physical violence, often wife battering. Much violence is connected with sex. This is not to be a path to liberation in the winning of women's rights.

In securing the economic rights of women, such as equal opportunities in education, employment, and property ownership, the means may be similar to those used by the oppressed classes: creation of public opinion, trade unions, collective bargaining, lobbying, demonstrations, picketing, fasts, strikes, general strikes, all leading to changes in law and in practice.

The struggle for political rights will depend much on the stage of political evolution in a country. In politically democratic societies the methods may be more legal and ''parliamentary.'' In the dictatorial countries the questions of women's political rights would be closely linked to those of the rest of society as well. Here methods may have to range from passive resistance to active struggle for the alternative society. In all countries women can refuse to join the armed forces or to work for arms manufacture.

In the cultural sphere women should not agree to be used as objects of pleasure, attraction, advertisement, or even of mere beauty. School curricula, the mass media, newspapers, films, and TV need to be contested in this type of sexist presentation of women. This is an extremely difficult level of struggle because of our internal subjugation by the prevailing values. Women are the largest consumer market in the world. Their refusal to participate in such domestication will also be a contribution to the other struggles of world justice.

4. *A Common Loyalty to Humanity and Nature.* For a holistic approach to an integrated human liberation we must transcend the limitations of the ghettos to evolve a common loyalty to the total human cause and the care and destiny of our planet (and universe). New world economic order, including a just and peaceful redistribution of land and resources among the peoples of the world, is essential for this.

In relations of women and men the personal conversion is essential and primary. It has to be ongoing for each person, relationship, society, and generation. In this sense, the women's struggle can make a contribution to a permanent and ultimate transformation of persons to accept the other in her or his otherness. In so far as this is realized we can approximate the society freed of oppression and exploitation and build on human understanding the new community of women and men, that is, the substance of the kingdom of God on earth.

All women are half of humanity—will they be together in the struggle to transform this earthly home for survival itself and for justice? This is not easy—*a deep personal conversion and a radical transformation of structures are required:* a transformation and a revolution such as the world has never seen before. It is, however, a very hard task fraught with much suffering.

The Sense of Self in Women and Men: In Relation to Critical World Questions

JEAN BAKER MILLER

I am extremely happy to be here with you and to present to you some ideas that I have developed in the course of my work. Because these ideas must inevitably reflect work that has been done in one country only, they are probably limited by national modes of thought. They are probably limited also by the tradition of thought which has developed in Western culture. Therefore, I am especially grateful to have the opportunity to hear people from other traditions and to experience their comments and criticisms.

Certain social and psychological dilemmas plague contemporary Western ''man.'' One oft-sighted issue is the lack of a convincing higher purpose, an interest beyond self-interest. A related issue is the inability to find a sense of community or even a sense of communication with others. A third is the failure to organize our knowledge and technology for the maximum benefit of human beings. And a fourth is the inability to encompass the development of others and to act on a basis of belief that one's own interest is synonymous with the interests of others. I mean by this—to truly encompass the development of the disadvantaged and oppressed peoples of the world and within one's own country. These themes run through much of modern social commentary and literature. As a psychiatrist, one can often observe that they are also prominent in clinical work with men; and in clinical work one can see their relationship to the sense of self which has shaped men's development.

I believe that these dilemmas relate to our culture's conceptions of the kind of persons men should be and the kind of persons women should be. Perhaps one way to think about these issues is to ask as a starting point, but only as

52

a starting point, what happens to people when they exist in unequal relationship to each other—that is, when there is inequality of not only material resources but the usual concomitants: inequality of authority, of power, and also of value in terms of how a culture values its people.

A great many things happen, and these have been written about in many different ways. To take one aspect we might say that in most societies certain parts of the total human potential—those parts which are held to be most important, most valuable in any culture—tend to be kept in the domain of those people who are considered the full-fledged members of that society.

In our culture the most valued and rewarded positions and functions (or jobs) are those which have been almost exclusively white men's, as is the encouragement of the psychological characteristics which are *considered* most valuable. So too is the power as well as the acceptable ways of using power.

Those parts of life which a culture needs but doesn't value highly tend to be relegated to other people, and these people are usually considered less important or inferior. These parts of life can range from, and usually do include, such obvious things as cleaning up for the full-fledged people or providing bodily comforts, such as comfortable surroundings, clean clothes, feeding, and the like. But they also include certain other much more complex aspects of existence.

In general, all groups of people who are seen as less important—women, in certain particularly complex ways—can then become the "carriers" for the social group as a whole of certain necessities. They become carriers of necessary aspects of the experience of all, of things which pertain to the group as a whole, things that are crucial but tend to be considered of less importance. Usually they are hidden, unsolved, denied, distorted.

Precisely because women have lived lives in the domain of these essential but less-valued areas, women as a group have tended to develop psychological motivations and characteristics which we have not been able to recognize fully and which we are still only beginning to understand. I would like to give some suggestions of what these characteristics and motivations are. I want to emphasize the two-sidedness of these characteristics. I think, too, that they all should eventually be defined and described in more appropriate terms. For the moment I should like to say that I see them as the basis of psychological strengths, and also, as a basis for a more advanced form of life than either sex has yet known. Yet, these characteristics have been defined as weaknesses or worse, and women themselves have generally thought of them in that way.

Some, or perhaps all of these characteristics, apply particularly to the dominant, white, United States culture, but perhaps to other cultures as well. In any case, I believe that it is important to try to understand them because this culture effects the structure of the total society with which all people have to deal in the United States. This structure, along with other Western cultures, has also had a major effect on the rest of the world.

One large topic involves an area that is a central one in psychological fields today, that of feelings of weakness, helplessness, vulnerability, and neediness. These are feelings which we have all known. In the extreme they are most terrifying. In the realm of psychological theory, they are feelings that most schools of psychological thought postulate at the root cause of various major disastrous psychological problems.

It is clear that men are encouraged to overcome but also to dread and deny feeling weak or helpless, and women have been encouraged to cultivate this state of being. One brief example may illustrate this contrast. A young woman whom I'll call Mary, a very good and very low-paid hospital worker and married mother of two children, was offered a new and difficult job as coordinator of a new medical care team, still at quite low pay. She immediately worried about her ability to carry out the work and felt weak and helpless in the face of the formidable tasks required. She would easily convince herself that she was really unable to do it, and she should probably forget the whole idea. Incidentally, Mary was a working-class woman but I have seen these same feelings in many women who hold advanced degrees including women in high positions in some of our most prestigious institutions.

Mary's worry was in some measure appropriate because it was a difficult job, if one is really aware of what patients need and if one tries to attend to these needs in hospital settings as they are constituted today in the United States. Mary was, however, extremely able. She had some remnants of common women's problems. She had trouble admitting to, and could easily deny and lose sight of, her strengths. This image of herself as inadequate and weak was one to which she still held on even though it was in contradiction to her true competence and resources.

In contrast with Mary and many other women who cannot really see their own strengths is another common example—a man's situation. A man whom I'll call Charles sought a higher position at work, and when one did come through for him, he seemed initially pleased. Just before the job began, Charles developed some physical symptoms, but characteristically he didn't talk about them. His wife, Ruth, herself a full-time worker, immediately suspected that these symptoms were due to Charles's anxiety about facing the new job. Knowing him well, however, she didn't say so directly. She did open up the topic in the only way she felt able. She suggested that perhaps they should make some changes in their diet, their sleeping habits, and the like. Charles's initial reaction was to become angry, sarcastically telling Ruth to stop bothering him and to leave him alone. Only later did he admit to himself and then to his wife that he could see that when he feels most uncertain and most in need of help—and especially if anyone should act as if she or he perceived his neediness—he can only react with anger.

Ruth's attempts opened up the possibility of dealing with these feelings. Charles couldn't have initiated the process at all. He couldn't even respond to Ruth's initiation in the first instance, but this time, fairly soon afterwards, he could catch himself in the act of denying his own experience. Otherwise, Ruth could easily have remained rejected and hurt and the situation might have escalated in mutual recrimination or withdrawal, as it had many times before—all times when Charles was feeling most vulnerable, helpless, and needy.

It is important to note here that Ruth was not being rewarded for her abilities. She was demonstrating several abilities which I shall spell out further in a moment. Instead, she was being made to suffer for them by anger and rejection. This is one small example of how some women's strengths are not only not recognized but punished; not only in the public world but within the family, and even here Ruth was not stating her real perceptions openly. She was still using sensitive so-called feminine ways or wiles.

In all societies no one emerges full-blown or full-grown. The most valuable of human necessities and the thing that makes us feel alive, I think, is the ability to grow psychologically. Incidentally, however, this is a statement that I would like to ask people from other cultures about. It may be only a provincial North American way of thinking. This necessarily involves an ongoing process. A necessary part of the process is the ability to recognize and allow oneself to know feelings of weakness when these feelings exist and to know that these are not shameful, but rather feelings from which one can move on—but can move on only if the feelings are to some extent experienced and examined. Only then can one hope to find some appropriate path away from weakness and helplessness. That women are much more willing to admit to feelings of weakness or vulnerability may be obvious, but I think that we have not recognized the importance of this factor. The forced flight from vulnerability forecloses large parts of growth and consciousness for men. Women then, in this sense both superficially and deeply, are more closely in touch with the experience of living, at least living as we have known it so far—that is to say, in touch with reality.

There is a further social point here—the fact that these feelings have been generally associated with being "womanly," hence unmanly, serves to reinforce the humiliation and the silence of men who have such experiences (and this is, of course, all men) and to encourage the attack on women who have been made to embody weakness. This process reduces the culture's serious consideration of the whole matter. Removing the feelings from the realm of the acceptable and the recognized keeps the total society from admitting that we all experience too much danger and doubt as we attempt to grow up and make our way in the difficult and threatening circumstances in which we live.

Women, meanwhile, have provided all sorts of personal and social supports which help to keep men going. These props enable men, and therefore the total culture, to sustain a mythology and refusal to admit to the need for better arrangements for all. Everyone loses in the end but the loss is kept obscure.

As illustrated by this first topic all of the qualities of women are multisided. They reflect their origins in areas which were devalued; there are, therefore, qualities which some "advanced women" have sometimes wanted to cast aside or to get away from, believing that these were the hallmarks of inferiority. Indeed, that is how they have been labeled. Also, these qualities have been the sources of many problems for women. They become reasons for us women to devalue ourselves further for feeling these things—as in these examples for feeling the experience of weakness. On the other hand, these qualities represent women's greater and specific experience with key aspects of our total culture's problems.

Some of the other topics may illustrate these points further. One is the even broader subject of emotions in general. Women have been said to be "more emotional" and here too have been made to be the carriers of emotion, but there is no such thing as "more emotional." Every thought and action is simultaneously emotional. What is probably true is that women have been more attuned to the emotional aspects which are present in every event. Male culture has emphasized rationality, so-called problem solving, analytical thinking, and the like. The emotions have not been seen as an aid in this pursuit but rather as an impediment, often close to an evil. There is a long tradition of trying to dispense with, or at least control or neutralize, the emotions rather than valuing, embracing, and cultivating the contributing strengths of emotion. Being in touch with the emotions does not mean that one cannot be intelligent or analytical if the situation calls for it. In fact, one can analyze better. One can grasp the totality of a situation more fully. But that is not how it has been made to appear. Ruth, for example, grasped the totality of the situation when Charles didn't. But she couldn't bring this forward into the family interchange. There has been an attempt to push emotion into the realm of women whence both emotions and women are maligned.

Women have been encouraged to be involved with emotion and also to be concerned with personal relationships. But out of this women do have a greater ability to let themselves know and therefore to truly believe that doing something is important, is satisfying, only if it occurs within the context of relatedness—or more likely only if it is accompanied by the kind of emotion which leads to a heightened and increased connection with others and to an enhanced inner sense of emotional satisfaction and well-being. The point is that this is true for men too, but men have not been able to encompass this as a primary concern. The troubles have come from the distortions which both sexes have been taught, and for women the belief that full satisfaction should come only from relationships and often only from relationships at any price.

Another part of life which has been placed in women's domain is that whole part of life which we might call fostering the development of other people. It seems clear that our culture has said that men will do the important work; women will tend to the lesser task of helping other human beings to develop. This has often been called nurturing, caretaking, and the like, but I believe that these words don't fully define the complex activity of so caring for another person that you foster and enhance that other person's development, a forward movement. I think the terms, the very words which have been used to describe all of women's activity, tend to minimize and to hide the complexity and the worth of this activity.

At the outset, this dichotomy means that women do have greater experience with fostering the development of other people. It also means that from an early age women develop the sense that playing a part in the development of others is an essential part of one's identity, of what it is to be a person, and also a part that can be very satisfying and can enlarge one's own development. Men are not encouraged to develop this sense as an inner and thoroughgoing *requirement* of their sense of what it is to exist, to be a person.

Likewise, it is part of this dichotomy that our major institutions—our economic, political, cultural institutions—do not then embody this requirement as a primary principle. To the extent that it exists, it has been left for women to "fill in."

Now women are seeing that participating in the growth of others without the right and opportunity for growth themselves is one clear form of oppression. It leads to many complex kinds of problems. The dilemmas of our society may relate precisely to the fact that this requirement—this sense that at bottom one must participate in the development of others and must foster the development of others—has not been made of the male sex, the sex which controls the operation and the thinking of all of our institutions and, therefore, controls all of us. So long as only women practice this activity in their lives and incorporate this way of being into their psychology, and so long as this remains a devalued part of life—one that is only good enough for women to do—everyone will continue to live and work in places not devoted to the development of the people who spend their lives in them. And our culture will not be able to embrace as a primary guiding principle the concept that it is truly responsible for fostering the development of its people and all people. Our culture will not be able to even conceive of such a concept and it is placed in the realm of the inconceivable—the unreal. We will be led to believe that it cannot be done.

There is time now to mention only one more topic, although there are many more. This one might be called creativity. I am not referring here to artistic creativity in the gifted few, but rather I am saying that as a person goes through each stage of life that person has to keep breaking through to a new vision if she or he is to go on, to keep living. This is a vision of what a person is and how she or he relates to her/his vision of the world and others in it. This all appears very different if one is four years old, or twenty or fifty. We have to somehow construct these concepts so that we feel at least a minimum sense of worth, if we are to go on. This inner, very personal kind of making and integrating, this creativity, does not usually go on in open and well-articulated ways. But it goes on.

In recent years women are the people who are trying to do this creating in a more open fashion. Women are struggling to create a new concept of what it is to be a person. This effort extends to the deepest inner reaches. But even in the past women had to do more innovative work in an inner, psychological sense; that is, in a society in which the most valued qualities of that society did not apply to women, women have had to create some inner sense of what it means to be a worthwhile person, which was then different from that most valued in the culture. So, for example, the traditional woman had to effect enough of a creative, internal transformation of values to believe that fostering other peoples' development contributed to her sense of being a person even if the inner conversion was not sufficient and was often accompanied by many problems. In this sense even women who have lived in the traditional way have created an inner, and therefore a very real, set of advanced values. This doesn't mean that women were thereby rewarded or recognized for it. Quite pointedly they are not, and they have often felt themselves of little value, as for example, in that common phrase in the West, "I am only a housewife and mother."

Some women have created other kinds of lives, and all women have usually had to do work in the field or factory in addition. But a woman who has taken her work seriously, as did Mary in the first example, had until recently often felt herself in violation of the prevailing system of values that said there must be something wrong with her for even being so interested in something else. Any woman who has gone beyond her assigned realm has had to create an inner conception that guided and sustained her, however imperfectly.

Today women are struggling to go on from this point. In recent years it has become apparent to many women that we absolutely must create new conceptions of what it means to be a person if we are to deal with some of the key problems in our very own lives. Thus, women are today raising this struggle to a much more widespread, conscious, and accessible level.

Now in saying these things, so far, I may have created many misunderstandings. Let me examine just a few. I do not want to say that women are more virtuous or saintly, that these relations relate to anything that is biological, or that women should stay in their secondary place—far from it. What I do want to say is that our culture is, so far, an imperfect one, built on a restricted conception of the total human potential and that this affects women directly and deeply. Certain essential aspects of the human potential of women have not been provided or even recognized. These aspects have been "carried" by women, filled in and devalued, so that women have been unable to appreciate these parts and to bring them forward fully in action and in thought.

But there is another side to this dynamic. In the course of projecting into women's domain some of its most troublesome and problematic necessities, our culture may not have simultaneously delegated to women what it may have tried to call humanities "lower needs." But, rather, it has provided the missing pieces—those pieces necessary for humanity's attainment of its highest necessities—those things which we all need and want but have not been able to grasp. We have not been able to really believe in them as much as most of us often want to. I mean by "missing pieces" the ongoing growth of such things as mutuality, cooperation, and creativity. Truly these elements are in human beings and are always necessary for human life and growth. They have, however, been hidden and made to appear as if they do not exist, as if they were unreal. Still, women have been living them and practicing them. And men have been encouraged—forced—to leave mutuality, cooperation, creativity, and so forth to women and have been prevented from encompassing them. How could a dominant group encompass these things and encourage their flourishing? They inevitably act against a system of dominance.

Today, it is women who perceive very acutely that they must openly and consciously struggle for these missing pieces if we are to attain even the beginnings of personal integrity. As women put their struggles forward into the open social arena, they are inevitably raising issues which are at the core of the total culture's major dilemmas.

In summation, I would say that women are one major (basic) group of unimportant people. And the importance of unimportant people is that as they—we—search for the first basic requirements of human integrity, we inevitably bring to light the parts of life which we have been "carrying" for everyone. When we say that we will no longer carry these alone, then everyone will have to find ways to incorporate these parts of life into himself and herself and so create or change the total social order so that these parts of life become conceivable and doable.

As women continue to describe their lives accurately, and not in the distorted descriptions made by others, and as women define their *own* needs and put these forward, I believe we will find the clues to what has been entrapping everyone.

As women continue to work toward this goal and are joined by men and children who grasp these visions, we can move toward finding the paths out of our central dilemmas, those which diminish all and are threatening to actually destroy our planet.

4

The Energizing Force
of Tradition

Orthodox Tradition as
a Resource for the Renewal
of Women and Men in Community

ELISABETH BEHR-SIGEL

"What *resources*—or better what *inspiration*—for a renewed human community do you derive from the tradition of your church?" I was asked to respond to this question, in a paper to be presented at one of the plenaries, on the very day I was leaving for Sheffield, because the original speaker was prevented from attending our meeting. It was perhaps rash of me to accept the assignment, and I apologize for the improvised nature of my text. It will be a spontaneous response, there having been no time to think it over and to compose a well-balanced text. As we say in French, *"Faute de grives on mange des merles"* (which in English would correspond to: "Half a loaf is better than no bread").

When reflecting on the topic, I was first of all arrested by the word tradition and its meaning. What is the tradition of the church? Quite obviously—but ignored by some—a distinction has to be made between a multifarious tradition and *the* tradition of the church, a distinction which is not always easy to define. There are popular traditions, family traditions, religious traditions related to the various cultures; and these traditions are not to be discarded as such. Within non-Christian cultures, they have often been seeds of the gospel—*logoï spermatikoi*—preparing for the coming of the one Logos. Among the peoples that the church has evangelized—however imperfectly this has always been done—the popular traditions carry with them elements that belong to the genuine tradition of the church. But they are not identical with it.

An Orthodox will not consider the tradition—contrary to what was expressed here—as "a collection of experiences and hopes of the past." For him or her the tradition is the very life of the church and its continuity is an ever-renewed inspiration. Both are the work of the Holy Spirit. The tradition finds its expression in beliefs, doctrines, and rites, as well as in the popular traditions I have just mentioned. But at the same time it goes beyond them. The tradition is essentially the dynamic of faith, hope, and love. It has its origin in the event of Pentecost and even before that in the encounter of a few women with the risen Christ on Easter morning, and from there it has been propagated like a wave train throughout the world and the centuries. It is a conveyor of energy; it is a ferment unceasingly raising and activating the dough of the institutions; it is the place of an ever-renewed event, a place where each of us in community with all (e.g., the "communion of saints") can meet the Lord of the church in an ever-renewed way.

Faithfulness to the tradition does not mean sacralization of the past, of the history of the church. Tradition is not a kind of immutable monster, a prison in which we would be confined forever. It is a stream of life, driven and impregnated by the energies of the Holy Spirit, a stream which unavoidably carries historical, and therefore transitory, elements and even ashes and cinders. Sometimes it seems to stand still as if imprisoned in a layer of ice, but under the rigid frozen surface the clear waters of spring run. It is our task, with the help of God's mercy, to break through the ice, especially the ice in our slumbering frozen hearts. Then, when our hearts have become "burning within us" again, like those of the disciples of Emmaus, we will recognize the Lord and the Lord will explain to us the "passages which refer [sic] to himself in every part of the scriptures" (Luke 24:27, *NEB*). In us and from us, the tradition will become a spring of living water again. "From this ancient source," says a contemporary Orthodox spiritual father, "we will draw new strength" to respond to the problems of our day.

This renewal of tradition is also our concern as we are gathered here in Sheffield: a concern for a "new community," from which all forms of domination, of slavery, of exploitation exerted by a human being or group on others will be banished—a concern which the church is called to illuminate in the light of the gospel. The church must be the sign and the seed in humankind's history of this new eschatological community.

This aspiration for a "new community" is one of the signs of our time. But is it something really new? Is it not rather a renewed awareness—unfortunately often deviated—of the old baptismal faith, and a deeper understanding of the existential and ethical implications of the grace given in baptism as a participation in the death and resurrection of Christ and through Christ as an access to new life—this grace, which, according to the mysterious design of the Triune God, is extended to all humankind (''Go forth therefore and make all nations my disciples; baptize men [sic] everywhere in the name of the Father and the Son and the Holy Spirit,'' [Matt. 28:19, *NEB*]); a grace offered to all and gathering all those who receive it into one body, making each one of them individually, whatever his or her race, culture, sex, social status, an equally precious and necessary stone of ''God's building'' (1 Cor. 3:9).

''Baptized into union with him, you have all put on Christ as a garment. There is no such thing as Jew and Greek, slave and freemen, male and female, for you are all one person in Christ Jesus'' (Gal. 3:27, *NEB*). This proclamation of Paul, which does not abolish the differences but does away with all the contempt and enmity that may exist between them, has resounded through the centuries. In the Orthodox church, it is solemnly sung at each baptism and at the great baptismal feasts of Easter and Pentecost. But, you will ask, what about the empirical realities in our so-called Christian societies and nations? As Orthodox Christians, together with all other baptized Christians, we cannot but confess, collectively and individually, our infidelity to the ''celestial vision.'' This is the tragedy of our historical existence that is not yet transfigured by the light of Christ, though already recipient of the first fruits of the new life. *''Semper justus, semper peccator''* (''always justified, always sinners'') as Luther said, a statement that the Orthodox ascetics and fathers in some sense would make their own. ''The whole church is a church of penitents,'' said one Syrian father.

Yet we must not yield to a kind of morbid masochism by making a caricature of the teaching and the praxis of the church, as having as an aim the oppression of the weak by the powerful, as if God had abandoned his people. I am deeply disturbed by a certain way of criticizing, of globally and one-sidedly condemning the historical church as has been done even here in this meeting, though I am fully aware of the imperfections, errors, and sins of Christian people. This is a criticism and a condemnation not only with reference to the community to which I belong and in whose depths I perceive the fullness of the catholic church—of the *kat'holon* church—but also with reference to other ecclesial bodies in which apostles and saints have again and again been called forth by the Holy Spirit.

What I am referring to specifically is the patriarchal model which should be defined more precisely. The so-called patriarchal model has certainly influenced the institutional structures of the various Christian churches. It has marked their mentalities. The church, while anticipating the kingdom of God, is also a historical reality *in* this world and therefore has not escaped this influence. The patriarchal model is not *wholly* negative in its ideal view of the family and of society. It does not necessarily imply lack of respect toward women. Within its structures and through a language which seems to remain patriarchal, the church has brought forth a radically new message.

St. Paul is accused of having exhorted the wife to be submitted to her husband. But what is ignored is that this recommendation is made in the context of and following a much more general exhortation, one of lovingkindness and service. The chapter opens with these words: "Be subject *to one another* out of reverence for Christ" (Eph. 5:21, *NEB*, italics added). It is true that this verse is often forgotten by the moralists in the church. In the same way, Paul's preaching lifts the union of man and woman, even its fleshly aspect, to the dignity of a sign of the mysterious love of Christ and the church, for example, of supreme love, a love so deep that each one gives himself or herself up to the other, a love in which there is no room for either dominator or dominated.

In the patristic times, St. John Chrysostom, who speaks very disparagingly of the coquettish and prattling women of his time, solemnly states that the woman can be the "head" of the man, his guide, responsible for his salvation, when she surpasses him in courage and spiritual strength. He also recommends to the husband not to be led to ruling over his wife as over a slave and to ask of his wife, as the mother of his children, not lavish obedience, but the love of a *free* woman. To acknowledge this, to acknowledge that the light of Christ was thus able to transfigure patriarchal customs, does not mean that the church should perpetuate them. It is the ferment of the gospel that shatters the old oppressive and outdated structures. I recognize the genuine tradition of the church in a women's movement which claims that women are to be respected as free and responsible persons. It is in the dynamic of the authentic tradition (and not in ephemeral ideologies) that we find the source of eternal life, the source of our real liberation. In line with the energizing force of this tradition we are called (following the example of the scribe of the gospel who draws from his treasure new and old things—*nova et vetera*) to invent new styles of communal life, new styles of family life in our society and church.

Driven by the breath of the Spirit swelling the sails of the boat—the church, borne by the mighty stream of life and grace—true tradition, we shall sail forth with faith, hope, and love toward the new continents that God has designed for us. With discernment we shall make use of the human sciences: psychology, sociology, even of psychoanalysis and Marxist analysis. As interpretative sciences rather that exact sciences, these can enable us to disclose, up to a certain extent, the mechanisms of the behavior of the fallen Adam, the determinisms that hang heavily on a humanity entangled in its anxieties, its egoism, its contradictory desires. Real faith in God, the one who is *altogether other* and in the good news, the radical newness that he proclaims to humankind, need not fear these sciences. Yet these sciences prove unable by themselves, when not accompanied by a deep change (*metanoïa*), to create a new future. They prove unable to haul man out of the cave, in which, according to Plato's profound myth, he is shackled facing the wall. This strength of overcoming is given to the believer who in his or her faith freely clings to the word of God and the vision granted to the church. The believer receives it in the communion of the saints of all peoples and all times, in solidarity with those men and women still immersed in chaos, but over whom sweeps the wind of the Spirit like a dove (Gen.1:2).

What is this vision of a human community that faith opens up in the framework of the historical tradition of the Orthodox church? To describe it, or at least to suggest its essential features, two icons will perhaps be more effective than an abstract theological discourse which would also require more time than is available. Unfortunately I cannot present them in a way so that all of you can see them, but some of you may know them.

Icons, as you may know, are those pictures in front of which the Orthodox people pray because through the pictures of Christ and his saints the believer receives the mysterious presence of him who is beyond all images and in whose image humankind, man and woman, was created. A father of the church reports the following words of a heathen: "Show me thy man and I shall know who thy God is." In the perspective of the fathers of the Eastern church, this sentence could also be inverted: "Show me thy God and I shall tell thee what human being thou art called to become." For they say: "God made himself man so that man may become God." This God in whose image man and woman were created, according to Genesis 1, and in whose likeness they are both called to grow, is neither the impersonal one, the faceless absolute of the philosophers, nor the solitary sovereign of a certain form of theism. He is the one God in three persons of the ancient symbols of Christian faith; he is the "Lord of love," as a modern Orthodox father has called him. Such is the mystery of communion, of the fullness of personal life entirely shared, given, and received, that a fourteenth-century Russian monk tried to give impression to by creatively renewing an old iconographic theme. Inspired by the Old Testament story of Abraham welcoming three men to Mamre (Gen. 18: 1–6), Andreï Rublev, following a traditional allegorical exegesis of this passage, represents the persons of the Trinity as three angels of marvelous youth and beauty sitting around a table. They bow to each other in a most graceful attitude which expresses both the absence of all constraints and the total giving up of one to the other. They do not touch one another, but their three figures form a circular movement in a kind of dance. One stream of life runs through them. They are distinct and yet one. Each is himself in the very gesture with which he bows his face to his neighbor and in the convergent movement of their heads. In the middle of the table there is a cup. It stands for the sacrifice of the Lamb "slaughtered from the beginning," the cross of the Son with whom the Father and the Spirit sympathize in the full etymological meaning of this word. Around the three in the center of the picture, trees, cupolas, and roofs can be recognized. They represent the physical universe and the historical world of humankind. They too seem to be caught in the same circular movement. Led by its coryphaeus, Christ, reconciled humanity and together with it the whole world join the divine dance. In the light that emanates from the center, they are not engulfed in the divinity, but, at their level, for example, the level of the creature, they participate in the Trinitarian life. This Trinitarian life—through the ecclesial vision of which the iconographer is the interpreter—appears both as the foundation in which any genuine human community is rooted and the fulfillment to which it tends. The icon transmits a call; it invites us to enter the mystery of communion, without confounding and annihilating personal existence, a mystery of self-denial without servility, of mutual love and giving up in total freedom.

To conclude I would like to mention rapidly another iconographic theme: that of the so-called *Deesis*. It is an icon that is traditionally to be seen in every church, above the "royal doors" of the iconostasis. Together with that of the *Trinity* it represents one of the major expressions of Orthodox spirituality. In the center, there is Christ in majesty. Converging toward him and heading a procession of men and women who represent the saints of all ages, there are, on one side, John the Baptist and, on the other, the praying Virgin, the Theotokos. Both processions move toward Christ as toward a fulfillment: the fulfillment of humanity in God, in which neither male nor female is denied, but in which their opposition is overcome by their conversion to the Lord in their mutual relationship as well as in their individual personalities.

Meditating on this icon, I read in it a message that we have to make ours more and more and to translate into reality: God, in his infinite respect for and love of his creature, wants to associate with his work of salvation, man and woman, or in a deeper sense, the male and female principles. They are represented by John the Baptist, the violent one, whose violence turned inward finds vent in his struggle against the possessive and egoistic self, and by Mary, the humble servant, who by accepting the Spirit as her bridegroom became Theotokos, the mother of the *Theos-Anthrōpos*. The Baptist, as the archetype of the law, in all its strictness, and of bitter and fruitful repentance, prepares the way and straightens the highway. But it is a woman, whose very femininity is a sign of the acceptance of the other, the supremely other—who is the beginning of the new humanity in which God makes himself flesh. "There is not a mother's son greater than John and yet the least in the kingdom of God [for example, the least of those born in Spirit] is greater than he" (Luke 7:27-28, *RSV*). And it is a woman who represents these "little ones," the "poor" of whom it is said that "the kingdom of Heaven is theirs" (Matt. 5:3, *NEB*). All this means that the humble acceptance by faith of the divine Word, wondering humility at the mystery of God's love manifested in Jesus Christ, is the evangelical value par excellence, whose symbol, according to scriptural symbolism, is feminine. In this essence the church, which includes both men and women, is essentially feminine, whereas each of those who compose it is called to take up his or her part in Christ and also the part of the "other" who is in him or her.

What connection is there, you may ask, between the mystical vision expressed by an icon and our daily struggle for a real community of men and women, between all human beings, whatever their race, culture, economic standing? I believe that the "celestial vision" can be a powerful source of inspiration in the struggle. It will prevent our struggle from getting diluted in a utopic immanentistic humanism, or from sinking into the moving sands of violence, sometimes denying the reconciled community toward which we aim. I say that it can be an *inspiration* for and not a solution for the specific problems set by specific situations. The "celestial vision" must inspire action. It does not exempt us from the effort of understanding and analyzing the problems, an effort which must precede and guide any action. The Western temptation is to neglect or to ignore the vision; while the temptation of the Orthodox is to dodge the effort necessary to translate it into the present situation. One finds pleasure in it and it is sometimes an alibi for laziness, a justification for a sclerosed conservatism, pretending not to examine the questions raised by modern peoples both inside and outside of the church. And yet the apostles and the "fathers," in their times, did not refuse to respond to these questions. They responded with the spiritual achievement of a "crucified intelligence," as Father Georges Florovsky said, which dared to invent new words and to inspire new attitudes in faithfulness to the evangelical and apostolic nucleus of the ecclesial faith. It is in the same faithfulness, according to the spirit of the "fathers," that we have to go forth here and now.

Resources in the Tradition for the Renewal of Community

ROSE ZOÉ-OBIANGA

"The urgency of radical changes needing to be carried out in order to improve the life of millions of Christian men and women in the world cannot be denied by anyone."[1]

There is no denying that we are living in a very difficult period, afflicted as it is by many different crises, inasmuch as the most obvious fact is that the traditional models of organizing community life of Christians have become fetters on freedom, hampering the fulfillment of the faith of committed men and women; or again are on the point of falling into disuse because henceforth unsuited to the demands and needs of Christ.

Faced with this situation intolerable for all, some people, and in particular the WCC through its member churches, as well as the Roman Catholic Church, have set off in search of new and untried methods, with a view to promoting the renewal of the Christian community.

The failure seems complete in the matter of the normal and harmonious integration of women in the decision-making bodies of our churches, and in respect of the demystification of structures and education of domination inherent in them. Frustrated, women find themselves "limited to special and secondary roles; their status often seems higher in the surrounding society than in the churches themselves."[2] The impression this state of affairs leaves on non-Christians and alert observers is that, strictly speaking, there is no place for women in the church.

So "women today like other groups of the oppressed find themselves on the point of protesting against the injustices which dominate our different churches"[3] and of asking, indeed demanding, a change for the good of all, for the fulfillment of all, for relations between women and men which are a little more "Christian."

The African context in which I live—to return to the tradition so as to try there to draw upon elements which are capable of responding adequately to this urgent need—tends at once to resolve two interrelated problems, that of our identity and that of our participation.

But, first of all, there is a fact which cannot be ignored. The African culture and tradition have long been neglected, even denied, not only by the colonizers (and the missionaries) but also, and above all (and the whole tragedy of the situation lies here), by the completely alienated first African Christian elites.

In the absence of any appropriate theological reflection, these elites had contributed (unwittingly) to the destruction of their African cultural personality in order to become Christians. For them, to follow Jesus meant completely abandoning one's own and putting on another. If we are to link up again with the tradition, therefore, we have to do so with only the scraps of all that constituted our originality. But the need for such an effort is now recognized by all, especially when it is noted that Western Christianity is in no way exempt from the cultural elements of European and North American peoples which have channeled it in the whole world throughout the centuries.

For Simone de Beauvoir the fundamental problem for women (and I would add for us Africans) is the problem of identity. The present image of women is only a complex and complicated fabrication of male-dominated societies. This is all the more true for us because we have lived and experienced it at two levels, as Africans and as women.

God created man and woman for a community life. And if there is conflict, if the participation of women has been denied, this was after and not before the Fall. The deplorable situation which exists in my society at the present time does not derive from the tradition. The regression noted should make us reflect on our real and sincere acceptance of Christ's message of liberation for all human beings.

If then it is up to women themselves to define their own identity—as men have done, as the African men have done and still do according to Awa Thiam in her book[4]—and their own participation in the community life, this is by 'no means to say that women will transform themselves into men, still less make the world solely and completely feminine. But rather, they will incite and lead men and women to play the card of *complementarity* to the very end.

Language

As all of you know, language is the supreme instrument for expressing human thought and philosophy. But here again "the tendency of the colonialist was to suppress the local languages, to despise them both in practice and in speech. . . ."[5] Yet language offers us the depths of the mentality of peoples and especially of oppressed peoples.

Take two simple examples in my language which will be able to help us to understand that the reference to the structure of our different languages in Africa proves that the utilization of the language is one of the "final defenses against alienation."[6] First, in the story of the act of creation, we are confronted with three essential and fundamental human units. The text of Genesis says (Gen 1:27): "God created *môt* in his own image. He *NyE* created in the image of God. He created *fam* and *minga*." There is no confusion, therefore, a term which refers to the ambiguities which we are familiar with in French and in English. In face of the divinity of God, *fam* and *minga* together constitute humanity. *Fam* and *minga* are not mutually exclusive. And when one or the other claims to be unique or the better representation of *môt* in God's sight, there is a falling away from what God really willed to do.

Second, another point which will require African theologians to think more deeply is the organization of most African languages into classes. In fact there is not at this level the pejorative connotation one finds in the following opposition:

> French: il/elle
> English: he/she
> German: er/sie
> Spanish: el/ella

The functioning of these class languages thus proves a different mentality in respect to the problem of relations between men and women in society. The same should be the case in our Christian communities. The Pahouin theologians, with an excellent training in linguistics, owe it to themselves to conduct an original theological reflection ending up inevitably in a concrete organization different from that which exists at present.

At this stage in our reflection, we link up again with the whole problem of promoting an African theology which still meets on the one hand with the laziness of those concerned who are content to swallow theologies from elsewhere and on the other hand with a lack of courage to accept the certainly revolutionary consequences of calling the status quo into question.

Social Life

The first example we offer to you concerns the Yoruba organization (Nigeria) of the market in the town of Ibadan as described for us by Dr. Zulu Sofola in an African meeting last September. It seems, in fact, that at the head of this huge market there is, parallel to the masculine structure of chiefs, a feminine structure in an egalitarian system which thus permits the women to act and to make very important decisions. Both structures in the leadership and control of the city of Ibadan do not express themselves without consultation with one another. Both are all the more respected. That of the women even seems to be the more respected and the more feared of the two.

As far as the Pahouin group is concerned, from which I come, the social organization fulfills a certain number of basic principles. We shall deal in succession with three of them.

1. *The Cohesion of the Group.* Everything is organized; the feminine and masculine initiation rites tend toward the maintenance of the cohesion of the group. The *mevungu* (for the women), the *ngil*, the *sô* (for the men), the bwiti train and educate their initiates in the protection of the community against all forms of attack, internal or external (war, sorcery, etc.). "The covenant of mutual *responsibility and obligation* is not merely between kinsmen but between the people and God."

2. *The Protection of the Individual.* While all efforts are combined to maintain the community and all possible means are used, the counterpart is also true. The group owes the individual (whether man, woman, child, old person) protection, love, support. All this being based on the idea of sharing. So "the Christian community affirms that the individuals are fundamentally dependent upon one another."[8] To love one another, to be one in Christ, these are the marching orders which underlie the existence of the Christian and "at the temporal level, human life is essentially a personal *relationship,* and the raison d'être of the whole development and the whole organization is to make this relationship possible, to support it, to give it its true character."[9] Julius

Nyerere sums it up excellently in this way: "We neither needed nor wished to exploit our fellowmen."[10]

3. *The Better Welfare of All.* All these conditions and many others are essential for the ultimate goal: the better welfare of others, of each member of the group. Everyone has the right to be respected by all the rest. It is normal, therefore, that *every* human being should play a part in this society. No one is excluded. This community was only possible with a common effort by every individual to come together and with the creation of objective conditions to facilitate this.

From what has been said it follows that in each community the participation of men and women is a duty and a right recognized by all. "I am because I participate."[11] In each community we are individuals within a whole. It is obvious, therefore, that "we take care of the community and the community takes care of us."[12] The African man or woman Christian owes it to his or herself to have the most "profound sense both of security and obligation."[13] He or she must be "ready to share."[14] A man or woman "exists not only in his/her identity but also in his/her involvement."[15]

To conclude it is nevertheless essential to recognize that the parallel between the Christian community and the Pahouin society cannot go very far. The two groups definitely do not coincide. The Pahouin society has its faults, and there can be no claim to perfection. The Christian community goes further and should go further, because it is in a sense the prefiguration on earth of the reign of God. Our efforts should, therefore, be in the direction of "witnessing God in solidarity with the poor and oppressed,"[16] but also in respect to Africans, in "assuming the African face of humanity."[17]

Consequently, the Christian community, while drawing upon elements in our cultures which permit it to be renewed, goes beyond this and widens its horizon in the measure in which it is broader and larger than the society or family type, such as the Pahouin society. The church should make prevalent the requirements of the faith in its own organization and in the organization of the city.

The speech of women has made possible the awakening of conscience of the situation which prevails at the present time. If then Awa Thiam gave the word to "negresses," they do not accept it at all. How to act then? We must act together, for history teaches us that nothing has ever been achieved without courage and obstinacy. It is at the level of action and commitment that change will be possible. It is for women and men of good will to denounce the situation of domination and discrimination and distorted relationships. We have need for the solidarity of all men and women. I remind you that for the Pahouin there is no humanity in face of the divinity of God in the *fam* alone or in the *minga* alone. It is in the complementarity of the two that our problems will be resolved.

So then, "every man, every woman who wishes to be faithful to the gospel should have a historical vision. At the present time, to serve humankind is to seek to construct a society with a human face. The authentic faith must identify itself with the historical process in which men and women, on the basis of our certitude in Christ's victory over our alienated condition, contribute to the liberation of which God, in the last analysis, has the first initiative."[18]

Notes

1. Jean Marc Ela, *Le cri de l'homme africain* (Paris: Harmattan, 1980), p. 70.

2. Constance F. Parvey, oral presentation to the African regional consultation in Ibadan, September 1980.

3. Joan Arnold Romero, "The Protestant Principle: A Woman's Eye View of Barth and Tillich," in *Religion and Sexism: Images of Women in the Jewish and Christian Traditions,* ed. Rosemary Ruether (New York: Simon & Schuster, 1974), p. 320.

4. Awa Thiam, *La Parole aux Négresses* (Paris: Denoël, 1978).

5. Louis-Jean Calvet, *Linguistique et Colonialisme* (Paris: Payor, 1974), p. 154.

6. Ibid., p. 155.

7. John V. Taylor, *The Primal Vision: Christian Presence and African Religion* (Naperville, Ill.: Alec R. Allenson, 1963), p. 113.

8. Aylward Shorter, *African Culture and the Christian Church* (New York: Orbis Books, 1974).

9. J. A. Malula, "Le chrétien dans la société," in *Revue du Clergé Africain,* p. 81.

10. Julius Nyerere, *Ujamaa—essays on socialism* (Oxford: Oxford University Press, 1968) in Shorter, *African Culture,* p. 197.

11. Taylor, *Primal Vision,* p. 85.

12. Shorter, *African Culture,* p. 197.

13. Taylor, *Primal Vision,* p. 100.

14. Ibid., p. 87.

15. Ibid., p. 109.

16. Ela, *Le cri,* p. 72.

17. Ibid.

18. Ibid., p. 126.

PART THREE

THE WORD OF GOD AND THE HEARERS OF THE WORD

5

"Woman, Why Are You Weeping?" (John 20:15)

Sermon Given in the Sheffield Cathedral

PAULINE WEBB

In one of the opening addresses of this conference, Elisabeth Moltmann-Wendel reminded us that church history began, not on the day of Pentecost, but in the resurrection garden. So it seems to me appropriate that this evening we should take as our text the very first words which the risen Lord spoke to the church. We often pay very close attention to the last words of a dying person. How much more important then are the first words of one who has risen from the dead! So I take my text today from John 20:15, the very first words of the risen Lord, "Woman, why are you weeping?"

Those words too echo something that was said in our first session last Saturday. Philip Potter reminded us that as he had read through the reports of the study on the Community of Women and Men in the Church, reports that had come in from all over the world, he had heard over and over again the cry of pain—deep pain, pain that is often not understood. It was the yearning of women to find their true identity, as they struggle to discover what it means to be full people, people in relationship with men, in relationship with children, in relationship with other women, in relationship with themselves, in relationship with God. For women are so often defined only by their relationships.

In a report recording pressure points in the lives of women and men published here in Britain just last month a researcher said that the findings showed that in the majority of cases of nervous breakdown or severe depression in women, the cause could be traced back to the ending of some relationship—either through bereavement or separation or breakdown. The main causes of distress in men have a different origin. More often they are related to failure at work, to frustrated ambition, to defeat in competition. Some would say this is all because of our conditioning in our sex roles. Men are taught from the beginning that they must succeed in their career. Women are taught to invest their whole being in loving and nurturing others. So for a woman a broken relationship can mean a broken heart. There seems nothing left to live for.

So Mary stands in the garden weeping, believing that her relationship with her Lord has now come to an end. She has stayed beside Jesus right to the last moment, even the moment of death. And now she has come to do what she can to tend his dead body. No man would do that. In the culture of her time, tending a corpse would be regarded as an act of defilement, fit only for a woman to undertake. It's an irony, isn't it, that the only people we know who actually handled the earthly body of Jesus were women. They were there at his birth and his death, at his cradle and his tomb. And yet the only people now not allowed to consecrate the sacred elements of Christ's Body and Blood are, again, women. And behind the prohibition lies deeply hidden the fear that somehow the female brings defilement into the holy place.

But Mary comes to the tomb and then finds that they have taken away the body of the Lord. And, like many women from whom that body is withheld, she searches and almost gives up. But Christ seeks her out, asking: ''Woman, why are you weeping?'' She doesn't recognize his risen body at first. Her eyes are too blinded by tears even to see those wounds that she had watched the soldiers inflict. But then Christ speaks to her by name—''Mary.'' And here is the first great truth that comes out of this text for us.

Jesus Speaks to Each One of Us
by Our Own Names

In this conference we have been reminded in our Bible studies about the importance of names. We have pondered on the meanings of ''Adam'' and ''Eve'' and ''Mary.'' We have observed the importance of the identity that is given by a name. The church has always recognized that. That is why right through our tradition, the Sacrament of baptism has been associated with the giving of a name, a Christian name, the one name we keep to the end of our days, and even beyond. For it is our Christian name that is written in the book of life, not our family name. That may change when we marry, but the unique name that is given to each one of us remains with us to all eternity. And yet many women hardly ever hear their own name used. I confess that often, even when I've been given hospitality over a weekend during a preaching tour,

I sometimes find when I come to write my "thank you" letter and begin "Dear David and . . . ?" that I actually don't know the wife's name! I've often never been told what it is. David introduces me to "my wife," the children all call her "Mother," the neighbors speak of "Mrs. Smith." But who is *she*? What is *her* name? There's a poignant story told of Queen Victoria, who said, when her beloved Prince Albert died, "I've lost the only person in the world who called me by *my own name.*"

So one of the great questions women face is how to affirm their own identity, not only in relationship to others, but in their own self. And this search for one's unique identity can be very frightening and lonely. So for Mary standing there alone in the garden is indeed a terrifying experience. Then she hears Jesus speak to her by name. And her first instinct is to hold him fast. Then come the even more surprising words of Jesus: "Do not cling to me." He won't allow this woman to be fettered, even by her love for him. She must be free to be herself.

I think one of the temptations of women is sometimes to love "not wisely, but too well." We tend to bind ourselves to those whom we love in an embrace that imprisons them and stunts our own growth. You see it often between wife and husband, sister and brother, mother and son, friend and friend. Our loving can be so protective as to be suffocating. And when for one reason or another that loved one goes, our arms are left empty and our lives as well. In the group where I was doing this study one woman expressed this vividly when she said, "My husband has died and my children have grown up, and I don't know who I am anymore."

So Jesus says, "Do not cling to me." Dare to be free. And then comes the second lesson from this text for us all.

Jesus Sends Mary to Join
the Community

"Go and tell my brethren," he says. The community of the church was defined even then in male terms because the men had gathered themselves together in one place apart. But Jesus sends this woman to join them, to bear the good news. I imagine Mary must have gone with some trepidation. Women had of course been present in the company of the disciples right from the beginning. I can never understand those people who place so much store on the argument that Jesus is not recorded as having called women to be disciples. Certainly women were always there in the company, but very little of what they said or did is in fact recorded. Even when Jesus pays great attention to their deeds or words, the men disciples almost always show misunderstanding. You remember the story of the woman who poured out her perfume at Jesus' feet. Only Jesus really understood what she meant by that action and immortalized it by saying that wherever the gospel was preached, her story too should be told. And so I'm sure Mary knew that the men would give little credence to her story. After all, what authority did she have? Only the authority of her own experience of the risen Lord.

And that is all the authority we need. That could give her the courage to go and join that new community which is about to be born, where the Spirit would be poured out on men and women alike and where sons and daughters together would prophesy.

So Jesus Gives This Woman a Message to Communicate

"Go and tell my disciples," the risen Christ says to Mary. And even though the disciples dismissed her tale as "the idle talk of a woman," I'm sure that didn't silence her. Have you noticed how all the great announcements of the gospel come through the lips of women? At the annunciation itself it is a young woman who recognizes that this is indeed the advent of the world's liberation—"He has put down the mighty from their seats and the rich he has sent empty away."

Now we remember the meaning of Mary's name—not only does it mean "the sorrowing one"; it means too "the one who rebels." And it is not only young women who recognize this liberation. The next great announcement comes from the Temple when the infant Jesus is presented before two old people who have prayed and waited long for the coming of the Messiah whom now they recognize. We all remember of course the prayer of the old man Simeon, "Lord, now lettest thou thy servant depart in peace." But the old woman, Anna, is often forgotten. She wasn't going to "depart in peace." She went out and told all her neighbors that the one who should liberate Israel had come.

And at the resurrection it is a woman who announces the good news. Even on that road to Emmaus when surely it must have been a man and woman, husband and wife, walking along the road home together, they speak of their longing to see the one they hoped would liberate Israel, and then at last in their home together in the breaking of bread they recognize the one of whom they spoke.

And so it has been throughout history. Women have been the "gossips"

79

of the gospel. The word "gossip" literally means "one who tells good news." What a terrible indictment it is that the word has come to mean one who delights in spreading bad news instead!

We were reminded by one of our Orthodox sisters that the gospel spread to Georgia through the "gossiping" in its literal sense of a saintly woman, St. Nina. And all our histories can tell of women who have spread the gospel in a variety of ways.

One of the things I've noticed as I've traveled around the world is just how many are the ways in which women manage to communicate their message— not always through the spoken word, but through other means of expression too. Go into the main square in Buenos Aires and see the courageous women there making their silent protest, as week by week they await news of their missing relatives. Or go to Chile and see the women making their brightly colored collages, depicting their situation and protesting about the social injustices in their land. Or go to South Africa and see women being bundled into police vans and drowning the police sirens with the sound of their freedom song. Or go to Australia, where I've just been, and listen to the aborigine women telling the legends of their "dreaming time" that warn of underground monsters which may destroy the earth if they are disturbed, in the very areas where men are now mining for uranium!

Yes, there's a kind of subversive gossiping going on among women all over the world, the telling of the good news of one who has come to turn the world upside down and reverse the order of things. And we need to communicate that gospel together in the community of women and men, as a sign that the new order has already begun. We need to share both the traditional teaching and the new insights, the authenticity of scholarship and the authority of experience so that we can together witness to our many-splendored gospel, a gospel of liberation not just for women, but for women and men and for the whole creation.

"Woman, why are you weeping?" The day shall surely come when hunger and sorrow and death shall be done away with and Christ shall wipe away all tears from their eyes.

Amen.

6

The Voices of
Sheffield

Preface at Dresden to the
Sheffield Recommendations

MERCY ODUYOYE*

The Central Committee discussion on the Sheffield recommendations will begin in the Unit meetings—with recommendations directed to all three units of the WCC, the General Secretariat, and the Vancouver Assembly Preparations Committee.

Certain findings at Sheffield stand behind these recommendations of which I will mention seven:

1. The first and most powerful, is that something happened at Sheffield. A new quality and freedom of spiritual/human life happened as we worked out our tensions, expectations, and real differences. In our confrontation, we found that we were not struggling against each other, but that we were committed to becoming a people, in search of a common goal; in that pursuit we discovered community.

This experience helped us to realize that in fact the Community of Women and Men in the Church study is just beginning. With the three years preparation we are just beginning to experience what this study is all about—not an ideology of equality—but a new life in Christ, a life of partnership, solidarity, unity, and renewal.

Though we know the program phase of the study ends this year, what is behind the recommendation (A.2) is the means to continue the momentum—

*The Sheffield Recommendations were presented to the Dresden Central Committee by Mercy Oduyoye of Nigeria. The response of the Central Committee, as it planned for the Sixth Assembly in Vancouver, can be found in the August 1981 Central Committee Minutes, published in Geneva by the WCC.

the approach and spirit of the community study—as part of the impulse and integral life of all aspects of our WCC work and of our planning for Vancouver and beyond.

2. It was realized that the final report of this consultation, in which there was so much grassroots participation, and in many languages and cultures, must not come out "speaking English only" when already by the end of 1978 it was in four languages and later in thirteen. *Recommendation A.2(c) addresses this.*

3. The consultation was deeply aware that a main hindrance to women and men in seeking new community has been our theological tradition itself and that one could not simply take a narrow view of ecclesiology, but that women and men becoming human in new community requires a view of the unity of the church as it is related to the profound eschatological framework of the renewal of human community. *Recommendations (A.3)* to the Commission on Faith and Order are from this perspective.

For example, the recommendations concerning ministry include fundamental considerations of teachings regarding the nature of the ministry in the body of Christ, placing the ministry in the context of its diaconal and prophetic dimensions, not limiting or focusing the discussion on ordination of women, or of men. The recommendation where ordination of women is mentioned has as its basic concern Christian unity, asking that the differing policies of churches regarding this issue be respected and not be a barrier to genuine movements toward unity.

Further, recommendations regarding issues of authority and worship also concern themselves with a deeper issue: *communication.* The question posed is: how do we find the language, images, and symbols to communicate new ecclesial realities of our Christian life? If we are living more salutary relationships, where is the creativity in our words and structures to realize this more fully as is God's intention in creation? When we speak of man and mankind, does it include an equal space for women? This is not only a question of language, but also of policy and of structures.

Since the community study as a program has its base in Faith and Order, it is natural that more recommendations are suggested for the Lima Commission meeting in January 1982 than are directed to other sub-units with the exception of the Sub-Unit on Women, the partner in this post-Nairobi venture.

4. Because the consultation realized that the search for inclusive community cannot be exclusive and that issues of sex, race, and class are intimately linked in a "web of oppression," issues of world economic disorder and its particularly oppressive effects on women came vividly to the surface, particularly

the issues of prostitution, a model of *sexism, racism* and *classism*. Delegates from rich and poor countries, seeing the linkage in international tourism, recognized prostitution as a blatant exploitation of the poorest of the poor, who are women, with its ugly dehumanizing effects on both the *user* and the *used*. The consultation felt that the churches have been too silent to touch the root causes of this growing dehumanization and hence the recommendation to Unit II—that it be seen in the context of global economic *dis*order.

5. Underlying the cycle of vulnerability and subjugation of women is not only a lack of education, but also attitudes in education that put women in fixed stereotyped roles and limit the development of the full human capacities of both partners. This has implications in every area of learning from early Christian education to the most advanced theological training. It also has broad implications regarding our attitudes toward human sexuality and, in its extreme, issues of violence (structural and personal) including violence in the home. Therefore the *recommendations to Unit III, C.1 and 2*.

6. No renewal of human life for women and men can take place without preparing more women as full partners in the dialogue. It is this main point that is the thrust behind most of the recommendations directed to the *Sub-Unit on Women in Church and Society (C.4)*.

However, the consultation realized that preparing women is not enough. Guidelines must also be developed to measure the work in the WCC so that we do not, by default, benefit only half of the partnership by our policies, at the expense of the other half. This affects our own employment procedures as well as our relationships with our partners in ecumenical sharing and development.

The Community of Women and Men in the Church: The Sheffield Recommendations

A. *Recommendations To Programme Unit I Committee*

1. We recommend that the Central Committee endorse the 'Letter' from the Sheffield consultation and transmit it to the member churches of the WCC.

2. We recommend that appropriate funds, staff and other resources be made available for effective implementation of the following recommendations:

a. that the Advisory Committee (plus two persons representing Unit II) be continued to monitor follow-up progress and help assure an effective implementation process through Vancouver;

b. that a staff task force be constituted with representation from all units to:

    i. assure that issues and recommendations of the Study be adequately dealt with in all units;

    ii. assure that these issues and recommendations become a part of the Vancouver Assembly programme and actions;

    iii. assure that continuing responses of churches to the initial invitation to the Study be properly handled;

c. that the authorized book emerging from the Sheffield consultation be published in Spanish, French, German and English.

3. We recommend to the Faith and Order Commission:

a. that the Report from Sheffield and other study materials produced during the CWMC Study process be incorporated, where appropriate, into all on-going study programmes of the Commission, especially into "The Unity of the Church and the Renewal of Human Community"

b. that the following theological issues, highlighted at Sheffield, find a place in the future work of the Commission:

    i. the significance of the representation of Christ in the ordained ministry, particularly in relation to the ordination of women;

    ii. the diaconal dimensions of all ministries, especially their understanding of the diaconate and the place of women and men within it;

    iii. the possibility and implications of churches being in communion when they have different policies concerning the ordination of women;

    iv. the variety of ways of offering ministries, such as ordination, consecration, commissioning, and accrediting;

    v. the relation of fundamental human rights to the Christian understanding of the calling to the ordained ministry.

c. that the following issues dealing with "tradition" be carefully examined as part of the Commission's on-going study "Towards the Common Expression of the Apostolic Faith Today":

    i. the significance of tradition in the search for a new community of women and men in the Church;

    ii. the evidence in scripture and tradition with regard to the participation of women and men in the Church;

   iii. the importance of various cultural traditions in the shaping of this community in the church (should be carried out in conjunction with the Sub-Unit on Dialogue with People of Living Faiths and Ideologies and with the Sub-Unit on Renewal and Congregational Life, Unit III);

   iv. such questions as: Is patriarchy a cultural tradition or part of normative revelation? Is there continuity or discontinuity between the "Abba" of Jesus and the Father of the Trinitarian dogma, the "Fathers" of the Church and church structures based on "fatherhood"? Who decides what sorts of experiences constitute tradition?

    v. theological insights of the Trinity in relation to the male-female language and imagery of God.

  d. that the Commission initiate programmes dealing with one or more of the following issues after the WCC's Sixth Assembly:

    i. power, authority and the structures of the church with particular reference to:

      a. full participation of women and men in the life, worship and ministry of the Church;

      b. the recent experience of women with regard to power, authority and structure in church and society;

      c. the manner in which our experience of power and authority and the character of our structures either express or obscure the community life of the Gospel;

    ii. the problems of language, imagery and symbols of God in worship and theology.

  e. that a woman be appointed to the Faith and Order Secretariat.

  f. that the Commission make fuller use of liberation theologians, woman and men, in its work, and that the issues raised in liberation theology (both in method and content) be given a fuller place in the work of the Commission.

B. *Recommendations to Programme Unit II Committee*

  1. We recommend that Unit II, as it joins in this process of follow-up on the issues of the Community Study, give special attention to the perspectives and experiences of women and their legal, civil and

human rights throughout each of the Sub-Unit's programmes, especially with regard to refugee, migrant and handicapped women and young girls.

2. We recommend that the WCC in its disarmament programme explore with other sub-units how the arms race distorts our roles as women and men and blocks our efforts toward new community; further, that the WCC encourage member churches to involve their communities and leadership in understanding the anti-development nature of armaments, to participate in regional and local disarmament efforts and to urge their governments to immediately resume disarmament talks.

3. We recommend that the WCC set up a world-wide programme of study and action for the elimination of organised prostitution by international firms whereby:

   a. member churches of countries concerned (both sending and receiving tourists) be requested to:

      i. gather accurate information and statistics on the subject, such as methods of promoting offers to clients, recruitment of prostitutes (women, young boys, etc.), sanitary provisions, consequences for the future of women and boys involved and for the surrounding community;

      ii. sensitize their respective public opinion on the problem;

      iii. share the insights and experiences gained through the program on women in development regarding the hardships encountered by women in oppressive, tight economic situations where women are often driven into prostitution as the only means of livelihood, and where organized tourism capitalizes on this reality.

   b. the Churches Commission on International Affairs be urged to work with the relevant agency of the United Nations on the most appropriate international action to be taken against this specific traffic.

C. *Recommendations to Programme Unit III Committee*

1. We recommend to the Programme on Theological Education that:

   a. as an important aspect of renewal in theological education, it encourage seminaries to re-examine their policies and curricula to ensure that they take account of the issues raised by the Community

Study and encourage courses with special emphasis on theological education for women;

b. it seek to integrate the areas of Biblical studies and practical theology so that clergy are trained to work with lay people in critical study of the Scriptures in relation to contemporary contexts;

c. it organise consultations and foster the development of programmes on women in theological education;

d. a woman be appointed to the Programme on Theological Education executive staff, to follow up suggestions growing out of the Study, and to work with the growing numbers of women in theological education.

2. We recommend to the Sub-Unit on Education that:

a. it request the member churches to monitor their own educational Sunday School and other materials to ensure that they are not re-enforcing stereotypes through the languages, illustrations and concepts used;

b. in the light of insights emerging on new and changing patterns of family life and partnership relations, it incorporate, together with the Sub-Unit on Women, women's experiences and perspectives into the study of all aspects of sexuality opened up by the Community Study;

c. it collect and share material from a women's perspective to facilitate education within and between churches on sexuality from theological, psychological, sociological, ethical, and legal perspectives, and that it encourage member churches also to produce materials;

d. it encourage churches to be aware of special needs of single women and men and lone parents, and of the handicapped in relation to both church and society;

e. in light of increasing violence in many societies, it continue its educational efforts to emphasize the responsibilities of women and men in the specific areas of violence in the home and in the community, including concerns with regard to prostitution, teen-age pregnancies and issues of family planning;

f. it produce understandable Bible Study materials and worship materials for use by small groups and local churches wanting to study the issues of community developed in the CWMC Study.

3. We recommend to the Sub-Unit on Renewal and Congregational Life that:

   a. it collect models of new community including experiments in new partnership and also models of shared leadership, and lift up the contribution of women for the renewal of the Church and the ministry;

   b. the issue of internationally organised prostitution by the tourist firms be put for consideration on the programme of the forthcoming consultation on tourism organised in cooperation with the Church of Sweden.

4. We recommend to the Sub-Unit on Women in Church and Society that:

   a. it collect case studies of the experiences of lay women and men as they relate to ordination and hierarchical church structures and that this collection be a basis for further discussion;

   b. it work to build a network of women in ministry, both ordained and non-ordained ministry, so that women in all parts of the world can share their experiences and that it take seriously the burden women carry in a discussion which needs to be shared equally by men and women;

   c. it study in cooperation with Family Education the causes of psychological pre-conditioning of violence against women and children which is increasing, and that it urge churches to enact their pastoral responsibility by caring for the victims of personal violence, by supporting activities already existing and by adopting a lay team approach to train those involved in counselling and social work, including class analysis;

   d. it take initiatives in developing guidelines for measuring the performance of the WCC, its units and sub-units and its member churches in achieving equal participation of women and men in the church;

   e. a study on the theology and liturgies of marriage be carried out in conjunction with the Programme on Family Education;

   f. in cooperation with the Programme on Family Education and the Commission on Faith and Order, it begin a new study on marriage and partnership following the Sixth Assembly.

D. *Recommendations to the Assembly Preparations Committee*

1. We recommend that the issues raised by the study be fully integrated into the Assembly planning process in the following ways:
   a. that the Assembly Planning Committee in cooperation with the staff task force investigate fully ways in which the issues of the Study are related to, or developed in relation to the main theme, "Jesus Christ, the Life of the World";
   b. that full use be made of all persons who have already been involved in the Study at local levels in preparation for the Assembly;
   c. that people who are knowledgeable about and have contributed to the issues of the Study be utilised as members of pre-Assembly visitation teams;
   d. that the *Risk* book emerging from the CWMC Study can be used as part of the planning for the Assembly so that dialogue can be continued with those already engaged in the Study process;
   e. that a slide set or film strip of Sheffield be produced with multi-lingual tapes to be used in pre-Assembly visitations;
   f. that in the preparations of the Assembly structure and style, the experience of the Study be taken into account.

2. We recommend that at the Sixth Assembly in Vancouver:
   a. the CWMC Study be selected as one of the issues of the Assembly and that a plenary be devoted to it;
   b. the substance of the Assembly demonstrate more evidence of women's perspectives so that the Assembly as a whole reflects more adequately the community perspectives;
   c. that 50% of the speakers, moderators and other leadership be women.

E. *Recommendations to the Committee on the General Secretariat*

1. We recommend that the WCC establish procedures to monitor and evaluate its own programmes and practices with regard to sexism, racism and classism. This monitoring of policy and implementation should include all levels and all units of the WCC with particular attention to recruitment and personnel practices; further, that the WCC recommends to regional and national councils of churches and related services and development agencies that women and men in their networks establish similar procedures to monitor their own policies.

2. We recommend that at the Sixth Assembly:
   a. 50% of all membership elected to sub-units and committees of the WCC be women;
   b. three of the six Presidents of the WCC elected at the Assembly be women.
3. We recommend that the language in all WCC publications and republications (not only the CWMC Study) be inclusive.

The Letter from Sheffield to the Churches

Introduction by
JEAN MAYLAND*

It was a great joy for the people of Sheffield to welcome into our midst the participants in the international consultation on the Community of Women and Men in the Church. We are delighted that the name of Sheffield has entered the list of the names of cities especially associated with great ecumenical events. We are happy and honored that the title of the letter which I am now to present to you is as a "Letter from Sheffield to the Churches." I personally am particularly thrilled that the letter deals with the question of the Community of Women and Men in the Church which to me is a vital one as it concerns the very life of the church itself and the witness which the community of the church may have or may fail to have in the world.

Work on the letter from Sheffield began early in the consultation when a small committee of six persons from very diverse backgrounds was appointed to consider the possibility, content, and form of a message from the consultation to the churches. Using the material prepared in local, national, regional, and specialist conferences, the committee drafted and circulated to all participants a summary of issues and concerns. This was a balanced and rather detached, descriptive document and the committee asked for comment both on content and on style.

It soon became clear that members of the consultation were happy with the content, but not with the style of the document which was described as a "typical ecumenical statement." Participants demanded a fresh style which

*The Letter from Sheffield was transmitted to the Dresden Central Committee. Jean Mayland, a member of the Central Committee from the Church of England and moderator of the Sheffield Local Planning Committee that received the consultation, read the Letter, prefaced with these brief remarks.

would enable not only the issues, but also the feelings of pain and joy involved, to be briefly and effectively communicated.

A new draft of this kind was prepared, circulated, and discussed in plenary. Careful attention was given in plenary to points raised. For example, there was a strong call to prepare a letter to the churches which could speak for all participants without dividing them into subcategories according to confession, nationality, or racial context, and this desire was met.

There was also a clear wish that the particular situations of different churches should be sympathetically recognized; that, for instance, the reference to the ordination of women should reflect the problem actually experienced by some churches without attempting to give a normative theological judgment or a comprehensive view of the whole situation in all churches, or requiring any church to accept a description of its own situation made from outside that context. Again, the committee strove hard to give fulfillment to this wish.

In a further plenary, the participants accepted the Letter as their own statement of the central thrust of the consultation and expressed their desire that the Central Committee should read it with commendation to the churches.

A Letter from Sheffield

Sisters and Brothers in Christ, we long that you may hear us, for we belong together with you in the church and in a common humanity.

Brothers, can you not hear the ''sighs too deep for words'' of women who suffer war, violence, poverty, exploitation and disparagement in a world so largely controlled by men? Sisters, can you not see how the lives of men have been trapped by the effects of their having this power and a supposed superiority?

We speak as those who have been seeking to listen anew to scripture and to live the tradition of the Church in its many forms. Thus we have heard a word of God for today about a vision for our human life—a renewed community of women and men. We speak with urgency. In a world threatened by nuclear self-destruction women and men are made more sharply aware that they need a new partnership as equals before God; in churches and societies which men have dominated in ways deeply damaging to women and to men, we need both repentance and faith to move forward at God's call through the gospel.

What did we in Sheffield hear the Holy Spirit saying to the churches? We learned:

how deep are the emotions involved in any reflection on our being as women and men;

how hard it is to address and envision God in ways that respect the Christian understanding of personhood rather than suggesting male superiority;

how great is the need for education on the issues of our consultation;

how radical may be the changes needed in our societies.

We received:

a foretaste of a global community of women and men vulnerable to the pain of all forms of oppression and united in struggle against them.

We gained perspectives:

seeing that for many women and men struggles against tyranny, militarism, economic exploitation and racism are the immediate task;

that Christians in many places need to call on governments to overcome exploitation, particularly where women and men have become victims of wrong patterns of development, through cheap labour, migrant labour or tourist-oriented prostitution;

and that for many women and men there is real pain in the frustration of a church life controlled by male leadership, where, for instance, women feel called to the ministry of word and sacraments and ordination is not open to them or where the Church has not responded to creative developments in society.

We recognized:

the importance of including Christians from every continent and culture and from all churches in this Community Study in order to achieve a perceptive hearing of all concerns.

We rejoiced:

to recognize that sexuality is not opposed to spirituality but that Christian spirituality is one of body, mind and spirit in their wholeness.

We sang at Sheffield:

the Magnificat of Mary that celebrates God's liberating intervention; the praise of Jesus in whom we look upon the human face of the Triune God.

We invite you to pray with us:
> Eternal God, as you created humankind in your image, women and men, male and female, renew us in that image:
>
> God, the Holy Spirit, by your strength and love comfort us as those whom a mother comforts:
>
> Lord Jesus Christ, by your death and resurrection, give us the joy of those for whom pain and suffering become, in hope, the fruitful agony of travail:
>
> God, the Holy Trinity, grant that we may together enter into new life, your promised rest of achievement and fulfilment—world without end. Amen.

Sisters and Brothers in Christ, we long that you will join us in giving reality to the vision which we have seen.

PART FOUR

SEEKING A COMMON BASE

7

Third World Statement— European Response

Women and Men in Community for Humanity

Since the delegates from the Third World presented a statement to the plenary, there has been a variety of reactions. Some friends from the First World have leaned over backwards and insisted on having a Third World voice on every discussion topic in the sections. Others have remarked that the statement was a brief flare-up and has died a quick and proper death. Still others have declared their support for the concerns expressed in the statement. Thus, there has been genuine solidarity, as well as a recurrence of paternalism and outright indifference. It is to be expected that in any human group there would be this diversity of response to the human voice of a human cry. But it is also to be hoped that in a community gathered together in the name of Christ, there would be greater solidarity, and an honest effort to understand the human voice, and the need for raising it at this time.

Let us try to understand this need. This study was initiated as a result of the consultation on "Sexism in the 70s" held at Berlin in 1974. After the Nairobi Fifth Assembly, it was formally launched by sending out study booklets in 14 languages to member churches. About 200 responses were received; significantly, 80% of those from local groups were from North America and Europe. This might have been an indication that the questions in this study may not have had the urgency and priority for the other areas. Those of us from the Third World who are here are grateful for the awakening of our awareness to sexism in our own churches. We are here, representing two-thirds of the world's women; they are the most exploited people on earth. We are from nations in Africa and Asia where the Church is a minority among other faiths and ideologies. Most of us have come here with no prior opportunity to share our concerns. When we did so here, we realized that they are not confined to women and men in community in the Church only, and that our perceptions about the global context are affirmed as urgent. We felt that dealing with such problems in section has precluded an overall view of our concerns.

Some members of the Third World have said that sexual discrimination is not a reality in their church life. Sisters in some denominations in Indonesia have been serving the churches there as ordained ministers for a couple of decades. We all, however, share an experience of being subjugated, controlled and exploited by men within the larger social context of our countries. But when we began to share our experiences as concerned Christians, we were forced to see beyond our noses, because behind those men who dominate with their so-called superiority, we became aware of a faceless, formless beast holding them by their skinny throats, threatening and making objects of us all, women and men. We had to ask what can we do.

We are all of us engaged in a process of exploitation of the less fortunate. We Christians in the Third World are the privileged minority: we exploit and oppress; we grow fat from the labour of thousands. Our rich women make slaves of our unfortunate sisters. We share in this guilt of dehumanizing.

We have been invited here to explore a concept of new community—a new community where there is equality and justice, where there is an equal sharing of resources and responsibilities, where there is food and shelter for all, where one human being does not control, subjugate, or in any way oppress another human being. We believe that this concept of new community cannot be pursued without including all the dehumanized and exploited humanity. Therefore, we invite you sisters and brothers, in humility, to engage in this exploration of the new community, by educating ourselves, seeking information, finding facts. The process of dehumanization that goes on in our world is not only allowed but encouraged in the name of progress and the pursuit of life, liberty and happiness.

As a start or reminder for the education process may we present a few facts:

1. Capitalism uses cheap labour all over the world, not only in the Third World. This kind of use results in loss of identity for women and men; they become cogs in the wheels of technology.

2. In the name of economic expansion, cigarettes, drugs and alcohol are dumped on Third World countries. When women in the First World stopped using baby formulas, these were sold to ignorant, weak, poor mothers with no consideration of the consequences to the infants. Contraceptives that are

not fit for use in the First World countries are sold to Third World women with no compunction.

3. Changing patterns of tourism encourage a thriving business in prostitution. It is dire economic necessity that drives the young women and girls into this life of horror.

These facts are only the tip of the iceberg of exploitation that we are all guilty of. While the WCC itself has published these and other well-documented facts and tried to encourage action against these dehumanizing patterns and structures, have not we, the member churches, largely ignored them?

While we seek to remedy conscious or unconscious sexual discrimination within the fellowship of the Church, let us also look to ways of ending the equally sinful exploitation of the powerless by the powerful, whenever that is found, whether it be power appropriated through the presence of hormones, hard cash or hair colour.

There is a further concern that all of us in community together, the ecclesiastical Church, the ecclesial, invisible Church, with our neighbours of other faiths and ideologies, dare not ignore. It is the mindless proliferation of nuclear arms and other arms that is going on. There is an increasing urgency especially for women, the nurturers of life, to gather in strength to stop this growing evil and threat to life.

Let us therefore appeal to all gathered here in the words of St. Paul in his letter to the Philippians: "So if there is any encouragement in Christ, any incentive of love, any participation in the Spirit, any affection and sympathy, complete my joy by being of the same mind, having the same love, being in full accord and of one mind. Do nothing from selfishness or conceit, but in humility count others better than yourselves. Let each of you look not only to his own interests but also to the interests of others. Have this mind among yourselves, which is yours in Christ Jesus, who, though he was in the form of God, did not count equality with God a thing to be grasped, but emptied himself, taking the form of a servant. And being found in human form he humbled himself and became obedient unto death, even death on a cross. ... Therefore my beloved, as you have always obeyed, so now, not only as in my presence but much more in my absence, work out your own salvation with fear and trembling; for God is at work in you, both to will and to work for his good pleasure. Do all things without grumbling or questioning, that you may be blameless and innocent, children of God without blemish in the midst of a crooked and perverse generation, among whom you shine as lights in the world, holding fast the word of life."

A European Response

We Europeans know how much the questions you of the Third World have put and the way you have spoken out has helped us. You have made us reconsider whether we have really accepted that each continent and each cultural group has an identity of its own. Therefore we take up your questions and problems, which differ from ours, and we become conscious of your priorities, which you are setting in your own way, e.g., in the matter of feminism, on account of your specific struggle for liberation.

1. We are a continent divided politically and economically into northern and southern Europe, into East and West. In the capitalist countries there is a Third World right in the midst of wealth, e.g., the migrant labourers who have no citizens' rights, the unemployed, women and men without hope for the future. We especially want to mention young people. Because of their utter frustration, they often become aggressive towards established society or they refuse cooperation altogether. We are thinking of women. Many of them are ill-trained. In times of a flouishing national economy, they are lured to the labour market; in times of recession, however, they are fired. Economic interests determine which goals and roles the state and Church assign to women: home-making and family care, or being part of the labour market.

The same economic mechanisms work in the Third World, mainly through multinational and transnational corporations. Therefore, if we Europeans want to develop and enlarge our solidarity with the Third World, we must overcome our ignorance in this field. We feel it imperative to launch comprehensive programmes of conscientization and learning amongst our population, programmes which help people understand the interests, mechanisms and consequences of the so-called old economic order. If we understand these, then we will be better prepared both to understand and to give political support to those demands of the Third World related to the new economic order.

2. Our struggle is not merely for equality within the old structures which we experience as rigid, oppressive, alienating and destructive. We have experienced their destructiveness at the local level, as well as at the national and international levels. They destroy the identity of adults and children, the relationship between individuals and peoples. They alienate people at work, orient people's minds to capital, militarization and the exploitation of the earth's resources.

We want to come to an end of this destruction and we want to work in our churches and in our localities and countries towards this end. We have begun to discover our own little strength and power, and we have made first steps to protest and demonstrate against injustices. We want to admit (sisters and brothers of the Third World) that we have not listened early enough to your cries for justice. In our personal encounters and by listening to your stories, we have discovered you.

3. We have become aware of the fact, for example, of how many forms of tourism have become means of oppression. We want to work both in our churches and in our societies so that tourism will no longer deform the landscape, change beyond recognition the way of life, and destroy the social structures of southern Europe. We want to report to our countries the devastating effects of sex tourism in your countries. We want to report how many women in your countries are driven into prostitution, and how many families suffer in consequence.

4. As Europeans, we appeal to our churches decidedly and explicitly to resist armament, and to demand gradual disarmament. We feel threatened by the new possibilities of a limited nuclear war. Last year $500 billion were spent for arms all over the world. Thirty billion dollars per annum would suffice to feed all human beings adequately for a year. In our countries, at present, governments reduce the benefits of the social security system in order to finance armaments. In order to save money on social services, the good will of people, predominantly of women, is being exploited through unpaid services to the Church and to society.

Resources of the Third World are being wasted mainly by capitalist countries. In order to safeguard their access to these resources (e.g., to uranium in South Africa), governments promote the arms trade with Third World countries. Third World governments linked to ours often oppress their people in order to protect their privileges. Very often these oppressive governments call themselves Christian.

5. As Europeans, we would like to build up solidarity with the struggle of our black sisters and brothers in South Africa. We know that often our actions can be no more than symbolic. We are aware of the fact that some of our European governments and our business people collaborate with the South African government both politically and economically. We regret that in spite of the analysis of the relationship between Europe and South Africa, made by the Programme to Combat Racism of the World Council of Churches, our churches do not always respond in the proper way.

In spite of this, we would like to assure our sisters and brothers in South Africa: we share in your sufferings. We commit ourselves to inform our countries and churches of the real situation in South Africa and we shall demand that they draw the political and economic consequences from the information.

We realize that your sufferings for instance in South Africa, in El Salvador and elsewhere demand of us efforts for peace. Peace is indivisible. But let us state it clearly: when we struggle for peace and disarmament in Europe it does not mean that we lose interest in your liberation struggles in the Third World.

We are learning how intimately related our problems are. Sexism, racism and classism depend on the way our societies are organized and ruled. We challenge ourselves with the radical question whether our social system must not be completely changed, aiming at a new system that sees peace and social justice as indispensable. Our Christian faith encourages our conviction that our world can be changed; we feel called to participate in this Christian revolutionary change.

8

The Section Reports

Identity and Relationships in New Community

This group worked in two sub-groups. Group A focused on "Identity and New Community"; Group B on "Identity and Society."

Identity and New Community

It was quickly apparent, in a group consisting of participants from Asia, Europe, North America, Latin America, and the Pacific, that our concepts of identity were as varied as the cultures represented. Our exploration of the subject revealed its complexity. Further, it was clear that not only do women and men see each other differently, but each individual gives her or his own emphasis—even two persons of the same sex and culture may define their identity differently. In addition, our individual identity may change at different stages of growth. Therefore, it seemed that absolutes cannot be laid down in our search for identity, yet it was agreed that our relationships with others and the values of the society in which we live do have a strong impact on our identity, self-awareness, and self-confidence.

We struggle to find our identity not only as individuals, but as different cultures, communities, and societies. We affirm that the Christian community must find its identity in relation to the whole human community. Further, mission must not be without love and a respect for the beliefs of others, and people must be free to find their own identity within their own culture, faith, or ideology, as well as in relationships with other people.

1. *Positive and Negative Signs.* In our consideration of the vision of a new community we were encouraged to find the following areas which support our search for this ideal:

- small groups emerging where the individual voices of women are heard, as well as large consultations such as this where we can voice our concerns together;
- indications in the reports from local study groups of a willingness to recognize each other's sexuality as integral to human wholeness;
- evidence that many young men now share in family responsibilities;
- church ventures which bring women and men together;
- cooperation between women and men in rural village life;
- people beginning to reexamine their values with regard to vocation and work, including unpaid work such as that performed in the home;
- new forms of worship in which language and content speak to all people and which express an inclusive vision of new community;
- women theologians whose insights offer a new perspective as well as a more "whole" theology, a theology which seriously considers the insights of women and other oppressed groups.

While we welcome these positive aspects of our situation, there is still a long way to go and much still exists that is nonsupportive of our search, such as:

- selfish individualism among sexes, races, and religions;
- the ignoring of individual personality and the tendency toward regimentation;
- unjust social and economic structures;
- discrimination against women by law in church and society;
- sexist attitudes;
- elements in different cultures which hinder women from reaching their full potential and playing their full role;
- sex stereotyping;
- a tendency to offer a place to a "statutory" woman, thus not recognizing individual worth but simply meeting a legal or other requirement;
- parental domination as, for example, in the choice of marriage partners or of careers;
- poor images of women presented in the mass media and in school books;
- lack of child-care facilities for those women who look for more self-fulfillment in work outside the home;
- women's own unwillingness to allow men to share in household work;
- church structures that are formulated according to male thinking only and theology and worship that are offered from purely male perspectives.

2. *Identity and Sexuality.* While we gave much thought to sexuality as a vital and inextricable part of our identity, this was found in some respects to be a difficult, complicated, confusing and even painful subject. But it was felt that sexuality must be an area that the church gives much more attention. Women and men should be able to share their sexual identity as part of their own and each other's identity. As church members, aware of sexuality as God's beautiful gift to us, we should be able to offer support to others in their struggle to accept their own sexuality and to find their own identity. We are aware that our churches, in many cases, are not yet prepared to listen to or to accept those of different sexual attitudes or orientations. We feel deeply about this and believe that opportunities for education and understanding will help us to reach a fuller appreciation of the richness of sexual identity in ourselves and others.

3. *The Churches and New Community.* There is a definite challenge to the churches to respond more positively to our struggles and aspirations. The "whole" theology we have in mind would have to be open to modern questions and insights and to feminist, in addition to other, interpretations of Scripture. In this regard we commend efforts such as the work of women theologians being done by the World YWCA in 1982 for the notice and consideration of the worldwide church.

It is hard to express in precise language exactly what our vision of new community is. We are reaching out toward a society in which we will be able to accept the fact that as human beings we are not all cast in the same mold and that there is no basis for placing one sex, race, culture, or class in a superior position. Alongside equal rights there must be equal value for all, irrespective of origins, occupations, sex, or race. The new community is not something we can ever hope to achieve by our efforts alone. It is only as we are filled with the love of God, the grace of our Lord Jesus Christ, and the communion and guidance of the Holy Spirit that we can help to build the reign of God on earth.

Identity and Society

1. *Internal and External Factors.* As a group from the following countries: Lebanon, Australia, the Netherlands, India, the Federal Republic of Germany, Hong Kong, Austria, United Kingdom, Kenya, Trinidad, we found from our discussion that the dominant values of the society to which we belong strongly influence our sense of identity. People receive a definition of self from the

subgroups within a culture, such as a tribe, caste, class, or a community of faith such as a church. Two influences work in the shaping of a person: external influences and self-discovery from within.

Out of these two influences a sense of identity emerges: one which may fit, feel comfortable, and be fulfilling, or one which may hurt, be damaging, or diminishing.

2. *Identity and North/South Issues.* In our exploration of the question of identity our group decided to look at the value system of each of our separate cultures and countries. This proved a fascinating exercise and highlighted for us the variety of experience within the consultation.

We began to understand the "gap" between the participants from the industrialized countries and their sisters and brothers in the "developing" countries. Some participants, particularly from Western countries, expressed concern about the re-valuing of women and their need for liberation, while for others the issues of famine, poverty, the arms race, and exploitation were of extreme importance.

Most Westerners spoke of a culture in which people were forced to find their identity within societies that are characterized by individual striving and competition, with high value placed on personal success and achievement of high status and income. On the other hand, participants from Africa, Asia, the Caribbean, the Middle East, and Far East pointed to societies where community values were still the most important. Their values were relational, that is, concerned about community, not simply about one-to-one relationships. The high values of the West however were individualistically oriented—values that lend themselves to the separating out of the individual and valuing him or her over against others, according to individual achievement.

We began to see that the protest of Western women and the protest of the industrialized countries coincide. Both are cries of a humanity that is under threat of death from inhumanity. We need to look at the way industrialization and its competitive systems—in which men and women both participate and suffer—poison world society.

Our attention was also drawn to the plight of refugees and displaced people. We acknowledge that such people suffer a tragic identity crisis. For them, the search for identity is full of anguish, perplexity, uncertainty. Today, they are joined by millions who are unemployed, those made "redundant," who feel they have to some extent lost their personal identities along with the loss of their jobs.

3. *Dialogue—A Process of Identity Discovery.* Following our discussion on values, we moved on to consider how culture gives us our sense of identity. Extracts from our dialogue have been included to highlight the issues raised and the process involved:

> What qualities do people foster in their children? What qualities make a person whole? The lack of identity is not only in women but also in men. Differences between persons are often greater than the differences between the sexes. We need to help each person to become, in keeping with the intention of God.
>
> —United Kingdom

> In my Indian society religious philosophy and traditions predominate. It is therefore difficult to understand a strong individualistic concept of community. Christian community must relate back to New Testament teaching.
>
> —India

> Christianity does not have a set form of behavior, like other religions—but refers us back to the principles laid down by Jesus. It tells how to live in relation to other people and to God and not how to live in a particular social form.
>
> —Lebanon

> The comparison we have made between East and West is valid. Social influences are shaping us all. The media plays a most important role in defining gender characteristics. We need, therefore, to respond as individuals in order to be critical of society.
>
> —Federal Republic of Germany

> Then, you are using individuality to escape from Western culture.
>
> —India

> No, to *confront* Western society.
>
> —Federal Republic of Germany

> Western culture is poisoned—it is less than human—we have to make a decision to break away—the individual has to decide to ''move out'' in order to create a new community.
>
> —United Kingdom

> Isn't it our [Eastern] responsibility to help our Western brothers and sisters?
>
> —India

> Now it's a case of the Black Man's burden?
>
> —USA

Yes, perhaps it is a reversal, missionaries are now needed *from* the East.

—India

Is it possible to transmit values? If so . . . is it possible to preserve values in industrial society?

—Austria

In Indian society values are not defined in gender terms. We have a safety valve which is our village community. People may go away to work as skilled laborers during the week but they maintain a strong connection with the home village. True, the suicide rate has increased, but not to the same extent as in Western society. We are concerned about the influence which Western society is having on our people. I am here today because the West sent missionaries to India to convert my grandfather. It is high time we sent out missionaries to the West.

—India

Women have a big role to play in social change. Women challenge men. If change is needed in the West, women must demand it. It is my belief that if there is to be a change, Western women have to come forward and say, ''We want this to be done.'' I'm not blaming women—but they must demand change!

—Kenya

You are saying that you are inheriting our problems? What are these problems? What is doing this ?

—United Kingdom

For example, sexual orientations, such as homosexuality, were not known in my country. This was introduced by white men. Individualism is now becoming evident. . . . And there is denominationalism within the church. Why should we quarrel? We are all one in Christ!

Another example—our educational system was introduced by the West to train people for jobs. Now there are no jobs and people in the cities are reluctant to return to the land. Nairobi is now a city like London.

—Kenya

People in Hong Kong are under Western influences which are conducive to conflicts within our Chinese culture. We have difficult problems to overcome in order to achieve a new community within our social system and economic context. However, it is important to define the objectives of a new community which we need to strive for.

—Hong Kong

In the Caribbean we are now developing a Caribbean identity. One must remember that we Caribbeans come from many different countries bringing with us traditions and cultures from outside. We are a migrant community. We now have to live, work, and worship together, and there is a desperate need for us to develop a united Caribbean identity.

—Caribbean

This is also true of Australia which is now a multicultural society faced with identity crises and the numerous challenges this presents.

—Australia

At this point an invitation was extended to our consultant from the U.S. to participate.

QUESTION: Can women take the initiative? Once in Western society division of labor and differentiation of roles did exist; now roles are not clear and men are more insecure and defensive.

CONSULTANT (speaking from her experience in Western culture): "Yes, women will take the initiative. Women have not been allowed to be the 'big' individuals in society—nor have 99 percent of the men—but there is a large middle class in the West and the possibility of upward mobility exists. Women are now becoming critical of the pursuit of status because it is alienating. The church tradition is also heavily dominated by male figures, with few heroines. It is my hope that a serious critique of West and East will be undertaken. I should point out, however, that women in the East are still below men in their culture. Is it true that when development comes, especially with Western ideas, the position of your women is worse than before?"

INDIA: "Yes, that is so."

QUESTION: "Where does this male identity—aggressive, achieving—come from? Is there some biological 'given'?"

CONSULTANT: "There is absolutely no evidence that it is biological. There is overwhelming evidence that such characteristics come from the culture. Studies in the West have shown that men do in fact stimulate little boys to become strong, to stand up for themselves, to be ready to fight. This is done by teasing, constant provocation to be aggressive. Men pay more attention to little boys—girls are often ignored. Often this stimulation is unconsciously practiced. Notions of community are seen as being unmanly weaknesses. Only now are we beginning to see how powerful this is."

LEBANON: "Our role as women is now to change that. We need to be stronger."

CONSULTANT: "Yes, too often we think that men know and that we don't know. Even I, a Professor Dr., an educated woman, doubted myself. I did not want our two sons to watch American football as it is a terribly violent game. But my

108

husband loves the game, and said, 'Do you want to make sissies of them?' So I did not fight—now I know more—now I *would* fight. I think that game prepares our boys for war, prepares them to become aggressive.''

QUESTION: ''Is aggressive conditioning promoted by fear?''

CONSULTANT: ''Basically I think it comes out of a tradition of war—that we must always be ready to meet attack.''

LEBANON: ''I thought the feminist movement was designed to assist women to become like men. But now I see. It is not like that at all. I was against the feminist movement because I thought feminine values were being undermined. We need to point this out more clearly.''

CONSULTANT: ''We need to see who it is that projects this image of the women's movement. It is the media on the one hand, and, on the other, men naturally assume that if you want to change your situation then you must want to be like them.''

HONG KONG: ''I believe it is fundamentally wrong to grasp at power.''

AUSTRIA: ''Men and women need to become more human, but in our society the human values are more realized by women. They should also be realized by men. . . . We need a common conception of human life for both.''

CONSULTANT: ''I agree. We are saying each sex, with its biological differences, needs the opportunity to develop its own potential. At this point in history one sex dominates the other. The other (female) sex has now developed tendencies which are valuable. There is a certain dynamic now; women do not want to be caught up in these dominant values. They have a potential to bring forward. This provides a basis for linkage with the dominant group.''

Our Vision for the New Community

The new community we envisage and hope for is an inclusive community, the supreme value of which will be that of loving relationships. It will be a unified community endeavoring to express itself as the body of Christ.

The new community will be based on love, a love that conveys itself in respect for all persons—children, women and men; the aged, physically and mentally handicapped persons; single and married people, families, orphans, and widows/widowers—and a love that conveys itself in mutuality and equality—without domination and subordination, and without superiority and inferiority. It will be a community in which people can find fulfillment in sharing and partnership. It will value differences and diversity. These should not be a justification for war and hostility, but an inexhaustible source of mutual enrichment and growth. The community will support, enable, and affirm

109

people in their development and provide them with a creative, dynamic environment in which to experience life. Above all, it will be a joyful community with a capacity to assist people in all times of sorrow and grief and to renew them through spontaneous activities. It will be like a seed that dies and regenerates with new life—one which becomes a creative force within the world.

This is our hope.

Marriage, Family, and Life Style in New Community

The exploration of this topic was undertaken by persons from Africa, Asia, Europe, Latin America, North America, and the Pacific. The topic was divided into three sub-sections, and these are reported as follows: the Christian Family; the Christian Family and Society; Changing Patterns of Family Life.

The background material on these issues was rich, and in addition each participant brought his or her own vivid experiences to the subject. In the plenary discussion of this report much dissatisfaction was registered. It was recognized that more long-term and intensive attention must be given to the plurality and seriousness of the topics here considered when approaching issues of the family on a global, ecumenical level.

The Christian Family

1. *Background of the Group Members.* In our discussion we became aware of the different situations from which we spoke. Group members came from Egypt (Coptic Orthodox), South Africa (Roman Catholic), Gambia (Methodist), Germany (Lutheran), and Switzerland (Baptist). Some came from extended families and strong traditional structures in which marriage and family are very important, while others were from nuclear families with fluid structures in society. Both, however, reported that marriage was marked by divorce and the weakening of social adhesion. We thus recognized that the wider community of persons must be part of our concern, and that single people, lone parents, divorced, elderly people, children, and people living in communes must also be part of our consideration. These issues will come up in the section concerned with changing patterns in family life.

2. *What is a Christian Marriage/Family?* We discovered that there are different points of view concerning what makes marriage "Christian." For some the quality of sanctity is to be seen in that marriage is grounded in the timeless

mystery of divine love, while for others a Christian marriage means to show a particular quality of relationship in the ongoing life together.

We found these common elements as a starting point to discussion: A Christian marriage is normally begun with a ceremony in the church or a blessing. It is marked by the will to life-long faithfulness and dedication to one another and to the well-being of the marriage/family, including the community of friendships around it and its many levels of social concern.

However, in the discussion we became aware that such a picture of Christian marriage/family life is questioned from many sides, although it may function in several socioreligious settings and in individual family situations. In areas of progessive secularization, a community of common faith or traditional Christian surrounding can no longer be presupposed as a uniting and determining factor. In addition, in such settings, family piety is often regarded as an imposition on the children, hindering rather than furthering personal and Christian maturity. For example, in the German Democratic Republic an analysis of family situations posed the question of whether a so-called Christian family is not merely a remainder of the bourgeois family in a post-Christian era. Also, in countries other than those that have been traditionally "Christian," religious pluralism occasions the problem of mixed marriages (two different religions), posing the question of the "Christian" element in familial relationships from a completely different angle.

So, in each situation the term "Christian" in relation to family and community life needs to be reflected on and redefined. In the plenary discussion of this section, several criticisms were made that the working assumptions of this report with reference to what constitutes a "Christian family" were too narrow.

3. What Impact Can the New Community Have on the Life of the Family in Community.

a. OBSTACLES. To begin with, we made ourselves aware of some existing societal problems. For example, there are often double standards for women and men with regard to fidelity. There are also many role expectations which foster an imbalance of personal freedom, dignity, and power. In addition, internal problems of excessive individualism, narcissism, and materialism put heavy strains on family relationships in rich countries and, among the poor, lack of adequate food, shelter, and work add to family stress.

On the one hand and particularly in the nuclear family, excessive demands on intimacy frequently lead to emotional exhaustion and disappointment. On the other hand, in many parts of the world the absence of the father or of both parents because of the work situation (migrant workers, greater distances between home and work place) has torn apart whole families, with children being left to the care of grandparents. In addition, the most recent movement for the liberation of women may have further loosened traditional bonds and confused sexual and social relationships in places where not enough attention has been given to concomitant changes in society as a whole. This has shown its effects, particularly on children. Thus, in the task of renewing family life, the double suppression of women—one coming from the wider sociopolitical and economic context and the other from the role expectations within the family—needs to be taken into account.

b. HOW CAN WE MOVE FORWARD? In many situations the starting point will be women's consciousness raising: that woman is equally loved by God and, as a member of humankind, is created, sustained, and guided by God. The raising of consciousness will raise questions that will challenge traditional concepts in family, society, and church which hamper the recognition of women's equality and dignity with men.

A next step will be to deal with myths concerning sex roles and roles of authority. The following statement was made by a group member: "The oppressor in church, society, and at home is the same." This is to say that the kinds of relationships and role-thinking that persons have within the church and society influence the family, and reciprocally the kinds of relationships and role-thinking in the church affect everyday life in family and society. Hence, there is a need for churches to rethink marriage and family education.

The church has a crucial role in educating the family about equality through:

• its preaching and teaching, especially in premarital counseling, so that positive aspects in the various traditions would not be neglected. The church should also take a fresh look at biblical interpretation of male/female attitudes and roles. Furthermore, the concept of the father as "head of the family" will need to receive an interpretation in terms of interdependence and mutual accountability ("being subject to one another"; Eph. 5:21). Other images of mutuality may be developed in existing cultural settings;
• its instruction by role models (couples/families/communities);
• the formation of a community that sustains people in the process of change—a community including women and men, marriage partners and

singles, children, widows, and aged people, as they must seek new identities and roles;

- its emphasis on personhood and mutuality rather than patterns of subordination in marriage ceremonies and in the selection of liturgical sermon texts for weddings;
- its emphasis that the nuclear family (where this is the predominant form) is not a means for the exclusion of others, but rather that it can become an opportunity for its members to build inclusive community.

c. How can we describe a vision in terms of new community in the family? Love, the prime virtue of Christian living, is based on mutual dignity and respect. However, love also encompasses a polarity: Love, on the one hand, invites and allows freedom for the realization of the self and the individual, for personal development, the unfolding of gifts, and the challenge of social, economic, and political participation ("finding oneself"). Love, on the other hand, also invites a voluntary limitation of freedom ("losing oneself") as commitment to the interests of partnership, family, and community. This polarity can be an integrative force in the personal and emotional nurture of an individual in relation to members of a family and persons in the wider community.

The tension between these two poles, besides various other factors, may cause social break-ups, isolation, divorce, and the neglect of children. These upheavals are often blamed on the new emphasis on equal opportunities for women. However, since traditionally freedom from the family has (contrary to the biblical commandment of mutual love [Eph. 5:25 ff.; Gal. 6:2]) been assigned to man and dedication to the family has been assigned to woman, the function of family commitment can become vacated when the mother and wife no longer fully dedicates herself to this assignment. In the new community the call to freedom and participation in society, as well as the call to devotion—to the sustaining of personal relationships—in the family and beyond, will be shared more equally by women and men. Freedom is thus not necessarily *from* the family; it can be freedom *in* and *for* the family. This was a constant reminder by African women in response to a Western attitude which they sensed downgraded family involvement.

The Christian Family
and Society

1. *The Christian Family and Family Systems.* Group members recognized that they represented, within the Christian community, two family systems—

nuclear and extended. Each has its own advantages and disadvantages; for example, for persons living under the extended family system there may be problems of space, privacy, and heavy economic responsibilities. However, these individuals also have the opportunity to live within their cultural and traditional background and to practice Christian principles of mutual help and interdependence.

The Christian nuclear family can also include persons regardless of marital status from the community.

In both family systems, the relationship between marriage partners is enriched not only by romance and sexual intimacy, but by friendship between themselves and with others.

2. *Specific Problems Faced by Families.* The group identified domestic problems and social pressures that families must face. The domestic problems included:

- alcoholism;
- breakdown in the relationship and communication between spouses, and between parent and child or children;
- lack of skill/education/ability to take on family responsibilities;
- infidelity;
- violence of any form—mental, physical, and so forth—by any member of the family;
- lack of education or false information about the use of contraceptives and about population issues.

The list of social pressures included:

- customs and culture that might pose an economic strain on young couples, for example, expensive weddings;
- mass-media pressures—especially programs which ''persuade,'' or show violence or sexism;
- racial, cultural, or religious language barriers faced by families within their own countries and by those who make geographical moves either voluntarily, or through force of circumstance. These might be oppressive acts by people in authority, creating uprooted settlements, or external foreign powers which threaten or forcefully occupy their homelands, creating refugees, etc.;
- misuse of power by those who are in authority, thus allowing conditions

of unemployment, exploitation of labor, miseducation and misuse concerning drugs, contraceptives, etc.;
• modern housing structures which force families into ghettos of isolation.

3. *Help for the Family.* The new community of women and men can and should help to salvage, preserve, and strengthen the Christian family. How?
• by providing educational and training programs to communicate more effectively; recognizing the importance of each other; generating a sense of "true community," such as looking to others' needs and improving the economic situation of family members by offering jobs, etc.;
• through the building up of support-systems for families, for example, married couples' groups, etc.;
• through conscious practice of Christian solidarity.

4. *The Christian Family as a Dynamic Force.* The group reaffirmed that strong Christian families can have some positive influence on church and society, their trends and structures. If well-organized, these families can lobby authorities in charge of education, mass media, and so forth, to change policies/programs which are detrimental to family life.

5. *Methods.* Christian lay members should be encouraged and trained to maximize the use of their gifts so that they move into decision-making bodies of the church and society and have the opportunity to directly influence their policies and decisions. Christian families should encourage their family members to be interested in and, if they so choose, to take up political careers.

Changing Patterns of Family Life

This section, related to the preceding discussion, wishes to stress that "isolated persons" are not to be considered as marginal, but that they can also constitute a family group. The "family" does not exist on one side with the "non-family" on the other. The isolated, the divorced, the separated, the widowed, the single—all are whole human beings, loved by God, called to oneness with God. We must seek theological images and theological language that give proper place to this form of "family." For isolated persons and for the whole community we must rediscover all the dimensions of friendship, love, and openness toward others. Some people will choose to live in community or in many personal emotional relationships. These forms have been

115

marginalized by being called "alternative life styles," implying that they are deviant or less complete than the life style lived by the majority of people. Each child of God has the freedom to choose the life style which will develop his or her full potential, for we are the "living stones" which make up the community. We are not fixed, but always growing and changing. We must exercise our God-given freedom with responsibility for others in the community. Every life style has the responsibility to embody the love of God and to reflect mutuality in relationships.

In each of our cultural and personal situations we identified these so-called alternate life styles of choice or force of circumstances: single people, lone parents, homosexuals, separated, divorced, and remarried persons, persons married outside of the church, persons living in communities and communes.

At a time when we call on the church to support families in the face of enormous societal pressures, the church must give support and guidance to these "families" as well. That support involves encouraging and enhancing the community's ability to make choices and, in those choices, to live out the qualities of mutuality, responsibility, covenant relationship, forgiveness, and reconciliation.

Scripture in New Community

The Authority of the Bible in
the Community of Women and Men
in the Church

The basis of membership of the WCC is as follows: the World Council of Churches is "a fellowship of churches which confess the Lord Jesus Christ as God and Saviour according to the Scriptures and therefore seek to fulfill together their common calling to the glory of one God, Father, Son and Holy Spirit" (WCC Constitution). The authority of Scripture is expressed in the basis of membership.

The Basis of Authority

We highly commend the document *The Bible: Its Authority and Interpretation in the Ecumenical Movement* (Faith and Order Paper No. 99).

For the church the Bible is the authoritative word of God. The document cited above deals with the different meanings of the term the "authority" of

Scripture. First, the Bible has weight and influence as literature. Second, the "authority" of the Bible "may be seen as consisting in its character as an indispensable source of knowledge for the church" (p. 46). There is, however, a third, and most important, meaning:

> When we speak of the "authority" of the Bible in the strict sense, we mean that it makes the Word of God audible and is therefore able to lead men [sic]* to faith. We are not thinking of its authority as a literary document nor of its literary value, nor even of its authority as the oldest documentation of the apostolic message, but of the fact that men [sic] are arrested by the message of the Bible, the fact that they hear God speaking to them from the Bible. Ultimately, of course, this authority is the authority of God himself and not that of the Bible as a book (p. 47).

The authority of the Bible has its basis in Jesus Christ, the author of our faith. The authority of Scripture "cannot be derived from any external criteria" (p. 53): it is derived from the activity of God in Christ through the Holy Spirit, and it is with the aid of that same Spirit that the Bible is to be read and interpreted today (cf. pp. 53–55).

The Diversity of Biblical Traditions

The Bible respects different traditions, each testifying to the same gospel, but no single tradition can in itself represent the Bible's full richness. *This diversity within the Bible neither detracts from its underlying unity nor counteracts its overall authority.* The Bible expresses the beauty of variety and the richness of human existence and divine mercy. It sanctions many forms of service based upon God's diversity of gifts and calls all of humankind to a future of hope and joy in the new community of women and men. On the basis of this affirmation, Christians and churches are called to reinterpret one and the same truth in their own culture and situation so that they encourage, correct, and complement one another, building one another up in Christ.

The reading and interpretation of the Bible is a task of the whole people of God—women and men, young and old. A female perspective is important because of the dominant male perspective of the traditional reading and interpretation of the Bible. In the community of women and men in the church we need to read the Bible together in a balanced and inclusive manner and in a way that is affirming for the whole people of God in the community of the church.

---

*See Sheffield Recommendation A.3d.ii regarding the need for inclusive language.

Biblical Authority and Human Community

For the church, the unique and central content of the Bible is the message of Jesus Christ. As a result there cannot be an equal authority assigned to every part or every simple statement that is found in the Bible. The Bible is a testimony of God's revelation in history and inevitably shows signs of the social and cultural surroundings, in which the different Scriptures were written. As the Word of God to people in particular situations the Scriptures are conditioned by their times both in their ways of expression and in their contexts.

It is remarkable that the Scriptures, written in a patriarchal setting, also contain antipatriarchal passages of great importance. This emphasizes the unique depths of their Scripture's authority: it is not the patriarchal framework (the sociocultural pattern of that time) that is authoritative, but the redeeming message from God conveyed within it.

Further, correctives to sexist attitudes within the Bible and church tradition are to be found within the Bible itself. For example, taking the historical context into consideration, most exegetes today hold the opinion that there is no sufficient argument against ordination of women within the Bible itself. Moreover, no act, attitude, or system of oppression can be properly legitimized by reference to Holy Scripture or by appeal to its authority. It is incompatible with any confession of faith in Jesus Christ as God and Savior according to the Scriptures.

The oppressive use of the "authority" of the Bible is not confined to the subordination of women; another instance in history was the appeal to the Bible to legitimize the institution of slavery. A contemporary example was cited in a response to this section report by a delegate from the Middle East. She called on the churches "to give due attention to the continual war and sufferings in the Middle East—a situation where such a misuse or misinterpretation of the Bible can play an important and dangerous role." She added that awareness of biblical authority and interpretation is necessary if the churches are to meet the Christian commitment to peace and justice.

Biblical Interpretation

Biblical interpretation involves the interaction, even the confrontation, of texts and contexts. While we might agree that the community of faith must listen to the word of God as it is communicated through the Bible, that listening process is conditioned by two types of context: the modern context (including both the overall socioeconomic, political, and cultural dimensions and the specific contexts, or conditioning, of individual interpreters) and the context of the biblical texts and their authors. Each of the extracts below is a quotation of a participant in the sub-section discussion.

1. *Modern contexts.* The churches' struggles to know what faithfulness requires and any interpretations of Scripture take place in the context of the pain and urgency of such issues as war and violence, economic oppression, ecological exploitation, racism, and sexism. In addition, one must also consider the influences of particular situations and the conditioning of individual interpreters. Each interpreter comes to the Bible with presuppositions, perspectives, methods, and questions conditioned by her or his economic, social, political, and cultural context, by gender, by theological traditions, and by educational background. These approaches *to* the Bible affect what word is heard *from* the text. This affirmation carries several implications, which are outlined below.

The task of biblical interpretation is a task of the whole people of God, not only of elites or professional experts. The Bible studies conducted in Nicaragua and reported in *The Gospel in Solentiname* by Ernesto Cardenal are examples of what can happen when people encounter the biblical stories in their own lives.

All that we know about the biblical message is conditioned by the questions people have brought. When new groups of people ask new questions, we discover a new richness in the biblical witness. Many times the Bible does not have a chance to say to us what it might say because we have been deaf to it. The exegesis of oppressed peoples from the Third World and the exegesis of women has brought new truths to light.

—a Latin American woman

We have the custom that after the sermon, there is a response from the people. The women weave songs from their interpretation of the Scripture readings in their experiences. The songs are beautiful and the insights are fresh and new.

—an African woman

Many of the unique perspectives that each of us brings to the reading of Scripture are invisible to us. We do not realize how our situations, experiences, or the methods that we use to study the Scriptures condition what we can learn from them. The involvement of women and men from different backgrounds in the task of interpreting the Scriptures can help each person become aware of blind spots and hidden assumptions.

119

When people are divorced from their contexts, they are not able to interrogate the text. For a long time I was not aware of how my personhood as a woman, and as a person living in the Third World, had been taken from me, and so I had lost my context from which to question the text.

—a Latin American woman

There will be a plurality of interpretations, not a single objectively verifiable, agreed-upon truth. This plurality of interpretations can occur *between* different socioeconomic or cultural groups (rich and poor; First, Second, and Third Worlds; women and men; etc.), or *within* the same group, church, family, or other context. For example, women from historically divided churches or denominations might discover common ground between them because of their experiences as women. At the same time, they might find themselves divided from others within their confessional group. These new divisions and connections profoundly affect the direction of ecumenical conversations in general, and particularly in relationship to the community of women and men in the church.

And that is good. There is no danger in such variety. Rather it helps us grow.

—a man from the Middle East

The fact of a plurality of interpretations raises the issue of norms or standards. If "the norm" is understood as that which the community of faith under the Holy Spirit finds acceptable, then it must be recognized that norms vary between particular communities of faith and undergo shifts within a particular community. One person, however, insisted:

As long as the church confesses the Bible as the criterion for the faith and life of the church, we must speak of the new experience of women in the light of Scripture. Though there are many patriarchal expressions in the Bible, the dynamic of salvation history points to their reinterpretation in the light of Jesus Christ, the radical liberator.

—a Japanese woman

Although it is sometimes suggested that the church must "let the Bible speak for itself," that suggestion was countered as follows:

The Bible "spoke for itself" on the slavery issue for years. When the economy changed and large numbers of slaves were not necessary or profitable, consciousness changed, and people began to read the Bible differently.

—an African woman

Orthodox respondents to this section report stressed the need to read the Scriptures in continuity with the generations of believers who preceded us, as well as the need to remind the churches of the importance of the unifying power of the Scriptures. (In this connection see p. 00, which attempts to identify a criterion for testing the integrity of our interpretation.)

The Bible itself can be the source of some norms of interpretation, such as the pervasive theme of liberation, or examples of Jesus' teachings or activity:

> Looking at the gospels, you have a sense that Christ wouldn't do a certain thing.
>
> —an African woman

This sense about Jesus might come from stories in which Jesus contradicted customs of his day (for example by including women among his followers) or when he sided with the poor and oppressed.

> We build on the clues to how Jesus responded to issues in his own day. We must study in order to understand the circumstances of his day and of ours.
>
> —a Latin American woman

> Just as for Jesus the proclamation of God's reign and of its values challenged the theologies of established religion, so also the community of the faithful always is engaged in self-criticism in light of the values of the in-breaking reign.
>
> —a European man

2. *Contexts of the biblical texts.* The biblical texts must be understood in their historical contexts. God's word is "incarnational," embedded in a specific place and time. This insight is the cornerstone of modern biblical criticism, but its implications for the task of interpretation must be both reaffirmed and expanded. In particular, attention must be paid to the social, economic, and political contexts of Scripture, as well as to the usually recognized issues of historical and literary contexts. Thus, for example, before drawing conclusions from 1 Corinthians 11 and 14 or 1 Timothy 2 concerning women, the major concerns of the church at the times of these writings must be examined.

> If Paul's concern in writing to the church at Corinth was that nothing impede the hearing of the gospel, and for that larger purpose women had to accept restrictions on their dress and behavior, then the interpreter must ask what factors today impede the hearing of the gospel. The conclusions we draw about women's roles might be the opposite of Paul's conclusions. If in the second instance Timothy's church was primarily concerned about the health, faithfulness, and survival of the church, and drew conclusions about certain issues of church order and ethical behavior, we have to ask the same questions in out contexts. Questions about the faithfulness, health, and survival of the church, if we really faced these questions, would push us to respond to issues of justice and liberation.
>
> —a North American woman

In the context of an understanding of the larger sociopolitical and economic frameworks that underly biblical texts, full account must be taken of the fact that Scripture was written down and edited in the midst of a patriarchial society and by men who were conditioned by their culture to view women as subordinate. What is remarkable is that, given this context, the message of liberation is heard at all. (See "The Authority of Scripture in Light of New Experiences of Women" [Amsterdam Report].)

Language, Imagery, and Symbols*

Language for God and humanity is in some cultures inherently inclusive. In several African languages as, for example, in Finnish, the word for "he" and "she" is the same (Rose Zoé-Obianga, "Resources in the Tradition for the Renewal of Community"). Nevertheless, although grammatical language may be inclusive words denoting gender are present in all cultures, and these terms are usually not inclusive.

Since languages in all cultures can be bearers of noninclusive words and connotations, many felt that terms for God and for people in hymns, prayers, sermons, Scripture, liturgy, theological language and curriculum should be carefully chosen to express inclusiveness.

1. *Language about persons.* In addition to sharing in the variety of gifts (1 Corinthians 12), we are as one body: children, women, and men, expressing the diversity of humanity. It is important, therefore, that all these ways of being human be *visible* and *functioning* within the body of Christ. Because we are all included in humanity, the church must include and nurture all of us by the imagery it uses in Scripture, teaching, worship, and theological language. When the church uses only male images in its works, this is a form of domination and exclusion painful to female members of the body. An Asian man noted the importance of feminine qualities such as mother love, inner peace, and concern in church imagery. These qualities are valuable and should be nurtured in men as well as women. A Danish woman said she felt there was a tendency in sermons for male preachers to use male imagery, such as weapons of war, to symbolize strength of faith. She suggested that to create a balance, women (and all lay people) be allowed to preach in the churches; thus the church would draw from a variety of human experiences.

2. *Language and images of God.* Of particular importance for the community of women and men in the church is the language and imagery of God. It should

* Note related discussion in the report on "Ministry and Worship in New Community (pp. 00–00).

be realized that in different traditions there are different perceptions of God, and this encourages the development of a range of diverse imagery which broadens the apprehension of God. However, a North American Orthodox woman said she felt that such diverse perceptions were dangerous to the unity of the faith, and some were so abstract as to deny divine revelation.

A Danish woman said that a variety of images was especially necessary for children. She proposed even the use of biblical symbols from nature to image God in order to avoid limiting God to a masculine image. A Canadian woman related her joy on hearing feminine God-imagery. She told how her use of feminine terminology for God allowed her to image and feel God as nurturing and caring—a mother image. A man from Taiwan related that in Japan, God was referred to in the Tienri-kyo religion as "parent."

Group members expressed concern for the pain women have experienced as a result of noninclusive language. An Orthodox woman from the U.S. explained that the terms "Father, Son and Holy Spirit" were never meant to connote masculinity, but rather to lead us to correct concepts of the inner trinitarian life. "All human terms are inadequate to express the transcendent, ineffable Godhead," she said, "but Jesus Christ gave us the name 'Abba' as an insight and not a block, and it is not easily to be exchanged. Patristic writers as well as some modern Roman Catholic and Protestant theologians have made this point."*

However, in each denomination inclusive language both of God and of persons should be implemented as far as possible in liturgy, theological language, and biblical translations.

3. *Symbols.* A woman from Latin America noted particular problems in the use of allegorical symbols, especially those which have traditionally been used in relation to women.

> Going from an allegorical symbol to the practicalities of life in the church has had disappointing consequences for women. For example, the church as a body has often been described in feminine symbols (Eph. 5:25–32), and women therefore have been taught that their place is in this feminine "body" rather than in clerical or headship roles. Such strong symbols have thus strengthened arguments for keeping women out of authoritative positions in church institutional life, although they are only allegorical.

*Gregory of Nyssa, *Against Eunomius* I. 14, in vol. 5 of *A Select Library of Nicene and Post-Nicene Fathers of the Church*, ed. Schaff and Wace (Grand Rapids: Wm. B. Eerdmans, reprinted from 1892 ed.), p. 51; Louis Bouyer, *Woman in the Church* (San Francisco: Ignatius Press, 1979); Gail Ramshaw Schmidt, "Lutheran Liturgical Prayer and God as Mother," *Worship* 52:6 (November 1978).

"Eve" also has been used allegorically to depict woman as the symbol of primal sin. The symbols for woman from mythologies of other cultures, however, have been sometimes edifying.

Among the Cherokee Indians of the Americas, a mythology also exists regarding the creation or origin of the man and the woman. The story goes that man was created first. Thereafter, the gods saw that he was incomplete and decided to create the woman. She was then created and summoned into existence through his head. She emerged from his head beautifully wrapped in corn leaves. The man looked up and saw this beautifully adorned figure and commenced with undressing her to see the beauty concealed under the leaves. But in his eagerness, he lost control of his sense of propriety, decency, and finesse, thereby offending her womanhood. She then hops to the ground from his head and takes to her heels. The man, realizing his guilt, runs after her as he pleads for forgiveness. But she is too angry to listen to him. Then again, the creator finding the man guilty of the offense but not in favor of disharmony between man and woman, caused berries to sprout on the woman's path. The beauty and aroma of the berries then arrested her attention whereupon she stops to admire and pluck them. In the process, the man catches up with her and pleads for forgiveness. She does so and offers him some berries. They share these fruits in a spirit of love, reconciliation, and joy. Afterwards the woman suggests that they take some home, but the man suggested that they uproot them and take the plant home. They did and with that, mankind's initial relationship of joy, love, and harmony was established.

—From the African Regional Consultation Report on the
Community of Women and Men in the Church study

Many of the group felt that basing existential conclusions on allegory was simplistic and even insidious for the community of women and men. All agreed that biblical accounts involving women need to be recovered.

Positive Uses of Scripture in
the New Community of Women and Men
in the Church

This discussion was based on two questions. They are quite closely connected and not to be considered in isolation from each other.

1. *How should we be interpreting and using Scripture within the community of women and men in the church?* Scripture must not be read in isolation. Both its historical context and the contexts of modern interpreters must be taken into account if biblical passages are not to be misunderstood. It is important to understand the social, political, economic, and religious contexts in which a given passage was written. Similarly, the various modern contexts of readers

and hearers of the Word must be considered in the process of interpretation. Thus, for example, the situation in Corinth must be taken into account as part of our understanding of Paul's instructions to women on the subject of the headdress (1 Corinthians 11). So also, however, we must take into account the contemporary context within which that teaching is heard. For many societies, the headdress itself is not an issue, though in others (as for example southern India) social and economic considerations still make it an issue. Furthermore, insofar as Paul's real concern was the way the sexes related to each other in the community of faith, the questions underlying this text continue to address the particular agenda of this consultation.

It is most important that the whole community participate in interpreting Scripture. Very practically, this means that in the worship life of a congregation biblical interpretation should not only be done through the monologue of the preacher, but also in a dialogue within the community, in meditation, and in inclusive groups copreparing the sermon.

Broadening the community of interpreters of the Bible adds an essential element to our understanding of Scripture. Especially where men have dominated biblical interpretation, a strong participation of women would make the difference clear. Women reading with their own eyes, from their own experiences, are often able to see what has escaped men for centuries and to identify with what men could not feel or recognize in the texts. Women contribute a whole new expertise to the task of interpreting Scripture. For example, at the Amsterdam consultation mentioned earlier, a Danish woman employed dance and pictures to present her interpretation of the story of the woman who was a sinner in Luke 7. Participants at that meeting found out how strongly previous readings of this story had been stamped by a focus on the theologically interesting words at the end of the story about "the forgiving of sins" and "love." A woman, however, seeing with her own eyes and from her own experience, was able to open up a new meaning of the beginning of the story. It became no longer an introduction to a theological debate, but a reflection of the painful suffering that the woman of the story had been going through and the courage with which she decided to go to Jesus in the house of a Pharisee.

2. *How does Scripture help to establish the community of women and men in the church?* Passages like John 20:30 ("Now Jesus did many other signs in the presence of the disciples, which are not written in this book," *RSV*) show us clearly that the Scriptures have a very specific purpose. For the

church, they are meant to be about *life in Christ*. This purpose should define our use of Scripture: it should be the criterion with which to test the integrity of our interpretation.

Thus, for example, we can recognize the distinction between two ways in which Scripture is reinterpreted *within* Scripture itself, and we can make a judgment about their relative power to address us. On the one hand, there is the way Genesis 1 is interpreted in Galatians 3 to show the liberating effect of Christ's restoring of creation in the new community. On the other hand, there is the reinterpretation of Genesis 2 and 3 in 1 Corinthians 11 and 14, when Paul curbs the freedom of the Corinthian church in the light of the particular Corinthian situation and under pressure of the "last days." Only what supports real community *(koinonia)* remains within the overall purpose of Scripture.

Scripture is addressed to persons created in the image of God, male and female, in community, not to men or women exclusively. In 2 Cor. 5:16ff. we find a clear illustration of the profile of the new creation in Christ. When the original Greek is read with a patriarchal perspective, misleading translations, such as "if anyone is in Christ, *he* is a new creation," suggest false limitation. Rather, this passage shows clearly the broad implications of the new creation. In the new creation the old has passed away, and, in our present context, injustice to women *has* disappeared. Furthermore, it is the whole world, and consequently the "old things" of the whole world that have passed away in this new creation.

Acknowledging that it is God's ultimate purpose to include all in his love, we must not forget that within history God's concern for justice sets God on the side of those to whom injustice is done. Within our present context this would mean that speaking about God's love for all must not in any way weaken our conviction that God is partisan, that God sides with the oppressed. We cannot speak about a new community of women and men as long as injustice to women prevails. We must not, in the name of universal love, conceal injustice. Rather we must act justly in order to affect love. Without justice there can be no true unity in a community of women and men.

In the context of this overall purpose of Scripture, we do find many more specific insights as well which bear on the new community of women and men. We can see much that has escaped us for a long time, for example, the crucial role of women in Israel's liberation from Egypt. In the past, whe have concentrated only on Moses, but now we see also the important participation of the midwives, his mother, his sister Miriam, and the Pharaoh's daughter.

We can learn the painful way of suffering by which we are to follow Jesus (see Heb. 2:18 and Phil. 2:5ff.*) in order to reach the new community. We can learn that such suffering does not mean that we are to accept a victim's life. Our Christian suffering is for the sake of Christ, which means that it must be seen in direct relationship with the overall purposes described earlier.

Ministry and Worship in New Community

Witness and the Prophetic Ministry

Coming together at this consultation in a great diversity we are once more struck by the variety of situations in which our churches find themselves. Many times churches are scattered and divided in changing societies that suffer because of political violence and/or economic exploitation. These phenomena pertain not only to the Third World but to most urbanized societies with permanent or temporary migrant workers, refugees, and students from different faiths, confessions, and cultures.

We acknowledge that the WCC has made efforts to raise consciousness on these issues in our various churches and that some work is being done. However, there is an urgent need for a prophetic ministry which meets specific human needs.

The minister and all others who have responsibility in our churches must take the risk to denounce all forms of oppression, especially of women. They need to seek the partnership of lay people, of other social groups, and of peoples of other faiths and ideologies. They must seek solutions and engage in action.

The churches, as well as each individual Christian, must commit themselves

*Note the two different translations/interpretations of this text in light of the present awareness of inclusive language:

Have this mind among yourselves, which you have in Christ Jesus, who, though he was in the form of God, did not count equality with God a thing to be grasped, but emptied himself, taking the form of a servant, being born in the likeness of men. And being found in human form he humbled himself and became obedient unto death, even death on a cross *(RSV).*

Let your bearing towards one another arise out of your life in Christ Jesus. For the divine nature was his from the first; yet he did not think to snatch at equality with God, but made himself nothing, assuming the nature of a slave. Bearing the human likeness, revealed in human shape, he humbled himself, and in obedience accepted even death—death on a cross *(NEB).*

to justice which is a foundation for the new community of women and men in the church (Amos 5:24; Mic. 6:8).

Worship as well as the structure of our churches should bear witness to this community of liberation, justice, and love. In fact, according to the Bible true worship requires the doing of justice.

Lay Ministry

We affirm the Christian truth that through initiation (baptism, confirmation, Eucharist) all persons become part of the whole people of God, with responsibility for the church and in the church. Each person has a gift of the Holy Spirit for the benefit of the whole body, and that is true regardless of sex, race, or class.

We affirm that "as many of you as were baptized into Christ have put on Christ. There is neither Jew nor Greek, there is neither slave nor free, there is neither male nor female; for you are all one in Christ Jesus" (Gal. 3:27–28).

We affirm the equal dignity and joint responsibility of all Christians through the diversity of their ministries. The Scripture still challenges us: "There are varieties of working, but it is the same God who inspires them all in every one" (1 Cor. 12:6).

We affirm that "grace was given to each of us according to the measure of Christ's gift. . . . Some should be apostles, some prophets, some evangelists, some pastors and teachers, to equip the saints for the work of the ministry, for building up the body of Christ" (Eph. 4:7, 11–12).

Based on our understanding of Scripture and Jesus' ministry we look for a time when all members of the people of God shall be recognized as having discernment and an effective voice in the common search and in the organization of the church.

We envision:

- a church structure that recognizes the authority of service, but guards against confusing ordination and hierarchy;
- more involvement of laity throughout the church structures in the development of theology, worship, and liturgy. We support those places where even now laity is involved with clergy in preparing sermons and the weekly worship;
- alternative mission ministries for laity, with eventual official and financial recognition for involvement of laity in bringing about justice within society;

- a church in which everyone encourages, supports, and compensates laity in full-time vocational ministries within the church;
- a church in which everyone respects the unique gifts and functions necessary for revealing the kingdom of God among us. We encourage an exploration of a variety of ways of affirming ministries (such as ordination, consecration, commissioning).

We confess that the reality of practices in many of our churches all over the world is not fully in accordance with the Scripture. All churches constantly have to measure their practice according to the gospel message.

We admit and confess the inadequacy of our present church administration and organization. In most parts of the world, laywomen are the majority of membership, but they are in few positions of responsibility in governing bodies in the churches. Instead they have positions as fund-raisers, cooks, cleaners, decorators, educators, and secretaries. Women often experience a high incidence of discrimination, for instance with regard to pensions, job security, benefits, and so forth, and little opportunity for job advancement. Often they are used for cheap or unpaid labor.

We recognize that laity, women and men, are restricted in their theological development by lack of proper training and opportunity for placement. This leads to the hesitation of laity, especially women, to accept positions of responsibility.

The Ordained Ministry

The group was made up of representatives of the Lutheran, Reformed, Orthodox, Roman Catholic, and Anglican churches. It recognized the need to continue a discussion of the ordination of women to the presbyterate within the unique ecumenical context of the WCC. It was aware of the complexity and diversity of the existing situations both within and between the different churches. The state of the discussion is also at different stages in different cultures. Amongst the churches there is a plurality of practice embracing those who do ordain women, those who do not, and those who are hesitant for ecumenical reasons.

Theological and sociological reasons always need investigating. As our knowledge of sociology and theology develops, we are offered a chance to deepen our understanding and practice of ministry and our relations with one another.

The issues involved in this matter touch us at our deepest level, embedded as they are in liturgy, symbolism, and spirituality. There can be no real progress if church, state, or any group within the church seeks to force a change in practice without taking this into account. At the same time we should never forget that all problems of the ministry are related to the social and cultural context where the identity of the church and of individual Christians is constantly being challenged.

Our discussions began by listening to the reasons for the ordination of women, advanced by women who wished to be ordained in churches which prohibited this. Three reasons were given by the women: (1) Their present experience of ministry led to a realization of the need for ordination to create a wholeness of ministry—a combining of word and sacrament; (2) Some women believed that they were being called by God to the presbyterate and looked to the church to recognize this calling; and (3) The growth of feminist consciousness demands a response by the church at all levels of symbol and structure.

We also listened to the arguments of those representing the Orthodox and Roman Catholic churches, churches that do not ordain women to the presbyterate.

The discussion did not take into consideration the experiences of ordained women from churches that do have this practice.

It was clear that the process of listening to and questioning each other among these various groups must continue without prejudice to the actions of those who ordain women and those who do not.

Worship

In order to help create meaningful worship many things need to be taken into account. In addition to the function of the ordained minister, there is the experience of the whole congregation and its particular context.

Some religious symbols appear to be universal, connoting almost the same meaning in all cultures: for example, water, light, fire. They can be used in a Christian context. The cross is a traditional Christian symbol universally accepted and understood.

Other religious symbols, such as colors, project quite different meanings within different contexts. A Sudanese man explained that even the color of clerical dress could make a vast difference. In his country, black (a color symbolic of clergy in Western culture) gave the impression of mourning for the sins of the world, instead of aid or service. Some symbols, meaningful in one culture, may have the opposite connotation in another.

Further, symbols from the past tradition may be elusive, even misleading, to the modern mind. A Canadian woman, discussing clerical dress, stated that this particular symbol—once signifying service and celebration—is now often connected with male authority and domination. The very word authority has lost its original connotation and produces distorted imagery in the modern mind. The question was raised: "When Jesus Christ said in Matt. 28:18 'All authority in heaven and on earth has been given to me,' did he mean it as tyranny or as the Lord of love?''

It is important that a culture should not consider its religious symbols as universally expressive; many areas of the world need to be educated to that fact through the rich examples already in existence. In some cultures hymns can be used to show the changing seasons of the year through using agricultural imagery, while in a modern industrial city hymns that reflect urban experience and life may be more appropriate. An Asian man told how rice, the staple food, and not bread, had been used for the Eucharist in Taiwan.

The churches must be cautious in using and proposing new symbols; the people in different contexts should be free to create and use meaningful symbols that reflect their experiences.

Authority and Church Structures in New Community

Introduction: Vision and Reality

Many Christians, both women and men, feel uncomfortable when confronted with questions of authority, power, and structures in the church. These words have acquired a negative connotation and the temptation is to avoid them. However, we recognize that living in community always involves the exercise of authority and the structuring of life together. We are convinced that as Christians we have, in the life, ministry, and teachings of Christ and in the demands of the kingdom of God, a particular understanding of power and authority and of the structuring of the church's life. We know that the historical expression of the life of the church often runs counter to this understanding. In particular, our section looked at this question from the perspective of women and recognized that the issue is not simply one of the location and exercise of power and authority. There is a deeper issue, expressed in one of our reports: "Women, historically the powerless, know that their quest is not for power on the male model but for a new model of power. Thus even though the women and men are talking about the same reality, it holds for them a different meaning. . . ."* Our primary concern is to find a structure in which neither women nor men feel oppressed.

Our thinking about authority and structures has therefore been set within the *vision* which we share of the church as the new community of women and men and children, believing in and baptized into Christ, being made whole.

In our vision the *structures* of the church have as their function to make possible a new community in which each individual can use his or her talents to the full.

In our vision, the *style of life* is living together as sisters and brothers in the church, as the family of God (Eph. 2:19): sharing money and resources; creating an atmosphere of learning and solidarity; living the gospel and witnessing in society; standing for justice and compassion.

In our vision, the leadership of the church is the model of Jesus Christ, who always entered into dialogue.

In our vision, the church community in any part of the world is called to be the salt and light of the society in which it stands. Thus its structures ought to be a model for that society.

In reality we see churches with: structures alienating individuals, communities, and the church itself; life styles that are often based on economic structures rather than on Christian solidarity; styles of leadership that on the whole do not make full use of the capacities of women.

In writings ascribed to St. Paul and St. Peter there is a teaching of the subordination of women and the restriction of their participation in the life of the church. In many church laws and structures the full participation of women in leadership and power sharing with men is not possible.

Women are assigned in many churches to work among women and children. Women are seen as a threat to men unless they are marginalized.

In many churches, the style is nonaccommodating, cerebral, obsessed by organization, lacking in relaxation, contemplation, and sensitivity to feelings and emotions. We ask if this is connected with the subordination of women.

Already for the future the Holy Spirit is speaking and bringing about the

* *Authority in Community,* U.S. Faith and Order Commission (New York: National Council of Churches, 1980).

renewal of the church. Examples mentioned were: Mother Teresa's work in Calcutta, the Aladura movement in Nigeria, the Sojourners' movement in the USA, the charismatic movement in the West Indies and Britain, and the basic community movements in Latin America and Europe.

There is also a new impulse to explore prayer and contemplation, including integrating the body in our worship, under the urgency of the Holy Spirit.

Power and Authority

Power has often been seen as possessing control or command over others. We believe, however, that power is *the ability to implement action, to bring about an effect, sometimes a change.* It is always operative in relationship, whether intended consciously or expressed unconsciously, for loving purposes or for the demeaning of others, for good or for destructive ends. Therefore, the first thing is to be conscious of the dynamics of power which operate in all relationships, particularly between men and women: when there are opportunities for choosing options, people experience the power they have as individuals.

The traditional male view of power is that it is something very precious, to be defended at all costs, or to be fought for—as if the quantity of power in the world were limited.

On the other hand, many women experience power, like love, as something limitless: the more one's power is shared with others, the more power there is. When persons both contribute and receive power, all are enriched.

Authority has often been defined as "power to enforce obedience." However, we believe that authority is merely the right or claim to exercise power. Sources of authority include the model of Christ according to Scripture and also through tradition. As men have shown in the past, women are also showing that their life-experience, so often unrecognized, can be a source of authority. This personal experience includes the body, the emotions, and the consciousness of insights which, when added to reason, enable one to grasp the totality of a situation more fully.

Women who have experienced multiple oppressions of racism, classism, and sexism learn to survive in each of these oppressive systems by knowing their rules and how to operate within them. This experience of living in multiple oppressive systems brings special insights and claims to authority. Yet women often unconsciously negate their own authority and that of other women because they are unable or unwilling to recognize the wisdom and strength they have developed in the face of demeaning subordination and the contributions which they can therefore offer to the prevailing culture. Now women as a part of their Christian duty are being called to claim their authority so that they might assume their full share of responsibility.

Genuine authority is exercised, according to this perspective, when its existence is recognized and authenticated as a *gift* to the community. It is therefore both present in the person and willingly received by the community for its own good.

Therefore our vision for a new community of women and men includes this unique contribution by women concerning authority—a new perception of the limitlessness of power, a power that is mutually shared and always expanding for the use of the human community. When this perception of authority is present, there is no need for power to be hidden or power games to be played. Thus, both women and men are afforded the space to be more human as they make choices about their lives. When women act out of this new perception, they cease to rob men of their humanity by either shielding or manipulating them; and thus, the accusation against feminist women that they want to dominate others (by reversing the pyramid) can be dispelled. This perspective on power should therefore contribute to the lessening of men's fear that they will "lose" their power; instead, they should find power returned to them.

Structures

Empowerment involves more than decision making; it involves the preparation of Christian women and men for Christian life, witness, and ministry. It acknowledges that "our structures preach more loudly than our sermons."

There are structures in the churches that block the empowering of women and men in the church; for example:

- Rigid hierarchical structures as they often operate now make full participation by women and men difficult if not impossible.
- A conservative or fundamentalist interpretation of Scripture that stresses Pauline injunctions against women supplies a foundation for structure that excludes women from full participation in the church.
- The conservative stance of people in the churches hinders the reform of oppressive structures that stand in the way of empowering women in the church.
- The structures and nuances of the language that church people use often fail to express fully the respect for people which is part of the gospel.

Church structures need to be liberated from anti-Christian cultural values and reshaped by the values of the gospel. The structures that enable and empower are those that:

- provide for maximum participation for people in the life of the church;
- enable corporate decision making by the whole people of God;
- fulfill the purposes for which they were created while remaining relevant in today's situation;
- do not impose importations from another culture or context;
- have built-in checks and balances against the concentration of power in persons and roles in the structures of the church.

The experience we as participants in this consultation had with its structures illustrates much of what we feel about their importance. Did the structures of our conference at Sheffield give enough time for response to the main papers in plenary session? Was the agenda too rigid? Since we work not only with our heads, should not more bodily movement and relaxation, more fun and spontaneity, be part of the agenda? How could we be helped to exchange and share things from so many cultures?

The same criteria should be used regarding women's organizations, concerning participation, leadership, and so forth. In addition, there is the need to examine the role of women's organizations in relation to the church: Do they have an opportunity to influence and revitalize the church? Are they free to determine their own programs? Are they a force for conscientizing women and men, empowering them for action in the community of the church and for its ministry and mission in the world?

Basic to such empowering are opportunities for education and experience in Christian learning and witness. For example, in the Church of South India a strong theological education program for men and women has been developed entitled Theological Education for Christian Commitment and Action (TECCA). This is an extensive program that takes two years and prepares people to think and act theologically. Action is the key to the program, which stresses being a Christian within your own particular life style. In the Church of South India, they have also developed weekend teaching missions which help Christian people build a new community for a new style of life.

Styles of Leadership

We looked into past traditions to find inspiration and insights about the way in which women have exercised leadership as part of the people of God. There is much material in the Scriptures that contemporary biblical scholars, especially women, are discovering. In Africa there has been a tradition of priest/priestess, which is found today in indigenous churches, in the form of "prophet women/men" who are endowed with special gifts of wisdom and healing. They have no hierarchical power/status. There are traditions in the Near East and in Europe of special status and leadership of widows and deaconesses who set up households for virgins.* In the United States for the first time, a women has been elected bishop (United Methodist). Will she conform to the male elements in the present role of a bishop in her church or will she develop female ways of exercising her episcopal ministry?

We looked into *present models* of leadership favored by women.

1. *"Leadership from below"* does not change the power structure and dominance unless people "from below" deliberately try *not* to imitate the image under which they have suffered. For instance, in *Fiddler on the Roof* the milkman and his wife dream of a time when they will become wealthy and then they too will chase their domestics! The pattern to follow is Jesus who remained at the bottom of the human hierarchy.

The aim must be to serve the needs of the community. "Soft" leadership does not exclude some form of organization, structure, and planning; it includes rational decisions, but it takes an integrative, or holistic (*ganzheitlich*), approach.

2. *Teamwork at the top of the hierarchy of organizations.* The peak is flattened; for instance, three women, or two women and one man, share in the leadership as equals. Teamwork at the highest level of an organization can encourage teamwork on all layers of organization. In the cases described, this is deliberately intended. The instruments and goals are: sharing of information, sharing in decision making, promotion of the personality of everyone, complementary use of gifts, and participation. We see this as an example that can work with women, but is not confined to female leadership.

---

* Earliest deacons/deaconesses seem to be undifferentiated, that is, male and female deacons. They served the needs of the community practically and liturgically and were go-betweens of the bishop and laity; they took communion to the sick and collected offerings from people. Gradually women specialized in ministering to women only. Some fourth-and fifth-century deaconesses had been widows with experience in managing large households. Bishops put them in charge of households of choral virgins. They eventually developed into abbesses. Today, in some cultures mature women—as a second career after raising their children—become deaconesses.

3. *Model of nonhierarchical leadership.* A useful model of such leadership might be one with a reciprocal style. There might be a small team at the core; around this there would be, on the same level, lateral leadership reciprocating with itself and with the core. The core would be a resource to the rest of the circle for leadership. Limited terms of office would encourage participatory style and give more people skill in exercising leadership.

Solidarity and Competition

Women sometimes oppose efficient female leaders. This should not be taken as an excuse to discourage female leadership. Moreover it should be studied and laid open that sometimes men in power misuse women to fight efficient women. By disguising their own interest in the conflict the men keep their own dominance.

Leadership Training for Women

We felt that women's organizations and single sex colleges help to train women for leadership. (Women, when permitted to join mixed groups, should not too readily disband their own groups.) Much more emphasis, however, should be put on training women to lead their own organizations toward more influence and share in the power structures of the churches. WCC and national and local groups should study in more detail the question of what enables women's organizations to exercise power and influence in church structures.

If women disband their own organizations prematurely, their less able members and less articulate members will lose their only opportunity to participate.

We need to modify our existing women's organizations so they will provide alternative socialization and training especially in leadership. We need more solidarity between women in the First, Second, and Third Worlds so they all can benefit from each other toward a greater humanization.

Women need the opportunity to be more responsible for the use of the money they earn.

Mature and experienced women at the stage of life after homemaking and family raising should be encouraged by church and society to work outside the home and to contribute to public and church life. We heard of a model in West Germany where housewives received a sociopolitical training before going back to work. The intention was to help them to struggle for their own rights in solidarity with others, for instance in a trade union. After twenty or thirty years of family life they were in danger of falling easy prey to isolating and exploitative structures.

Conclusion

The church of God cannot do without structures and cannot live without the exercise of power and authority in its corporate life. The church is always part of history and composed of human beings who must find ways of working together to achieve its purposes. The problem is to bring power and leadership under the control of the Spirit of Christ and to order the structures so as to liberate people: for structures are made for people and not people for structures. For Christians the structures of the church should reflect the relational model of the Trinity.*

Both men and women are called to wrestle with these problems. By the emancipation of women from every kind of discrimination, the church will be freed to witness more fully in the world. This study provokes us to work with renewed energy for the transformation of our churches.

Tradition and Traditions— A Chance for Renewal?

Tradition is God's reconciling word and act in Jesus Christ as witnessed by the community of women and men in the church. It functions to maintain the continuity in the developing experience of faith throughout history. Its fundamental elements are Scripture, creeds, liturgies, and the lived experience of the people of God in the Holy Spirit.

Meeting together at Sheffield we realize anew that the church and its traditions have been shaped by the churches' milieu (*Sitz im Leben*); and the milieu is not outside God's concern and creation. So today, as in the past, as God's people seek to be faithful, they find that the tradition they are living derives both from the tradition they have inherited and the experience of their own time and place.

The churches have always recognized that the authentic tradition is rightly accompanied by expressions of Christian life which are appropriate to a particular time and location, but are not of universal obligation. Each of the churches has its criteria for distinguishing the tradition from what is thus tem-

---

Authority in Community, U.S. Faith and Order Commission, (New York: National Council of Churches, 1980).

porary, localized, or distorted. In speaking of tradition in this report such continuous assessment by each church of its own life is presupposed.

Tradition thus understood is important in our search for a new community of women and men in the church. We are embedded in it. ''The tradition of the church is not an object which we possess but a reality by which we are possessed'': (cf. *The Bible: Its Authority and Interpretation in the Ecumenical Movement*, WCC, p. 23). The issue is how we can live our tradition as a basis for envisioning and effecting a renewed community.

Why and When We Question Tradition

We begin to question tradition more as we discover possibilities of new forms of community of women and men in our everyday lives. For example, we often join in partnership in our professional and political commitments and in a sharing of responsibilities in the family. Where male and female contributions are balanced, the new community is experienced. More and more women find the opportunity to make contributions in every area of the churches' life and society. Other women join together to work for peace and international community and suffer because they unite in solidarity to share in the suffering and injustice of the world. The United Nations' conventions against discrimination of both men and women are definitely providing measures for a society based on equal partnership between women and men in the social, economic, and cultural sphere. The same motive lay behind the recent passing of the Sex Discrimination Act by the British government. The churches in Britain are exempt from this Act on the ground of ''doctrine'' and ''fear of offending the religious susceptibilities of its members.'' This exemption causes some women to suffer and the community of the church is hampered.

On the other hand the new community of women and men has already begun in some churches. Some do give women equal opportunities in resource and governance and ordain them to their ministries. Some even have women as their moderator, for example, the United Church in Canada. In Africa some of the new charismatic churches are open to and live this new community of women and men.

It is important to stress that though the ordination of women is not *the* issue for this consultation, it is *an* issue of real importance. Many Sheffield participants represented communities that ordain women, and they felt a responsibility to express their solidarity with those women who long for ordination and with those now ordained who face problems of acceptance and placement.

This is not a contradiction of the section report on the ministry which embraces the viewpoints of Orthodox, Roman Catholic, Anglican, Lutheran, and Reformed participants. That report gives suggestions for how we can speak together in an international ecumenical context. Both statements, one that affirms the ordained ministry for women and the other that attempts to find a middle ground on this sensitive issue, need to be heard in discussions on unity.

In most churches we see a tension between the opportunities that society provides for the partnership of women and men and those provided by church life. This leads us to ask the questions: why do some churches make it impossible for women and men to experience the growing human partnerships which are often encouraged by the social structures? Is not the gospel calling women and men to full human growth (Luke 4:7-9)?

Important Aspects of Tradition
in the Search for a Community
of Women and Men

1. *Images of the Church.* The understanding of the church as body of Christ needs to be reconsidered. This image has shaped a hierarchical view of the church in which the major emphasis is that of Christ as head of the body (cf. Ephesians and Colossians). Throughout history this image has been reinforced by other images culturally acceptable in particular situations (for example, the emperor, or king, as head of state). It thus has strengthened power structures in the church controlled for the most part by men. However, Paul has another vision of the body of Christ (1 Corinthians 12) in which all members are indispensable and interrelated as a *koinonia* (communion) to their head who is the source of life and authority. Christ is also referred to as foundation and cornerstone, so office in the church is understood in terms of service rather than rule. Considered in this way, the tradition of the body of Christ opens up possibilities for a new community of women and men in which there are indeed gifts of varying values ("seek the greater gifts" [1 Cor. 12:31]), although the holders of the gifts, whether women or men, are equal before God in the mystery of Christ.

The tradition of the *royal priesthood,* as expressed in 1 Pet. 2:9-10, describes God's subject people, those who have received mercy. Their priesthood does not serve the purpose of self-glorification and authoritarianism, but rather it consecrates them to declare God's word among humankind. This image can inform our vision of the creative community of women and men by the dignity which it bestows on all God's people without cultural, sexual, economic, or racial distinctions. All those who have received God's mercy have a place in this priesthood in order to make the gospel known. For example, former "untouchables" in India, both women and men, "who once were no people" have found in this text that they are now God's people in Christ—"a chosen race, a royal priesthood, a holy nation."

The tradition of Mary is being reappropriated today by more churches. Her life as recorded in Scripture is being explored more fully. She is seen as the sharing woman who seeks out Elizabeth to tell the news of her pregnancy; as being in the tradition of prophecy bearing the Magnificat; as the mother neglected by her son in favor of his mission; and then as a disciple, journeying in partnership with Jesus along with other women and men. Then we witness her profound grief at the death of her child under the judgment of religious and political powers, her faithfulness to follow him to the tomb, and the divine gift bestowed upon her to be a witness to the resurrection of the "flesh of her flesh, the bone of her bone." Mary is no longer seen as the model of submission and subordination, but rather as a woman who has fully lived her partnership with God in the Christ Event.

2. *Images of God.* When the new community of women and men in the church speaks of the triune *God,* we will be aware that all words are used as analogies. Any one word or image used in isolation is incomplete and all words combined, even though complementary, cannot describe the living God. Even Christ discloses God as hidden and revealed. Biblical images such as creator, lover, nurse, judge, potter, and so forth, reveal the variety of analogies available, including "feminine" and "masculine" ones. The traditional use of mostly or exclusively male images has made the churches' understanding limited and prevents the rich diversity of God's people from particularizing their own identity in relation to the community of the whole people of God as female and male, poor and rich, colorful and bland.

Jesus the man is accessible to women as well as to men for self-identification. There are several ways in which we might describe this accessibility. In the informal tradition of the church, many if not all cultures have appropriated the Christ-child in their own image out of their own cultural context: Asian, African, North American, Indian, and so forth. In its best sense, this may be seen as evidence of each people's need to discover in Jesus' particularity their own identity as well, rather than as an effort to deny Jesus' concrete historicity. Women and men need to know that the maleness of Jesus as such is not essential for the self-disclosure of God, as though masculine expression of human nature were capable of mediating the divine or sacred in a way that the feminine is not. Similarly, we understand that his racial identity does not mean that people of other races are in essence farther from God.

Jesus disclosed his own identity in symbols not essentially male or female, but common to the experience of both sexes. Thus he reveals himself as the bread of life, the light of the world, the good shepherd, the vine, the *ego eimi* (I am) of John's Gospel. He is also related to both the servant and the New Jerusalem in Isaiah as the redeemer incorporating the redeemed.

An attempt to find the feminine nature of God only in the Holy Spirit is limiting. Various languages have accorded different genders to "spirit." Separation of Holy Spirit from the wholeness of God in this way denies trinitarian unity. Yet many traditions have understood the Holy Spirit as feminine. The Holy Spirit came to all flesh, "sons" and "daughters" together (Acts 2:17ff.), and called all into an equal intimacy of relationship with God. The Spirit came to liberate in truth and for action both women and men. Both rational and emotional dimensions are integrated in the Spirit, so denying identification sexist lines.

How We Question Tradition

Tradition is also expressed through cultural and historical factors and thus differs from time to time according to the historical situations. For example, Paul distinguishes in his writing between "what he has received from the Lord" and his own views which are colored by the concrete situations of his day (cf. 1 Corinthians 7). Many interpretations of the church fathers of the undivided church which have become normative were influenced by the dualistic and androcentric thought of their day. We notice that this dualism corresponds to what is now considered to be male (the stressing of objective formulation) and female (the importance given to life). By "androcentric" we mean "man-centered" thought. These considerations lead us to ask: (1) Is patriarchy a cultural tradition or a tradition of God's will? (2) Is there a relation of continuity or discontinuity between the "Abba" of Jesus (Matthew 23, Mark 14, Galatians 4, Romans 8) and the father of the trinitarian dogma; the "fathers" of the church; and other church structures based on fatherhood? (3) What kind of experiences does tradition retain? (4) Who retains tradition?

Tradition and Local Traditions

Many of the missionaries who preached the gospel in foreign countries frequently presented the Christian faith in a way which enshrined occidental culture and ignored local traditions. The local traditions were destroyed, or changed into Western ways. Now churches in Africa and Asia struggle to free the expression of Christianity from its occidental elements and renew it for their own culture. For example, the local traditional sense of community was often destroyed. (An Indian participant informed us that this was especially so in Assam.) Now this sense of community is being rediscovered and expressed in new ways. Questions are also raised about the rightness of enforcing foreign forms of worship. In Western countries a post-Christian situation accepts new patterns for married life, and traditional behavior is being challenged. There are new ways of choosing partners which foster a new vision of community; on the other hand, there is promiscuity which devalues sexuality. These considerations cause us to ask: (1) When Christianity influences or dismisses a local tradition, does it do so in faithfulness to Jesus and the gospel, or only out of its attachment to cultural traditions which it has sacralized? (2) How do churches identify what in Christian tradition must be kept?

We recommend that the Christians, especially in the Third World, encourage exploration of local tradition which can be used to build the new community of men and women.

A Way of Renewing Tradition

The parables of Jesus may be a useful paradigm for the understanding of tradition in the new community of women and men. The parables as storytelling deal with both women and men (cf. the pairs of parables in Matt. 13:31–33 and Luke 15:3–10). As storytelling they include the listeners in the storytelling (cf. Matt. 21:28–32, 33–43; Luke 7:41–43); all concerned take part in the tradition making. The metaphors of the parables are open to different interpretations in different communities; for example, ''the lost sheep'' is interpreted differently in Luke than in Matthew.

Toward a New Community as
New Humanity in Christ

Before we can describe and discuss the Christian hope for a new community of women and men as new humanity in Christ (cf. Eph. 4:22ff.), we are confronted by the methodologies, histories, and interpretations of what it means to be human. The biblical picture in Gen. 2:7 portrays human beings as both flesh and spirit. The fall described later in Genesis reminds us that humanhood expressed in community is subject to sin which creates hindrances to the formation of the new community in Christ.

These hindrances come in the forms of injustices such as socioeconomic systems which corrupt, as well as religiocultural traditions which may unknowingly exploit a race, class, or sex, so leading to a dehumanized existence where people cannot be responsible for their own lives. A vision of new community includes a conscious overcoming of these injustices so that the gift of humanhood is returned to us in the mystery of reconciliation.

Through trust in God's grace a new humanity is revealed for example in the renewed partnership between women and men, mutual support and self-giving, intimacy and a sense of belonging, in communion with God as (cf. the Katos in John 14—17) Jesus Christ himself has lived and called us to live. Human beings indeed have their limitations, just as when we are sick or handicapped. However, these limitations do not need to hinder possibilities for self-fulfillment. To the contrary, they witness to how much we need each other in the new community as new humanity.

The following poem is a reflection on theological anthropology from one of the section members.

HUMAN BEING

Human being . . .
Why are man and woman created in God's creation?
For the sake of being opposition and comparison?
Or being an enemy to one another?
Or being a manipulating-exploiting tool for one another?

Human being . . .
Woman-man exists for the truth of agape-living
Man-woman exists for the truth of power uniting
Woman-man exists for the truth of being whole
Man-woman exists for the truth of being one.

Human being . . .
To be man and woman is to be supportive to one another
Not for being enemies but co-sustainers
Not for despising but for praising
Not for selling-buying but for being dignified.

Human being . . .
Thou art mono and not duo
Thou art made co-sustainer and not solo
That's the truth of being
Human being.

M. Pongudom
July 1981

Justice and Freedom
in New Community

The vision of new creation in which all humanity may live in harmony with one another and with God impels us to struggle for change in a world torn by division and dehumanization. This struggle goes on in both church and society in every part of the globe among those who work to transform structures, including the ways in which we think about them. This struggle requires us to be involved in a continual process of action against forces of domination and destruction. At the same time we must be in a continual process of reflection on the ways in which these changes alter our mental picture, or our methods of thinking about reality. This continuing and interrelated process of action/reflection is called conscientization. As Paulo Freire has said, conscientization is learning to perceive the social, political, economic, and religious contradictions in our world and then engaging in action together with others to transform them.

In a global community of women and men in the church, we seek to understand more deeply the interrelationship of freedom struggles by looking at the interlocking "web of oppression." Having analyzed the relationships among sexism, racism, and classism, we present three concrete issues as an invitation to continuing reflection and action.

Racism, Sexism, Classism—
A Web of Oppression

1. *Seeing the Web of Oppression.* The struggle for change is *one* struggle. Racism, sexism, and classism and all other forms of domination, rejection, and marginalization are linked together in a demonic symphony of oppression. Any attitude, action, or structure to exclude persons from participation in power (economic, social, and political) and/or to declare them to be inferior because of their economic or family position is classism. The systematic process by which the rich become richer and the poor get poorer is one manifestation of classism expressed today in global imperialism. Any attitude, action, or structure that treats people as inferior because of race is racism. And a similar declaration of domination and exclusion based on sex is sexism. Together with other false ideologies that declare some persons to be less

than others, these form a "web of oppression," that is described by St. Paul as "a symphony of groaning" (Rom. 8:22).

Sexism, racism, and classism are both personal and collective manifestations of sin. Human beings were created in God's image. It was a good creation, and yet, we live with anxiety, greed, envy, and the lust to dominate and subjugate other people and nature. Human beings both male and female were appointed to be responsible servants. And yet people have become irresponsible tyrants of other people and of nature. The evils of our time—sexism, racism, and class conflicts—cannot be explained only by reference to cultural and economic factors or to social and political structures. While each of these plays an important role in human life, the roots of our struggles are primarily illumined by the biblical concept of sin. Therefore , it is an illusion to believe that the root of evil can be eliminated by the institution of a new order. Instead our struggle for justice and freedom must be unceasing. As we struggle we must ask which processes and mechanisms in the church and in society minimize and which promote negative attitudes and values for human beings. The struggle against evil in our hearts and in our world has to take place on the personal and the social level. We must begin this process with ourselves by asking for the gift of repentence as we acknowledge and confess our own complicity.

2. *The Universality and Particularity of Oppression.* These principalities and powers that rule our lives and world must be faced together. We cannot afford to work against one another for we then cancel out each other's efforts and, fighting among ourselves, we assist the forces of domination in preventing change toward justice and freedom. We also cannot afford to work against each other because we are so few and we need one another in the struggle. Most importantly, we must work together because the struggle against oppresion and for liberation is universal. No one form of freedom will in itself accomplish the new creation which is a gift of God. Yet each struggle toward freedom is a sign of God's intention for new creation in which true community is restored and exploitation brought to an end. The gospel message proclaimed in Mary's Magnificat calls us as a community of Christians to witness to the intention of God for the elimination of all that destroys human wholeness (Luke 1:46–55). This witness requires solidarity with the poor, the oppressed, the marginalized (Luke 4:18–19). God has created us as one human family, and we are not fully set free to be "children of God" until all are free (Rom. 8:21).

At the same time the struggle against oppression and for liberation is very particular. In different contexts and situations persons must struggle for the change needed in that place. Without neglecting a critical analysis of the interlocking web of oppression expressed through economic, sexual, and racial exploitation, we must each take up the struggle for change against the oppression that is forced upon us in our situations. For the starving, food is the first step on the road to freedom. For the rich, actions to betray our own class and stand in solidarity with the poor is the first step—and there are many more steps to be taken! The more steps we take, the more we see other parts of the web of oppression and come to understand our situation in a global context.

Persons and groups oppress and are oppressed in different degrees. For instance, a black woman from South Africa is oppressed by racism, classism, and sexism. Her first struggle will be against racism although sexism and classism are linked with it. A woman in Guatemala is among those who might be oppressed by imperialism, classism, and sexism. Her first struggle might be against imperialism, while the struggles against the other two must follow. A white woman belonging to the middle class might be oppressed by sexism, yet the beginning of her struggle in this area must be linked to her struggle against classism and racism, in solidarity with the marginalized in every society.

3. *International Tourism and Oppression.* In seeking to understand the interrelation of forms of oppression and to find areas of collective action toward liberation and new community, we turn to action/reflection on international tourism and prostitution. This one example reveals the way in which oppression is universal yet particular and concrete. In international tourism/prostitution we see the ugly face of racism, sexism, and classism. The prostituted, battered, and exploited woman becomes a powerful metaphor for the anguish of men, women, and children whose lives are destroyed. Her cry of anguish calls us all to joint action. The flood of tourism has been a boon not only for the hotel industry and airlines, but also to "pimps" who provide tourists with women or young boys depending on sexual preference. (We heard stories from every region of the world. Tourism and prostitution have become a multinational industry, which has spread worldwide and been made accessible on a a mass scale through cheap package tours.) This is not very new, but there is a further refinement. For instance, one woman described how men now come from abroad to India looking for "wives." Indian middle men and impoverished families connive to provide them with what they want for a consideration. Girls as young as thirteen and fourteen are sold in "marriage"

147

to men, often much older, frequently already married men. For many of the girls it is one way of lifting the family out of the hopeless depths of poverty, and they sacrifice themselves in the interest of the family. For others it is their only chance to get married since their parents cannot afford to give them dowry. Many of these girls end up as servants or even prostitutes back in their "husband's" country, or they are used for the duration of the tourist's visit and left to a life of prostitution.

Another delegate reminded us that the Philippine Department of Tourism has published statistics for travel and tourism which show the industry had become the country's fifth most profitable by the 1970s. "In the Philippines . . . sex provides a major incentive to the traveler. Whereas in the past Japanese all-male tour groups took night tours in buses which returned to the hotel with double the original number of passengers, a first class [sic] hotel now offers a room package which includes a female companion. For the more discriminating there are also co-eds, fashion models, movie starlets or teenage boys. It should be noted that the women included in the package deals normally get only 15–20% of the fee paid by the clients" (excerpted from *Compassionate and Free*, by Marianne Katoppo [Maryknoll, N. Y.: Orbis Books, 1980], p. 5).

Large-scale prostitution is organized by powerful tourist agencies. People described the way local girls are offered as part of the travel package bought by tourists planning to go to such countries as Thailand, Tahiti, Fiji, the Philippines, Sri Lanka, the Gambia, and the Netherlands. The profit remains with the tourist agency rather than going to the girls or the local communities.

Others told of South African laws that forbid sexual activity across racial lines. A tourist business for whites has emerged in the surrounding countries (for example, Swaziland, Lesotho, Mbotho) which includes the use of black prostitutes. The tourist business is organized by South Africans, not by the neighboring countries. The women are left further stigmatized in their own societies with biracial children and/or venereal diseases.

Before the Cuban revolution, Havana was known as the "playground of North America," a center for prostitution and organized crime. The "playground" has now moved to San José, Costa Rica, where "Havanatization" includes the establishment of organized prostitution connected with tour packages and with the large hotels and travel facilities. Devastating the local social and economic base, foreigners control these enterprises and continue to drain resources from the country.

Now that international tourism/prostitution is being recognized as a multinational business, churches around the world are taking it up as an issue even though these efforts are on a small scale and require an international network of action. Nevertheless, some steps are being taken to combat this oppression. For instance, women's groups in France and West Germany have started inquiries into the ''services'' offered in their countries by international ''package tourism'' and international ''club'' travel. The offer of prostitutes is never made openly so it is difficult to collect evidence. Churches in the area often do not dare to give information or to protest because they fear this would deteriorate relations with local authorities and would weaken their ability to speak out on other issues that church leaders (mainly male) find ''more important.'' Action against tourist agencies is filled with traps, as the campaign for disinvestment in South Africa has shown. Such action can lead to conscientization of public opinion both in the countries sending and receiving tourists.

Economic Disorder

1. *The Old Economic Order.* In the world today, we see an imbalance of world resources and powers. The smallest percentage of the world's people (the rich) control the largest percentage of the world's resources which are found in the poor countries. This system has brought about mass poverty, glaring inequalities, social injustices, militarization, ignorance, and fear among the people in every country.

The elite of the rich, as well as poor, countries dominate the economic, sociopolitical systems. The resulting exploitation and apprehension of three-quarters of the world's population defaces the image of God in each one of us. As the community of women and men in the church we have often been part of this system. We call for repentance and realize that we should be working together as women and men, identifying with the deprived, oppressed, poor, and exploited in order to bring about a new global community.

2. *Experiences of Economic Disorder.*

a. DIVISION OF FAMILIES. Imperialism divides us from our families. The effects of migratory labor are devastating for both women and men.

In South Africa, Mexico, Puerto Rico, and the Philippines, men leave their families to seek employment, sometimes traveling over eight hundred miles. The women are left at home to care for the children and find work to support the family. Sometimes the men never return. Similar problems are reported from Europe, the U.S., and from all parts of the world.

Men are exploited by either not being able to find work or receiving low pay. Women are doubly exploited by having to find employment and fulfill all the home duties.

In the rural area of Indonesia and Kenya the women work in the fields all day and take care of the children at night, while the men drink and converse. In these situations the women suffer from the inequalities in the division of male and female roles.

b. MULTINATIONAL CORPORATIONS. Women and men in various parts of the world suffer from the practices of multinational corporations.

In Kenya, banks are trying to nationalize and Kenyan business is building up. Yet multinational corporations abound, one employing as many as two thousand workers at low pay.

Asian countries compete for the location of multinational corporations and these corporations are booming in South Africa, while in the Netherlands and the United States factories are closing down, leaving women and men with no work. At the same time in Indonesia and the Philippines, raw materials are bought by the corporations at a very low price, then the materials return to these countries in the form of very expensive processed goods.

Advertising by these corporations increases the economic, social, and cultural problems in these countries. Multinational corporations build factories in countries where there is cheap labor and higher profit, at the same time closing factories in the Western world. The women and men of the working class in both the First and Third Worlds suffer.

c. CULTURAL AND RELIGIOUS IMPERIALISM. Economic disorder is experienced in countries of the Third World through cultural invasion. The religious and cultural fabric of the society is undermined where Western culture is more highly valued. The churches have played a role in this because missionaries have encouraged the indigenous people to abandon their culture and accept the Western culture.

In the Philippines, some missionaries sent by churches in the U.S. have taught the people to pray for the government leaders, but not to become involved in the struggle for liberation.

As we listen to these experiences we become aware that they call for change in the fundamental structures of society. They call us to work together in establishing a new economic order.

The Struggle Against Arms
and Violence

Violence is used to ruthlessly oppress the already exploited. It is used by oppressive regimes to suppress change and to support their own positions of power over the people. This is yet another aspect of the web of oppression.

Women and men should recognize their duty to express solidarity both with the victims of violence and oppression and, perhaps with more difficulty, with those who have to use violence as a last resort in order to overthrow the oppressors and to liberate their fellow humans.

Liberation struggle, even if forced to resort to violence, works toward an ultimate peace because "peace is not only the absence of war but the presence of justice."

1. *Struggle Against Violence.* Liberation struggles are often described as subversive terrorist insurrection and this misinterpretation is reinforced by churches who understand the message only in personal terms. Women and men in the churches in all lands are an ideal network for dissemination of information and for supporting the struggles. We recommend that women and men in the churches further develop their networks of alliances and solidarity to inform, motivate, and organize action.

This institutional violence is not the only form of armed inhumanity. Violence is used to struggle against oppression. We noted that the negative portrayal of freedom fighters is often a direct result of deliberate propaganda by the developed world in whose interests it lies to portray the forces of change as subversive. We noted that in some European situations protest violence is, in some measure, linked to liberation struggle, in that it too is often a reaction against oppressive structures and social injustice such as unemployment. Protest violence occurs when women and men are denied the opportunity to effectively express their opinions other than through violence.

With regard to violence against persons, especially against women and children (for example, rape, incest, beating of wives and children), we urge women and men to study the cause of this social evil and then to use this knowledge to combat both social causes (bad housing, inhuman living conditions, stress, and work pressure) and the psychological preconditioning and stimulants of this violence, such as pornography, violent publications, and television. We urge the church to recognize more fully its pastoral

151

responsibilities—not only by caring for the victims of personal violence, but also by adopting a long-term approach and more effectively training those responsible for counseling and social work, including class analysis.

Examples of *violencia blanca,* or violence by default include the false distribution of resources. As a result the citizens of the poor country often die because of lack of medicine or starvation while vast sums of money are spent on militarization. This is often the case, for instance, because the developed countries profit more by selling guns than by giving development aid.

2. *Struggle Against Arms.* Faced with these problems we talked of how to achieve peace. It was illustrated just how wide our understanding of the term "peace" is. For instance, a West European who advocates peace may mean the removal of the nuclear weapons which threaten his or her future, whereas a person who advocates peace in Central America may mean giving in to the dictatorship which guns down children before the very eyes of their mothers. However, it was seen that the violence of the nuclear holocaust and the oppressive violence of dictatorship are connected in that the arms source of the oppressors is always a greater military power in the developed world. We noted that this served a double purpose against the Third World. Firstly it allows the developed world to reap enormous profits from selling arms to lands where the more pressing needs are to provide basic necessities such as food and water; and, secondly, it allows the First World to keep down the forces of liberation in the Third World which would, if successful, break down the unjust system by which the developed world survives. (This includes the underpayment of Third World labor and the unjust exploitation of natural resources.) We call for a peace based on a new, just, and egalitarian economic order. We urge women and men in the church to speak out against the injustice and exploitation perpetrated against the Third World by an economic system which is dominated by the inhuman interests of the weapon-exporting countries.

We noted with alarm that the tendency to accept the theory of "limited" nuclear war (P.D. 59) has started to replace the traditional belief in Mutually Assured Destruction (MAD) thus making the prospect of a nuclear war more comfortable.

We recognized the fact that the established church structures have on many occasions sided with the oppressors, or have been indifferent to oppression.

But we also noted past and present Christian involvement in liberation struggles and urge that the WCC and its member churches support those struggling to change oppressive situations. We call women and men, in solidarity, to action with the oppressed.

Freedom and Justice
in Community

We affirm that spirituality is the wellspring of our activity on behalf of freedom and justice. Spirituality and action are not two separate or opposing dimensions of our life. Rather, as our action is inspired by our faith, so our spiritual life finds fulfillment as we engage in struggles for liberation and life around the world.

As Christian women and men we profess our faith in Christ as the truth that sets us free, as the one who liberates all those oppressed in body, mind, and spirit. We recognize, however, that the liberating truth of Christ is revealed not only in and through church institutions, but also is present wherever women and men are working on behalf of the world's oppressed. This means that we Christians must be ready to join hands with sisters and brothers of all living faiths who seek freedom and justice in a new community of women and men.

We affirm that all women and men ought to be free to develop their potential. For many people this means freedom *from* ignorance, exploitation, hunger, poverty, and repressive governments. These basic necessities of life must be available for all people so that we can then speak about freedom *to* choose and act as women and men.

Women and men in richer countries must become aware of the ways in which their freedom often limits and imposes itself on the freedom of women and men in poorer countries. As we seek a new community of sisters and brothers around the world, our commitment must be to work for the freedom of each and all. Therefore, steps toward freedom will assume different forms in different societies and cultures. We hear of women involved in the boycott of South African fruits in the Federal Republic of Germany. We hear of the work for women's education in the Sudan. We hear of Indian Christians rediscovering their own cultural heritage rather than the Western one brought by missionaries.

As we work for freedom we believe that we have much to learn from one another about the meaning of freedom. While in Western cultures freedom for the individual has been emphasized, in Eastern cultures freedom as a quality of life in community has been emphasized. In this communal context loving and sharing are more important than securing one's own rights.

This perspective on freedom in community illumines the Christian understanding of freedom which is the freedom to serve God and the community of sisters and brothers. We believe that for Christians freedom is freedom to grow into the image of God revealed in Christ whose body is the community of women and men.

Likewise, while we believe that the call for justice is crucial, as Christians we affirm that justice is only the beginning point toward life in community. Even as we seek an equal distribution of resources and rights we believe that Christ calls us to life in a community of love. While traditionally women have been the ones who nurture relationship and embody love, we envision a new community wherein women and men share all things in common and respond in love to one another's needs. Only as we live in a community of love will we move beyond relationships that are oppressive.

It is the message of love that we Christian women and men are to carry into the struggles for liberation, wherever they may appear in our world. This does not mean that we ignore or hide from pain and hurt and anger. The church must not remain in an isolated ghetto. Rather, as we walk into the darkness of oppression present in the wider human community, we are called to shine the light of love that transforms struggle into hope, even as Christ burst the bonds of death revealing new life.

PART FIVE

PROLOGUE TO THE FUTURE

9

The Community of Women
and Men in
the Ecumenical Movement

Held Together in Hope and
Sustained by God's Promise

A Personal Reflection

CONSTANCE F. PARVEY

Introduction

For four years I have had the privilege to animate this process. Like the talents of a gardener who plants the seeds and lets them grow and like those of a baker who prepares the dough and lets it rise, the skills needed for this task have been those of preparation and nurture, assuring the right starting conditions and being attentive—trying not to hinder, neglect, or overlook what has been set in motion. My work has been to enable others to speak.

Now, after so many other voices, I am asked to add my own. What I have learned over these years has had many mentors. Enrolling in the ecumenical education that this worldwide assignment gives is an action of expanding one's horizons through listening and learning with others and experiencing reality through their perspectives.

Though what follows are my own thoughts, almost every image, every impulse, comes out of the experience of the community study. Not to repeat what has already been said in the previous chapters, I will concentrate on some of the theological themes that have captured my attention through the reports, personal encounters, consultations, and deliberations about the study on so

156

many levels—from visiting local groups, to hearing regional discussions, to reflecting on the WCC Central Committee debate about Sheffield.

My comments are addressed to the next stage: to aspects of community, its definition and functions, in the work of human renewal and Christian unity. They begin with some reflections on the theological instruments that we, women and men in the church, use—our language, images, history. Then they move to thoughts on who we are with God and with each other, our nature and what is required of us. At the end they deal with aspects of our life together as *community* in the church. Divided into three parts: "The Process and the Means" discusses the community study, its method, and some clarifications needed regarding what theology is and how we go about it together; "*Theos* in Identity and Relationships" points to some of the ethical issues, made more apparent when we look for *theos* in identity, partnership, friendship, and family life; and "The Church—A Venture in Service" deals with the nature of the church and its ministry—how we find it, live it, recognize it.

If I speak in the pages to follow too much as a member of a privileged group in North Atlantic civilization, it is because that is where I come from. If some sisters and brothers feel that I have not been sensitive enough to all of their concerns, it is because, in a global setting, there are many pulls, and choices must be made. If I do not speak enough of Orthodox concerns, perhaps I have not heard all of the voices clearly. If I do not give enough place to the voices of men, it is because I still hear more strongly and remember more clearly the voices of women. Each one of us is an interpreter of texts and contexts; I bring the authority that comes from my experience and the human limitation which comes from whom I am.

THE PROCESS AND THE MEANS
A Trial Run

The vision of the church making manifest a new community of women and men has been tested. What happened, culminating at Sheffield, was the building of a kind of pilot project or "trial run" of a new ecclesial model. Innovative industries generate new models all the time. Airlines do not build one jumbo jet and then stop. If the first plane passes the demanding test of trial runs, then the word goes out to produce more. The Community of Women and Men in the Church study has passed its trial run. As the various materials brought into existence by the program are now being published and shared, the next study book ought to be produced, perhaps several in the different cultural and church contexts, and, in this way, the process set in motion will be continued. With the publication of the Sheffield report, women and men in the church are in the same position as the questioner in Lewis Carroll's "What the Tortoise Said to Achilles":

Well now, would you like to hear of a race-course, that most people fancy they can get to the end of in two or three steps, while it really consists of an infinite number of distances, each one longer than the previous one?

This is not a word of discouragement. The community study has enlivened discussion around the world—sometimes painful discussion—but its vision of new community in Christ has helped to overcome the many problems that are posed through it. From the beginning it has been clear that the study design was initiated by women and that the questions put forth for reflection and response were questions that women are asking.

It has meant an unfamiliar role for men. Looking at life from a woman's point of view is something that men are not trained to do, and the more power that men have in male-affirming structures, the less they may be able to understand the traditional subculture of women's lives from which men receive their support. Socially, in most cultures of the world, women are trained to adapt to men. The community study has been a reversal of this process, asking men to adapt to women. For men it has meant sometimes finding themselves not only a minority in numbers but also a minority in power. The method of the community study has not been to create difficulties but to find a means by which to face a reality that already exists in the churches: women around the world are less and less willing to accept subordination in church, family, work, and social life. Women are less and less willing to sacrifice their personalities, their education, their talents, their quality of life, solely in order to give support to their brothers, husbands, and other male authorities in church and society. This does not mean that women are not willing to sacrifice but rather that they now expect this process to work both ways. For example, in marriage, the emphasis is not on "wives, be subject to your husbands" (Eph. 5:22, *NEB*) but on "being subject to one another" (Eph. 5:21, *NEB*). New roles and perceptions are sought for both partners.

Because the community study, initiated by women, was placed in the WCC Commission on Faith and Order, which is given the specific task to work toward unity in church teaching and practice, it was essential to find a context for this reflection where the goal of unity would be underlined. The study was designed therefore not for a specific constituency in the church, for example, a program *by* women, *for* women, *about* women, but as a program *of* the church, *by* the churches, and *for* the renewal of the church and its fuller manifestation of Christ's wholeness of partnership and reciprocal sharing of women and men in community. It is not surprising that more women than men have been motivated to begin this work and provide the leadership. As the process developed, its major constituency has been women; and through their encouragement more official church and ecumenical bodies, as well as women and men in theological education, have taken up the study.

One criticism of the work thus far is that there is not yet a clear enough voice from men, not enough emphasis on what the changes of women and men in community mean for the reality of men's lives—their identity and roles in family, society, and church. Ecumenically, the responses of men are just beginning. Men are starting to take seriously for themselves the meaning of the new contributions of women. A fuller picture must be part of future work.

In the evolution of the study's trial run, the composition of the many groups who worked together across confessional lines has shown that the vision of women and men in community can become a common basis for renewal. Self-evident in the churches' pursuit of unity are disclosures of unity in practical experience.

A Radical Rethink

Different from some theological studies, this study is one in which everyone has experience and well-formed opinions. Everyone is an "expert" on what is "man" and what is "woman." A fear expressed in the preparations for Sheffield was that it would be a forum for "opinions against each other," but this did not happen. Instead, a new kind of listening took place that touched many levels of our lives and from which no one could turn away. Rather than becoming defensive, women and men were willing to risk some sharing and in the process to discover life in common. Yet, in the reading of the local reports, the regional meetings, the day-to-day worldwide correspondence, one was continually made aware of the deep gap in communication between women and men; between the different ways women and men are educated, trained, and socialized; between our expectations, starting points, and the faith-reality of our lives. Working in a global context where cultural underpinnings become relativized in multicultural dialogue, it is also possible to see more clearly how our personal and cultural experiences influence our theology and our interpretations of Scripture. In such a global setting what were once considered norms become questions. In countries of the Northern Hemisphere, centuries of assumptions about patriarchy in social, political, and religious life, about structures of power and authority, are being reconsidered. In countries of the South, where familial, communal life has long been the pattern, community ties are weakening with modern modes of industry, trade, education, and work. Worldwide, and on many levels, there is a search in society, as well as in the church, for models of cohesive associational life and for leadership that can enhance the gifts of each member, women and men.

The process of the community study has not told people what to think. The study method was not one of indoctrination that said, "We once thought B and now we think A," but rather it has invited women and men, young and old, professional and lay theologians to do their own theological work. Many people responded to this chance to reflect on the sources of their faith—in experience, beliefs, spirituality; in church teachings and structures and in forms of ministry. The study emphasized the importance of affirming different churches, cultures, and interpretations without losing the central vision of women and men in the ever-new community of the risen Christ.

The voices that have spoken are overwhelmingly the educated laity of the WCC member churches, as well as Roman Catholics and conservative evangelicals. What has come forth from the process is not a "theology of the laity" (which assumes a theology of the clergy) but a theology of the church, disclosing weaknesses as well as strengths in its practice. As one reads the materials, much hope comes through, along with a new awareness of the formidable obstacles, for example, the stereotyping of women's identity, decisions about what women can and cannot do, centuries of attitudes that have put women in a separate sphere, defined them as "unclean," or their biology as destiny. In spite of all this, women and men throughout the study and at Sheffield expressed their claim on the gospel and the church. What has been documented in this trial run is that the churches are undergoing from within a radical rethink. The community sought is old; the challenges facing it are new.

Community—The Woman's Side

In a period when all levels of relationship and community life are in transition and long-accepted values and customs are being eroded, there is hope that the churches, with their sense of past and future held together, will play a much-needed cultural and spiritual role in listening with discernment and aiding new human adaptations. As with the first Pentecost, there are risks involved; yet, peoples once profoundly separated by language, age, and sex—

Parthians, Elamites, Medes, young and old, women and men—broke through barriers of old identities and, filled with the Holy Spirit, found new community.

The questions set before the churches are not those of interpersonal relationships, of psychology alone, but those of the very concepts and structures of power and authority by which women are either left out from the beginning through custom, attitudes, and education, or given a special, complementary status that may include them spiritually but exclude them politically. In a poignant post-Sheffield reflection a Latin American woman wrote:

Our inherited ancestral "taboos" continue to constitute an almost insurmountable obstacle. If women outside of the church have historically suffered a double oppression, then those of us within the church have suffered, and still suffer, a triple oppression. A religious piety of devotion and sacrifice, falsely considered, keeps Christian women, at least in our case, in intolerable submission.

The word *community* is the key to opening up this "woman's side." To talk only about "women" and "men" is to position the issue on two parallel tracks, rather than to see that the problems of women have to do with the problems of men. Though both women and men need space to struggle with their own transformation (for neither their problems nor their solutions are the same) they reflect *one* common human condition in need of renewal. At the Faith and Order meeting in Accra, Ghana, during 1974, the question concerning the nature of the community that we seek was raised. It was felt that in the steps toward unity, the marks, dimensions, and quality of community life must be more fully explored.

In the community study process some women have said that it arrived too soon at an emphasis on community—that not enough time was given for women to clarify their own experiences and, out of them, to establish their own priorities before beginning a dialogue with men. They pointed out that few women leaders in theology and church life have ever had the opportunity to assemble and share their thinking on national, regional, or international levels. There are few role models and much to learn from each other. Women leaders work in predominantly male structures and environments with the exception of women who work in women's organizations. Women lack the experience of challenging and being challenged by other women colleges as is the normal pattern for men. This holds true for the ecumenical movement itself where women have much catching up to do because the ecumenical and ecclesial agenda has been so dominated by a fellowship of men, coming from structures of ecclesiastical, doctrinal, and ritual power. Many women fear that simply to enter these structures, without having first the opportunity to share and learn from other women in leadership, has the fate of becoming "like men." Because women are now more aware of this, much of the discussion of equal participation among women today is actually about difference—women, not men, trying to clarify what being different and doing things differently could imply.

The steps toward community involve the following:

1. Women with women, having the opportunity to reflect, develop, and affirm their own gifts, talents, and priorities;
2. Women with men, finding the ways to be partners where the women's side of the partnership can make a difference in the justice and quality of the relationship;
3. Men with men, discovering from this new dialogue with women the personal resources for their own self-critical reflection and renewal;
4. Women and men together, becoming more human in community.

Language and Symbols—The Chrysalis Opening

Along with the clarification of identity there is also a symbolic change taking place. There is a search for new forms of communication and language. Women, whose voices have been absent, not from history but from *recorded* history, are now speaking. Out of the silence, new images and uses of language are emerging: the concrete, practical language of names, communities, and vocations is emphasized more than the language of projection or generalization. Also, there is a reusing of the language of ancient faith, of memories returning to the sources. It is the language of insertion into the historical/theological process as well as the language of its transformation. Much of the writing of the community study is descriptive and spoken, tapping the sources of power within experience itself. Some of the poetry to emerge is a mixture of realism and fantasy, of history and myth. It speaks of vision before action, of pictures before prose.

These new images and appropriations of language do not imply that theological language is inconsequential or that the longing for an inclusive language of human community (including women and men) and for inclusive metaphors for God and God's presence are only provisional and passing. Rather, it means that our symbol words are in the process of redefinition. The birth of new theological and relational language today is like an open chrysalis. Like the larva coming out from its hardened sheath transformed, so fixed words and familiar phrases are undergoing a metamorphosis, generating new speech appropriate to new relationships.

For some, this change is a source of fear and uncertainty, even of open conflict, for language is not neutral but a product of culture, class, and power relationships. Not everyone is at the same stage or time in their awareness of this process. The images and symbols of language in one culture may have a different resonance in another. Many at Sheffield from the North Atlantic expressed dismay that inclusive language and symbols were not always used, especially in worship; many expected more from a community of women and men. Steps toward inclusive language must be taken, but they need not be seen merely in reaction to some Western language patterns. They can provide an opening to learn more from non-Western languages about how God, active in creation and in human relationships, is expressed, experienced, and understood. As women and men grow in new community worldwide, there is bound to be increasing awareness of what an open chrysalis theological language really is.

Theology and History: The Story and the Storyteller

Through the Holy Spirit, God addresses us in our time. This is the faith affirmation of Pentecost, recorded in Acts 2. And it is also the affirmation behind the question in the Sheffield letter: ''What did we at Sheffield hear the Holy Spirit saying to the churches?'' Our historical experience and God's experience with us, as people of God, are inseparable, yet quite distinct. Like the letters addressed to the seven churches in the Book of Revelations. God still speaks to our different social contexts. On the one side, theology is reflection on God and how God reveals God's self through peoples, in all their historical and cultural diversity, different time frames, and various dilemmas. Theology at its best is tradition with a capital ''T,'' addressing itself to a multitude of life situations, making specific replies, yet the integrity and authority of God's voice is maintained. On the other side, history begins with the voice of the ''storyteller,'' the historian and scribe whose task it is to make clear the particular sequence of events, to describe what has happened, and to lift up what is fundamental about events, people, and places that mark and shape the destiny of the long human journey.

The stories of the people of God have been influenced and shaped by storytellers coming from many social patterns—slavery, nomadic tribal life, the patriarchies of Rome and Byzantium, the ancient and diversely ordered cultures of Asia, Africa, the Middle East, and the Pacific. Today's storytellers are affected by modern transhemispheric communication and by global, political, and economic struggles for dominance and power. In Europe and North America where church tradition has been so linked with the development and spread of Western culture, theology is mixed and fused with Western social history and its languages. For Christians living in the many other cultures of the world, the spread of Christian stories has tended to suppress indigenous social patterns, their models and symbols of order and authority. Various African understandings of the roles of queens and chiefs, of extended familial life, of priestesses and healers is a case in point. Forms of contemplation and worship in Asia and the organization of social life and relationships to nature are another. In its beginnings, Scripture (the story of God's people) was itself sculptured from the words chosen by its faithful storytellers, editors, and scribes. Both Scripture and tradition through centuries of interpretation reflect and influence the special contexts, the "story life," in which the story lives.

There is no single homogenized theological or ecclesiological story. On this point, there is in fact a dynamic of great contradiction existing within the ecumenical movement itself. The closer we as churches come to one another, the more we are motivated to study, preserve, and cherish our own distinct identity, our special languages and stories. In the search for reasons why the churches can and cannot become one, the churches are challenged to their very roots and to their diversity. In terms of theology the experience of the community study has shown that the closer the issues compel the churches to come to their sources, the more likely they are to discover commonalities in theology, yet wide divergencies in history and tradition.

In addition, women and men in the churches today are aware that the telling of the story by the many storytellers has often been biased, restricted by the vision and experience of the teller. There is an overlooked side of the story—women's story in the people of God, women's history in the church catholic, the churches, and the ecumenical movement. Theology and tradition are being reshaped and expanded, as women, the other partners, are charged as well to give God's good witness in its wealth of understanding. The divinely given spiritual and symbolic power of *both* theology and tradition is needed to give full expression to our theological description and faith proclamation as we listen into God's future coming. For participants at Sheffield there was this posture of listening, a stretching forward to be attentive, trying to catch the meaning of their story in relation to the biblical *litteratura*— of what it could mean that the Spirit speaks to the churches (Rev. 2:17).

It cannot be said that "tradition," even with a small "t," is a nontheological factor. The story and the storyteller are not the same, but they do belong together. The storyteller's words are limited by space and place. They change and demand new interpretation. Women and men in new community experience the fact that the language which used to tell the story has often been too rigidly bounded by the concrete setting through which it was birthed. Like the languages of history through which theology finds its voice, theological language is itself part of an unfolding process. Theology requires a discovery of new and renewed words, symbols, and signs that point to God in Christ, to the Holy Spirit of God, yesterday and today, present and active.

The story, God's faithfulness, remains the same in time's eternity. History is always in tandem with eschatology. It is God's coming in fullness, as well as that God in Christ has come, that continually shapes and expands the churches' theological vision and helps to separate the essential story from the voices of its storytellers.

THEOS IN IDENTITY AND RELATIONSHIPS

Liberation and Equality:
Part of the Divine Anthropology

The phrase "human renewal" used often with reference to the community study has that key word "human." The statement in the Sheffield letter that "sexuality is not opposed to spirituality" is an attempt to underline the meaning of the word "human": the goodness in which God has created us and the liberation from corruption and exploitation from which God delivers us.

The first chapter of Scripture begins by making the fundamental declaration that "human" means "male and female." This biblical anthropology has two dimensions built into it: that both persons come into being in *one* single act and that the character of being human is *relational*, with God and with each other. Women and men are one humanity. We are partners in God's divinely fashioned means of human communication and generation. Together, by divine fiat, we are made *imago Dei:* our major distinction being related to our common task, but respective roles, in the re-generation of the human family. Genesis 1 deals with the question of our human anthropology, and Genesis 2 addresses the relational question of our anthropological identity as women and men.

The Fall, inaugurated, portrayed, and enacted in Genesis 3 signifies the alienation of the sexes from God, creation, one another, and from one's self. What follows in the later chapters tells the stories of the beginnings of domination: of men over creation, over other men, over women, over children, and women over women in a patriarchal ordering. Already at the start of the

Genesis history, even Sarah with all her matriarchal strength is shown to live dependent on Abraham's priorities. To provide Abraham with an heir, she is obliged to oppress another woman, Hagar, and she herself submits to the indignity of being ''replaced'' so that Abraham can have a son. At this beginning of patriarchal history, God, God's self, is seen to protest this act of indignity against Sarah by giving her a child when well past her years. For it was known and is repeated in tradition that the people of God cannot be born from a lineage of slavery. For the sake of the community and its future, birth from a free woman is seen to guarantee the children of future generations their right to full humanity through being bearers of God's covenant and promise. The liberation of Hagar—linking class and sex, a major concern at Sheffield—is not dealt with in this text. St. Paul picks up this Sarah/Hagar theme again in Galatians 4, calling those who are in Christ (those delivered from the curse of the Fall) the children of Sarah; but today we must ask, ''What about Hagar?''

As the biblical story begins God is creating the cosmos, the creation, and its creatures. God gazes on what is created and pronounces it ''good,'' whole as a physical/spiritual reality. The whole creation is vibrant in the spirit; the spirit is not disembodied, but everywhere concretely manifest in substance and matter. Body and spirit are seen as one psychosomatic unity. To many of the theologians of the ancient church, the biblical phrase ''image of God'' meant that true humanity (*anthropos*), manifest in Christ, was a theocentric self. Jesus, through the cross, manifests that being human exists in fullness through participation in and with God's goodness.

The stories about our encounter with God after the Fall focus, through covenant and prophesy, on how God helps humanity to maintain or attain its wholeness against all of the forces that destroy it. The *imago Dei* of the first woman and man is always in opposition to the chosen actions of the fallen Adam and Eve. The story of the Fall, of those who wanted more, who blamed each other, is a prism of our brokenness and alienation. It is this falling story with its myriad of human tragedies that is reversed for all humankind in Jesus, the Christ, who, incarnate as a person, lived God's goodness beyond the limits of what fallen human society would permit. It was not ''thugs'' or ''terrorists'' through whom Jesus suffered ridicule and violent death, but it was through the actions of those responsible for the exercise of civil and religious power.

In the suffering Jesus and the resurrected Christ, false exercise of power is condemned. Through Christ, God lives out the longing for the fullness of creation and of humankind, participating with us in the process of resisting and overcoming evil—false power relationships between women and men, poor and rich, black and white, weak and strong. Human wholeness, *anthropos,* is a becoming; it is to recover and discover in the body of Christ that divinely distinct, integral identity that is *imago Dei.* It is from this perspective of "second birth" in baptism's new creation that once again, identity based on sexuality is transcended and the church's affirmation can be, as in these words of Gregory of Nazianzus: "One same Creator for man and for woman, for both the same clay, the same image, the same law, the same death, the same resurrection."

Genesis 1 and 2 are thus not simply "myths of origin," but they describe divine anthropology: God's creative goodness that makes up the wholeness of our true humanity. These chapters express and signify the source of that repeated, sustained action of the divine Word, manifest in community, in equality, without distinction or partiality. Through Christ in community, covenanted in rebirth by the Holy Spirit in baptism and renewed in the eucharistic life, the tragic human story of the Fall—of wholeness broken into domination and submission—is turned around. Faith's conversion/liberation process discloses that through God's word and incarnation, humanity is once again "set free from its bondage to decay [to] obtain the glorious liberty of the children of God" (Rom. 8:21, *RSV*). Human barriers once erected—Jew or Greek, slave or free, male or female—are overcome in the God-given identity of human oneness and relationship: bone of bone and flesh of flesh, across race, class, and sex.

Sexual Identity: A Question of Justice and Human Dignity

In sharp contrast to human wholeness, one of the issues that emerged during the Sheffield consultation was that of prostitution and sex tourism—a sign of degrading human exploitation, linking sex, class, and race in one "web of oppression." Prostitution has been something of a taboo issue: all men know about it and all "good women" turn their eyes from it. It has been a subject avoided by Christian communities. At best it is identified as part of the immoral community from which, by conversion, one can be delivered.

Prostitution is not only a theological issue, a use of persons—and a being used—as things, it is also reinforced in Scripture by vivid pictorial imagery. In the drama of Genesis 3, woman (Eve) is the temptress. Man (Adam) is not responsible for his actions; he is under the power of Eve. She leads him astray. He gives his excuse for betraying God's ordinance: "The woman whom thou gavest to be with me, she gave me fruit of the tree, and I ate." But she too has her excuse: "The serpent beguiled me, and I ate." Already in this story of the Fall, depicting the beginning of human corruption, it is told that man is tempted by woman, and woman is tempted by a beast of the animal kingdom. Behind this story, some say, are remnants of Canaanite fertility cults, child sacrifice, "sacred prostitution," and idolatry. One such graphic example is the story of Oholah and Oholibah in Ezekiel 23. Not only does Scripture begin with this focus on the corrupting role of women, but the theme appears again in the prophetic tradition (Jer. 3:6–10; Hos. 14:13–14) and in the last book of the Bible, the Revelation of St. John: "Babylon the great, mother of harlots and of earth's abominations" (Rev. 17:5, *RSV*).

Here, the image of ultimate corruption is signified by the prostitute woman who receives God's divine judgment. In both Genesis 3 and Revelations 17 the woman's image is unredeemed. The Fall (sin, corruption) is associated with female sexuality. Hosea's unfaithful wife and the harlot of Babylon form part of a continuous theme of negative anthropology related to women, extending back in time to experiences during the conquest of Canaan and underlined later in church tradition through figures such as St. Augustine of Hippo who understood original sin as transmitted through sexual intercourse and, with it, the temptress role of women. And later still in scholastic tradition, St. Thomas Aquinas listed in his reflections on the order of creation that man is closer to the image of the divine and women nearer to the animal kingdom. This tradition lingers on in a multitude of ways in phrases like: "Man is the image of God and woman is the reflected image"; "Man is the head and woman the subordinate"; "Man has the capacity for self-control; woman is weak and readily influenced."

Significantly as women reflect on this history, joining the formerly all-male community of interpreters, there is beginning to be a reversal of this tradition of negative interpretation. One example at Sheffield was the Bible study of Phyllis Trible which demonstrated clearly that in Scripture sexual difference is linked neither with women's subordination or weakness nor with male privilege of primacy. In the Gospel of John the story of the woman prostitute who is brought before Jesus for judgment begins to change the temptress image. Rather than being quick to punish the woman, Jesus invites those men who are *not* guilty to cast the first stone. This passage provided a clue for a reversal of the male-influenced cultural attitude that women are the focal point of weakness and sexual immorality. Jesus addresses the men gathered. He identifies the problem as the men's problem. He calls them to own up to their own partnership in this indignity, for which they had projected blame only on the woman.

More and more documentation verifies the fact that prostitution is a big business today, linked to international tourism, hotel chains, government agencies, international "entertainment centers," and so forth. The "wicked Babylon" is now transnational. Many studies show how women (and even children—girls and boys) are forced into prostitution because of poverty, illiteracy, unemployment. For men who engage in prostitution, it is symptomatic of a socially approved duplicity of personality, for example, "good men" enter into it. For women who become caught in it, it is a gross sign of how the negative impact of their socialization further dehumanizes them when supported and maintained by vested economic interests. For both the sexual oppressor and oppressed, prostitution is symptomatic of world economic misdevelopment, giving some the possibility, the "privilege," to buy the "sexual rights" to prostitute another's body, as one might buy the "right" to take another's land or political, civil, or personal freedom.

In parts of the world fathers even sell their daughters into prostitution as a means of income. For the churches to be effective in confronting this dehumanization, they cannot simply condemn the victim. Much can be learned from the action of Jesus—to identify the guilty and to call them to responsibility. Those institutions that allow some people with economic power to exploit others for their own needs and satisfactions must be called by name. A campaign against sex tourism will only be effective as part of an analysis and action against those transnational and local elite forces that exploit poor peoples, wherein women and children are always the poorest of the poor and in the most vulnerable positions. At Sheffield, Maen Pongudom from Thailand put in straightforward language an affirmation of the human person which ought to be protected with whatever moral and economic means necessary: "Human beings are not selling-buying, not enemies to be conquered, but friends to be dignified, cosustainers in God's work." This ought to be the guiding practical principle of all development and self-help strategies—women and men as equal partners in the process.

In the area of sexuality and violations of human dignity, prostitution was not the only issue to emerge; the issue of rape was also discussed. If the military, an institution so pervasive in its influence on the socialization of men, uses training images of women as "enemy targets" to be destroyed, can people continue to say that rape is a "mad man's problem"? This is only one example of institutionalized brutalization of human feelings in women/men relational life. One could ask: why does the Book of Revelations not end with the rapist rather than the harlot of Babylon? Why, in Genesis 3, is it not the man who is tempted and made weak by the enticements of the serpent rather than the woman? We, women and men in the church, are responsible for our myths and for their consequences. We need to examine their origins. Symbolic miscasting and misinterpreting of sexual identity in history and theology must be seen against the backdrop of present forms of human oppression. We cannot rewrite the Bible, but we can understand that women and men today are called to be its interpreters, allowing God's word to address the conditions of our own time. We can actively oppose flagrant violations of human dignity, a corruption of the *imago Dei*, a destruction of God's most basic human covenant, without which social life cannot long survive. We, in the church, where Scripture is a basis for authority, bear a responsibility to transform the symbolic, structural, and psychological situations that perpetuate the diminishing of women's identity and foster an inhumanity between the sexes, contributing to the erosion of justice and human dignity.

Partnership, Marriage, and Family Life: Helper Relationships

No word transcends all of these categories of relationship better than the word "friendship." To be a friend to another, to have a friend, is to be, and to have, a "helper." A "helper" is a divinely given gift. As the psalmist says, God "delivers the needy when he [sic] calls, the poor and him [sic] who has no helper" (Ps. 72:12, *RSV*). To have one's basic personal and economic necessities and to have a "helper" is to the psalmist equated with God's redemption, with cooperating in God's actions of human deliverance.

Yet the word "helper" is much discredited and abused. At the African regional meeting of the community study it was asked: why is the woman the one who is always seen as the helper to the man and not the reverse? A helper, mutually understood is: woman, a helper to man; man, a helper to woman; woman, a helper to woman; and man, a helper to man. A helper is someone who lives equally with another in a mutually supporting, loving, sympathetic, trusting, well-wishing way. It seems so normal that all friendships, all partnerships in marriage, family, and work, should be those of reciprocal helpers.

For the psalmist to find a fit "helper" is to be delivered from isolation and loneliness, yet why should it be so difficult to find a helper? At Sheffield, the section report on marriage, family, and changing patterns of family life proved to be the most difficult one in which to find a common framework. In a worldwide ecumenical context marriage and family life exist in and are influenced by a host of different social forms with pressures on family patterns in a multitude of directions, that is, conflicts between traditional and modern family structures and expectations, modern industrial and commercial modes of work and unemployment, the legal rights of the partners in marriage, and so forth.

In countries with a socialist, economic, legal structure, obstacles to partnership are not so related to family law as they are to attitudes and conventional roles. A community study group in the German Democratic Republic had a session on partnership in the family. About ten couples gathered in the parish hall. One husband contended that he and his wife had worked out a good partnership, but, he said, it was clear that someone needed to be "in charge." He added that to live a biblical partnership, the wife must obey her husband and, in turn, the husband must love his wife. Though they both worked, he went on to say, "my wife is basically in charge of the household and I am the overseer of the total family." A couple sitting across the room was visibly upset. The two husbands exchanged strong words about the man's responsibility in the marriage. Finally the second husband said, "Both my wife and I work full time. We have two daughters. And I can scrub the kitchen floor just as well as she can, and she can oversee as well as I."

In many situations where women also work outside the home new psychological attitudes of "helpership" must evolve; social attitudes have not yet caught up with changed roles and economic rights. In places where the law protects and enables both women and men to be self-reliant, women still feel the social pressure that the home is their primary responsibility: its success or failure depends on them. Reports from Scandinavia show that the psychological and traditional socialization of women and men to their parental role models is very strong. Even when parental roles are fully shared, women find it hard to overcome their inherited sense of having entire responsibility for home and children. Regarding employment, a report from Czechoslovakia speaks for many. It states that full-time work outside the home "puts considerable strains on the women and leads to many tensions, sometimes breaking up the marriage. Yet, most women prefer to work and choose to be employed for many reasons: to keep a reasonable standard of living for the family, to make use of their own education, to develop themselves, and to make a contribution to public life."

For men, modern, industrial work structures shape their lives and determine their own and their families' role and fate—whether they are black workers in South African mines, migrant workers in Europe or North America, or industrial workers in sectors of socialist economies. Often the poorest-paid workers are at work most of the day. Some must spend up to eleven months of the year separated from wives and children, living in "dormitories," because work conditions demand it. On the opposite end of the economic spectrum, well-paid men in large companies and transnational work are also often absent from the home for three or four months of the year, living in hotels, eating in restaurants. For both, a great gap exists between their work and family life, often leading to family alienation and violence. No matter what the socioeconomic level, few people in industrialized countries escape the impact of this duality of life styles in which women and men live.

It is in a "macro" form a network of a hunter (male—absent from the home) and a gatherer (female—present in the home) economy, creating First and Third World structures of power and dependency within the "mini" society of the community and home. In caricature form, the First World "rich" need the Third World "poor." The rich justify their life styles by helping the poor. The poor need the rich so long as they cannot find for themselves a sustainable base of self-reliance. This caricature of world inequality impacts on families and on role expectations. Fathers justify their work and life styles as necessary in order to help their wives and children. Mothers become economically dependent on their husbands as long as economic, work, and legal structures are roadblocks to their own self-reliance; teen-age children are caught between two worlds.

Contained in the domestic sphere, "helper" rights for women are limited compared with those for men. If a woman has no access to ownership of land, property, credit, or a source of income, she is dependent on a father, husband, or welfare, where it exists. In societies where the economic base of the family is dependent on a man's earned income, the woman becomes the "Third World" partner from within. First World work structures interfere with a man's parental family role; family structures, as structures of dependency, interfere with the development of women and their self-reliance. The larger the economic gap between the "helpers," the more vulnerable is the relationship to becoming one of domination or subordination. Looking at the family structurally, in this caricatured way, one can see why it is so difficult for some partners to find a common language of understanding and a common basis that can sustain partnership and build relationships as mutual "helpers."

In parts of Africa where matrilineal family patterns have existed for centuries, modern forms of ownership of property and credit undercut the authority of the woman and the woman's family. Built into modern "development," law and strategy is a Western-influenced male bias toward the "male head" as the representative head of the household. This is reinforced by the church when it emphasizes the dominance of male headship. The result of this is catastrophic in matrilineal families which tend to be agriculturally based and related to traditional market systems. These family-oriented structures are not primarily motivated to the accumulation of capital but to distribution and providing for the basic needs of larger, open, extended families. Underlying First World economic incentives is the concept of self-interest, while underlying these Third World traditional structures is a social orientation of care for others, founded in a mother's role. There is much to be learned from traditional family structures where a village organization and neighborhood communication system protect and oversee the community's basic needs. In such a system all are interdependent. Children learn very young to help their parents and to care for other children. Older people continue to have valuable roles in supporting the family. Architecture, simple as it might be, is flexible and adjustable to changing family circumstances.

The tragedy today is that agriculturally based people the world over who are poor are becoming poorer. As land is bought out from under them by larger agencies and, with the help of mechanized farming, is turned into cash crops for rich consumer markets, less land is available for families and especially for women, most of whose work is marginal farming, gardening, and the sharing and selling of surpluses if they exist.

In the West, much is written today about the diminishing of "fatherhood." There is also in other parts of the world a diminishing of "motherhood," about which women are now beginning to speak. What is usually said about the diminishing of fatherhood is that is signifies the breakup of family authority. What is usually written about motherhood is that women are abandoning the home, being unfaithful to their children. Little is written about men abandoning their homes or about women losing their rights because of male bias in legal and economic life. Seen worldwide, both fatherhood and motherhood are in trouble. No matter what the economic system or social pattern, it takes all "helpers" to keep together marriage and family life.

It would seem natural that the church could be a helper in the midst of these many pressures. Traditional festivals of the church—Christmas, Epiphany, Lent, Easter, and Pentecost—could take on new meaning, seen as occasions of helpers, sharing and receiving, as times when the "household of God" becomes more transparent with the many forms of family and familial life in which women and men live.

In many Christian traditions the family is "the little church." As such, it could be more sympathetically engaged in nurturing the theological and spiritual basis for sustaining the covenant, trust, and faithfulness needed to make possible responsible relationships of mutual help. Where family and cultural structures weaken, the church as women and men in community could play a more significant role in sustaining changing patterns of family life and in enlarging the horizons in which isolated family problems are often dealt with. One sees some of this happening in churches among the poorest of the poor. Education, distribution of food, all sorts of community organization efforts are stimulated by families (mostly initiated by women) meeting together for worship and prayer. Gathered with the hope and the will to improve their human condition, they live in faith that God will sustain them in the process. Though problems in churches in rich countries are different, there is also a need for this hope, energy, and will to form "helper" networks.

God is "our help in ages past, our hope for years to come." Perhaps the sentiment of this seventeenth-century hymn can speak much truth to us today as a model of "God with us." Partnership can only be reconstructed if it works at becoming a model of mutuality, difficult as this is to attain. Symbolically, the model of God as "daddy" (Abba) so genuine to Jesus and his time has in our time become linked with other qualities—with male dominance and absentee fathers and with the diminishing rights of mothers. Both fatherhood and motherhood—as loving, caring, forgiving, and sustaining figures in family life—need reconstructing for these terms to signify more completely the qualities of the human family's helper God.

THE CHURCH—A VENTURE IN SERVICE
Participation and Headship

Local groups working on the community study addressed the subject of participation often, starting with an evaluation of women's participation in the churches. Their findings are not surprising; for example, women form the majority of teachers in Sunday schools, but their representative role decreases as they move from the parish council to districts or synods. In some churches, along with men laity, women are excluded from any leadership related to the eucharistic celebration, though young boys are included. In other churches, the exercise of ritual and decision-making power is limited to those who are male and also celibate, though the majority of the worshippers are women.

Because of new levels of women's participation, many churches are undergoing changes: allowing women to read the Scripture lesson in the Liturgy but not the Gospel; to read the Gospel but not assist with the distribution of the Eucharist; to assist with the distribution of the Eucharist but not preside at it; to preside but not to be head of a parish; and so forth. A voice from the Latin American regional meeting on the community study expressed this hope:

> We should be talking about a new church. Theology is usually presented by men with masculine ideas, deeply impregnated with societal traditions. Many churches "permit" women to do things, but the structures remain the same. There needs to be a renewed church, without sex and class discrimination. We do not need to form a new denomination; this is a job of transformation.

Sheffield itself had problems with participation. There was much criticism of its structures, for example, a high platform to look up to, long opening plenaries with little time for response, not enough input from the regions at the beginning or participation from the range of Orthodox traditions, too much head work and consequent neglect of the body, and so forth. Some expected more structural flexibility that would allow for more space and freedom for contemplation and more careful attention to concerns that required action.

Side by side with the challenges coming from expectations within the consultation itself was a challenge to the churches. In many ways it was stated that if community in Christ is authority for our lives then partnership with each other, as friends and coworkers with God, must fully include both women and men. Some questions asked were: "How is it possible for one partner to be 'head' over the other?" "What is the real basis in the church for the exercise of headship?" "Do our present structures reflect the true intention of the 'headship of Christ'?" "If headship is 'source' (beginnings, origin), then where and how do we look structurally for the source of authority in the church? How do we identify it?"

These questions were indirectly responded to by means of posing new models. Some called for hierarchy to be reversed; others claimed that hierarchy in its pure form is Trinity wherein all are equal parts of one dynamic relationship. Some quoted Jesus' response to the sons of Zebedee (Matt. 20:20ff., *RSV*): "Whoever would be great among you must be your servant, and whoever would be first among you must be your slave; even as the Son of man came not to be served but to serve." Still others used a model of mission, drawing on the parables of Jesus, especially the themes of the messianic banquet. The feast of the kingdom is not a company of those first invited, but of those who, after the others refuse, are gathered from the highways and byways—the outcasts, the poor, and among them, the widows, prostitutes, foreign and non-Jewish women, such as the Syro-Phoenician woman, and the Samaritan woman at the well. Still others looked to a model of the church in the Magnificat of Mary, not the church modeled on a woman who uncritically serves, but on a woman who is motivated as prophet/servant of God. Behind all of these ecclesial models is a vision of the church, transformed by the full participation of all God's people. It is a church that grows and is alive because it has learned to serve, share, and celebrate in solidarity with all. It is the church as an expression of God's self-giving partnership, not just with some, but with all classes and races, women and men. These models of the church reflect a new awareness of who participates and how its authority is validated. They lift up the significance of those who have been previously overlooked and of the servant role, reminders of the invisible status and the work of women in the churches for centuries.

To some extent, the Sheffield consultation ran into conflict with the "headship" model of the church when its recommendations were presented for discussion and action to the 1981 WCC Central Committee, meeting in Dresden. The participants at Sheffield included about two-thirds women and one-third men—lay leaders, theologians, and pastors from the member churches. The participants of Dresden were about nine men to one women, many of them either heads of their churches or carrying the responsibility for them. Given the different people participating in these two gatherings, what seemed perfectly normal at Sheffield sounded radical at Dresden. It occasioned, as reported in the press, "a clash of contexts."

Juxtaposing the two ecclesial realities of Sheffield and Dresden could become a worthwhile case study. The responsibility for this reflection is not only on the WCC but also on its member churches who shape its being and becoming. To move toward the realization of the church as one community, member churches might well examine more carefully and together their own internal patterns of authority and decision-making. Sheffield recommended that the churches do this, that they reflect more about the church as a community of women and men and about the obstacles to a fuller enabling of all its gifts in making manifest the one body in Christ. At Sheffield participation and the ordering of authority were not seen as two separate issues, running parallel, but as part of one movement toward the unity of the church as a sign for the renewal of the whole human community.

The first, large-scale meeting of its kind in the worldwide church, it was probably the first of its kind in any of the member churches. The impact of

Sheffield's glimpse of renewed ecclesial reality was not just that it was an event, but as stated in the Letter, it gave "reality to the vision." This can be seen in the recommendations to the Dresden Central Committee, particularly the one which asked that, for the committees and working groups to be appointed to the Vancouver Sixth Assembly, fifty percent of the members should be women. This was not Sheffield in a militant mood. It was not a simple asking to right past injustice. Much-debated at Sheffield itself, the recommendation finally passed with the argumentation that full dignity of partnership means fifty-fifty. This was seen as a principle of partnership, one that applies to race and class as well. It was acknowledged that it may not yet be fully feasible, and that not more could be asked of the WCC than must be asked of the member churches. Yet, in spite of the difficulties, coming from Sheffield, a community of women and men, it was felt that nothing less than fifty-fifty could be recommended as a goal. Women and men in the church are not servants, one of the other, but share together in authority and participation the church's servant role.

Ordination of Women

About fifteen of the women present at the consultation were ordained. Their presence was and is a reality to be acknowledged in the ecumenical movement. Ordination of women to the priesthood was not one of the priority items prepared for the common agenda. A special consultation had been held on the subject and its report was included in the background materials for the meeting. However, among the local group reports, those from the Orthodox made clear that priestly roles for women were not a part of their tradition, though they acknowledged roles for women in ordained ministries as well as in many other ministries of the church. The focus of the preparatory work for Sheffield was built on common concerns. This meant that "women in ministry" was the common subject, and ordination of women was one aspect of it. Attention to the ordination of women came as a surprise from the plenary floor. This initiative emerged because some participants felt that this painful struggle in some churches would be ignored, that the consultation would too easily draft a smooth concensus statement.

In the section working on ministry there was a carefully drafted statement about not allowing the ordination of women to be a roadblock for the churches in their efforts toward unity. This was acknowledged and accepted by the plenary, but still it was felt by many present that this was not enough. Then an intervention from the floor began with the preface, " . . . knowing that ordination is not the issue of this consultation . . . I feel we would default in our responsibility to those not here if we did not express our solidarity with those women who long for ordination and with those now ordained who face problems of assignments and placements." This intervention received a standing ovation. As a result it was requested that something expressing this sentiment, whether all agreed with it or not, be included in the Sheffield letter and in the section reports. This was the source of the reference in the Sheffield letter, regarding those who "feel called to the ministry of word and sacrament, but ordination is not open to women." The section work on ministry at Sheffield suggests how we can speak together in an ecumenical context—Orthodox, Anglican, Protestant, and Roman Catholic. The Letter describes an existential situation in some of the WCC member and nonmember churches, a situation with which many at Sheffield wanted to join in sympathy.

Historically, initiatives for the ordination of women have come from the Reformed and Free Church traditions of the Reformation; therefore biblical and theological considerations were of fundamental importance, along with pastoral concerns. In the 1950s and 60s, Lutheran and Reformed deliberations on this issue did not center on cultural, historical, and social questions. It was argued that the sphere of God's reign and providence has more authority than civil order. Care was taken that the decision on this question be made independent of societal pressures.

Presently, although close to one-half of the WCC member churches ordain women, in terms of numbers of Christians these together do not balance the three major church bodies that do not—namely, the Orthodox churches, most churches of the Anglican world communion, and the Roman Catholic Church. Though the debate is essentially settled in much of Protestantism, it is almost new in the international ecumenical movement, and there is considerable resistance by some to even consider the ordination of women to the priesthood as an item for discussion. Sheffield recommended that further ecumenical study needed to be done. The January 1982 meeting of the Commission on Faith and Order in Lima, Peru, received this recommendation. Difficult as the issue appears to be, it cannot escape being part of future work.

There is ample evidence, acknowledged by scholars of all churches, that women were ordained as deacons during the first four centuries of the church. What is not clear is whether women were ever considered for ordination to the presidency of the Eucharist during this period when the churches were in full conciliarity. If it were established that the ordination of women to the priesthood is a genuinely new issue for the church today, never considered nor rejected at one of the early ecumenical councils, then the present debate could find a focused direction as one of the issues for resolution in the larger process and steps toward one conciliar community.

If no early ecumenical council has dealt with this question, then the issues to be faced are primarily on the side of theology and not tradition. Among the theological questions that would need attention are: What is the nature of the eschatological Christ, the Christ to come, in relation to the celebration of the Eucharist, including eschatological dimensions of the Eucharist itself? Must the representative of Christ at the Eucharist be male, a physical likeness to the historical Jesus, and in the male line of the priesthood of Melchizedek? Or is the Christ of the new creation, neither male nor female, thus making sexual identification a nonissue? Or, is it essential that the Lord of the Eucharist, the priest of the royal priesthood, be representative of both women and men in order to reflect the full and universal character of being human? These are some of the questions asked by the various voices, questions yet to be studied ecumenically.

Concerns arise not only with regard to the ordination of women to the priesthood but also with regard to placement in those churches that do ordain women. There is little information on this topic. The general impression is that ordained women are rarely in chief positions as ''heads'' of parishes or synods. They are most often working in pioneer specialized pastoral ministries of mission and service and in team ministries; they are often paid less. More attention must be given to the positive side of what women and men in ministry actually do, and what new dimensions women now in ordained ministries bring to the church's life and contemporary role.

Ordination itself is also being reconsidered in some Christian communities. Men, as well as women, are questioning the relevance of its forms for today's needs. In some ministries of mission and service they are asking if ordination does not further separate the clergy from the laity rather than bind them together in one community. Similar questions are posed about celibacy in some cultural situations, especially in parts of Africa, Latin America, the Caribbean, and the Pacific. Many levels of dialogue are still required to clarify the meaning of ministry and ordination, and the functions of the ordained, a process well underway in the Faith and Order work on baptism, Eucharist and ministry.

Mary, Mother of God, and Mariology

A whole range of questions about anthropology emerged in the study: women and men as ''being human,'' women and men in roles of generation, parenting and partnership, issues of sexuality, of body/spirit human wholeness, of equality and human rights, of corruption in fallen community, and of becoming human in God's redemptive work. The list is long.

The question of Mary, Mother of God, and Mariology is a topic not yet treated in depth in the community of women and men. In the ecumenical movement great divergencies of experience, belief, and opinion exist on this. Some reflect traditional doctrinal differences between the churches. Others, within the churches reflect contemporary divergencies in biblical/critical and dogmatic studies. Still others point to a strengthening of Mary as a symbol of great power and promise for women in the church, and a symbol of human liberation for all.

In some churches there is no strong theological tradition around Mary. In the majority of Protestant churches, there is no developed doctrine or teaching related to her. In these churches, Mary is often consciously overlooked, a reaction to developed dogmas in other churches. In churches, however, where Mary is part of the doctrinal tradition—Mariology in the Roman Catholic tradition or the Mother of God in the Orthodox churches—the symbol of Mary combines many images of her to form an ecclesiology of the church. As the bride of Christ, she is linked to the prophetic tradition of the people of God. She is the opposite of Hosea's unfaithful wife or the harlot of Babylon. Her faith signifies God's triumph over evil and God's governance over all humankind. There has been some uneasiness expressed but not yet a serious new ecumenical reflection around the metaphor of the marriage imagery, of Christ the bridegroom of the church and Mary the bride. This biblical metaphor is sometimes used in tradition to describe the relationship of priesthood and laity, for example, priests (male) must be like the bridegroom, and laity (women and men) must be like the bride.

In all churches, those with and without a doctrine of Mary, there is a wealth of spirituality and popular piety surrounding her, particularly the image of Mary, the mother of the Christ. In contemporary biblical thought there are attempts to separate the facts about Mary from the myths, in piety and popular devotion, that encircle her. In some circles she is being demythologized, and in others there is a new critique and appreciation of her, a kind of remythologizing and appropriation of her image and role by women. In the Southern Hemisphere, both Protestants and Roman Catholics are examining her anew in areas of the world where Roman Catholic piety is deeply embedded in the folk consciousness. In the Northern Hemisphere among Protestant and Orthodox women there is a new inquiry about Mary and about the many ''Marys'' of the church. New poetry and preaching about her is being done by women. For the future ecumenical agenda Mary, Mother of God, and Mariology are sure to open up subjects of great surprise that can aid churches and persons to share and deepen their spiritual understanding of one another as women and men living the church, as well as the church's teachings, worship, and devotional life in a variety of ways.

Mary was singled out at Sheffield as one of the basic paradigms. In the section on tradition and traditions the consultation said:

> The tradition *Mary* is being today reappropriated in the churches. Her life as recorded in Scripture is being explored more fully. She is seen as the sharing woman who seeks out Elizabeth to tell the news of her pregnancy; as being in the tradition of prophecy bearing the Magnificat; as the woman neglected by her Son in favor of his mission; and then as a disciple journeying in partnership with Jesus along with other women and men. Then we witness her profound grief at the death of her child under the judgment of religious and political powers, her faithfulness to follow him to the tomb, and the divine gift bestowed upon her to be a witness of the resurrection of the "flesh of her flesh, the bone of her bone." Mary is no longer seen as the model of submission and subordination but rather as a woman who has fully lived her partnership with God in the Christ Event.

In popular religious piety, Mary is often associated with the woman in Revelations who flees to the wilderness. She is supported by "two wings of the great eagle that she might fly . . . to the place where she is to be nourished for a time, and times, and half a time" (Rev. 12:14, *RSV*). Like this Mary, the reality of the church as women and men in community requires support and nourishment as do all who venture into new spaces, fields, and places.

A Wilderness Community

Many have remarked that Sheffield was not just "against sexism," but that it was a thrust forward, an initiative toward a new realization in time of Christ's body in world community. The symbolization used for the nature of the community being sought was not that of the Exodus, an action of leaving, but of the wilderness of promise, an entering into and being nourished in community, guided in faithfulness, yet working within the demands and limitations of necessity. As the consultation looked back, in the reusing of the history of God's people, it was reminded of the many other struggles for human wholeness and their interconnections, of risks that come with vision, change, reordering. Tradition was understood as a foundation, an energy, a source of power to quicken the reality of the promised time when barriers caused by sexism, racism, and classism will be overcome. This wilderness theme was apparent in the final worship.

In the soft evening light, the assembly processed out over the green lawns of the university residence halls, passing by a pond and swampy area, filled with slippery rocks. Recovering herself from a fall, one person confirmed what others felt, "Entering the promised land is a joy, but it certainly is hazardous!" When gathered again at Earnshaw, rather than having a eucharistic service, the consultation chose a practice from an ancient baptismal rite; participants regrouped to partake of honey, sharing with one another. This was not an act of sentimental sweetness. For some it brought tears, for others it was the nourishment to go forward to a time when there could be a truly inclusive ecumenical feast. Some felt there should have been a final eucharistic celebration. Others did not want anyone to be left out. The model of eucharistic life style with this metaphor of sharing honey in a wilderness community of promise enabled solidarity; it welcomed and included all. And in remembering an ancient act of new community, it was a small foretaste of a future that can happen now.

A significant faith disposition of those participating in the community study has been the readiness to live tradition as a life style of anticipation rather than to see the past as only a burden from which to be delivered. The thrust has not been to dwell on what has not been done, but to concentrate on what can be done. With this was also the awareness that as an ecumenical community, women and men in the churches still have far to go to be liberated from that which separates and divides. There was, thus, a realization that this future character of faithfulness is vulnerable and uncertain; it must be nourished and sustained through a life of communion, through the "This is" of God in Christ, as bread and wine shared, food for pilgrims. Sheffield—with its emphasis on community as inclusive, on power-sharing, and on considerations of practical life—forged a new path between the churches' established traditions, customs, and structures on the one hand and their realistic transformation on the other.

To follow this path is no easy task. In a message from the European regional meeting, participants captured some of the words to describe its tensions and pains, existent not only within the churches, but internally in each person's experience.

> We are seeking new forms of being together but the old structures still exist. There is great tension between our dreams and our realities. We are experiencing different types of conflicting loyalties. Many times there is not room enough in the churches for the realization of our visions. Living between old traditions and new opportunities definitely means living in controversy. This ambivalence is not only

an external matter. It lives within us. It is part of the process which leads us to find a new identity both as individuals and as communities. The openness which we have felt so strongly is at the same time both promising and painful. But there is no other way. Even in the most difficult moments we trust one another and know that we belong together. We are aware of the fact that there are many individuals and groups, ourselves included, who may have to pay a high price for the transformation process which aims at a new community. We want to be in solidarity with all and to take care that nobody will lose her or his integrity and dignity because of our common struggle.

Much of the worldwide reflection about the church as women and men in community has been about the way, the process, the journey. Starting with identity, the members of community, it has raised questions about the methods often used in theological and biblical interpretation, about the ways in which the past is remembered, about history's biases, its lessons applied. It has asked ''why'' and ''what'' about the words that have been chosen in talking about God and our common life in *theos*. Reflection on the study has started with the ''where'' of the concrete, the experience of women and men in church and society and how they have seen the churches contributing to, or helping to overcome, human inequality and injustice in many forms. The problems dealt with are the real concerns of human dignity that people live with, that shape their lives, destinies, images of each other, and their expectations of partnership. Reflection on the church has been directed toward how structures and styles of ministry reordered could better support and enrich the churches' service and spirituality in its vocation of renewal of humankind.

Choosing the image of the wilderness community was not a vote for withdrawal, rather it offered a model for faithfulness. With wholeness as a vision and unity as a goal, it was possible to experience the church as women and men in community held together in hope and, step by step, sustained by God's promise.

APPENDIX

A

List of Participants

Delegates

Ms. Anne Abayasekara (Methodist),
Sri Lanka

Dr. Göran Agrell (Lutheran), Sweden

Rev. Hans Arne Akerø (Lutheran),
Norway

Dr. Elizabeth Amoah (Methodist),
Ghana

Ms. Lily Amirtham (Church of South
India), Switzerland

Ms. Daphne Joan Anderson (United
Church of Canada), Canada

Rev. Thomas E. Anderson (Lutheran),
USA

Ms. Irja Askola (Lutheran), Finland

Rev. Dr. Albert Aymer (Methodist),
USA

Rev. Father Tissa Balasuriya, O.M.I.
(Roman Catholic), Sri Lanka

Rev. Aziz Bassous (Presbyterian),
Lebanon

Dr. Elisabeth Behr-Sigel (Orthodox),
France

Ms. Deborah Belonick (Orthodox),
USA

Ms. Violeta Davyt de Bertinat
(Waldensian), Uruguay

Rev. John N. Boro (Presbyterian),
Kenya

Dr. Madeleine Boucher (Roman
Catholic), USA

Ms. Dora F. Browne (Anglican),
Barbados

Ms. Marta A. Bubeck (Lutheran),
Federal Republic of Germany

Ms. Jeanne Buster (Lutheran), USA

Rev. Raquel M. Caceres (Methodist),
Argentina

Ms. Julia Campos (Waldensian),
Mexico

Rev. Dr. William B. Cate (Methodist),
USA

Ms. Somsri Chaiyasate (Presbyterian),
Thailand

Dr. Sang Chang (Presbyterian), Korea

Ms. Pamela Pauly Chinnis
(Episcopal), USA

Ms. Eva de Carvalho Chipenda
(Presbyterian), Angola

Ms. Nerolei Chisholm (Presbyterian),
New Zealand

Prof. Andrei Ivanovich Chizhov
(Orthodox), USSR

Ms. Ellen Juhl Christiansen
(Lutheran), Denmark

Rev. Margaret (Peggy) Clark
(Christian Church/Disciples of
Christ), USA

Ms. Marie-France Coïsson
(Waldensian), Italy

Ms. Cecilia M. R. Cole (Methodist),
The Gambia

Rt. Rev. Martin H. Cressey (United
Reformed), England

Rev. Yaseda Daba (Ev. Church
Mekane Yesus), Ethiopia

Mr. Kuldip Thakur Das (Church of North India), India

Mr. Edgar H. Davidson (Methodist), Trinidad

Ms. Margaret Price Davies (Methodist), England

Ms. Suguna Devasundaram (Church of South India), India

Ms. Amal Dibo (Orthodox), Lebanon

Ms. Marjorie Dubarry-Cameron (Presbyterian), Trinidad

Ms. Kerstin Ekberg (Swedish Miss. Covenant), Sweden

Dr. Helmut Erharter (Roman Catholic), Austria

Rev. Lillemor Erlander (Lutheran), Sweden

Dr. Irene W. Foulkes (Evangelical), Costa Rica

Ms. Christiane Frühauf (Lutheran), German Democratic Republic

Rev. Dr. John Gaden (Anglican), Australia

Ms. Christa Golpon (Lutheran), German Democratic Republic

Ms. Susan C. Goodfellow (Anglican), Canada

Ms. Elena M. Gundayaeva (Russian Orthodox), USSR

Sister Madeleine-Marie Handy (Presbyterian), Cameroon

Ms. Maidie Hart (Reformed), Scotland

Ms. Astri Hauge (Lutheran), Norway

Rev. Helga Hiller (Lutheran), Federal Republic of Germany

Rev. Chen Huei Hung (Presbyterian), Taiwan

Ms. Comm. Pauline Hunter (Salvation Army), England

Ms. Femmy Janson-Oosterhagen (Old Catholic), Netherlands

Rev. Kathy J. Johnson (Baptist), USA

Ms. Isabella Johnston (All Africa Conference of Churches), Kenya

Very Rev. William B. Johnston (Reformed), Scotland

Ms. Lilian Kanyikwa (Anglican), Democratic Republic of Sudan

Rev. Timothy Kiogora (Methodist), Kenya

Ms. Gerda Kuhn (Reformed), Federal Republic of Germany

Prof. Dr. Elisabeth J. Lacelle (Roman Catholic), Canada

Mr. Wesley Lackley (Presbyterian), USA

Mr. Phillip A. Ladokun (Baptist), Nigeria

Ms. Kibobe Biasima Lala (Baptist), Zaïre

Father Dr. Hervé Legrand (Roman Catholic), France

Ms. Kathryn Johnson Lieurance (Lutheran), USA

Ms. Eva Loos (Lutheran), Federal Republic of Germany

Mr. Jan Lukaszuk (Orthodox), Poland

Dr. Florence Mahoney (Anglican), The Gambia

Rev. Charity N. Majiza (Presbyterian), South Africa

Rev. Thomas Maluit (Presbyterian), Democratic Republic of Sudan

Ms. Violetta Marasigan (Philippine Independent), Philippines

Ms. Jeanne C. Marshall (Presbyterian), USA

Ms. Rachel Mathew (Mar Thoma Syrian), India

Ms. Daw Tin May (Baptist), Burma

Ms. Melanie A. May (Church of the Brethren), USA

Deaconess Diana McClatchey (Anglican), England

Prof. Alberto Moisés Mendez (Baptist), Mexico

Ms. Jean Guy Miller (Presbyterian), USA

Ms. Rita Milne (Baptist), England

Ms. Bernadette I. Mosala (Roman Catholic), South Africa
Very Rev. Basil Stanley Moss (Anglican), England
Ms. Sheila A. Moyes, D. C. S. (Reformed), Scotland
Ms. Alida Nababan-Lumbantobing (Lutheran), Indonesia
Rev. David Ndongo (Presbyterian), Cameroon
Dr. Sijbolt Noorda (Reformed), Netherlands
Ms. Mercy Oduyoye (Methodist), Nigeria
Dr. Tamiko Okamura (United Church), Japan
Dr. Milan Opocensky (Presbyterian), CSSR
Ms. Marlene Pinto Pinto (Lutheran), Colombia
Rev. Nancy Van Wyk Phillips (Reformed), USA
Rev. Dr. Maen Pongudom (Church of Christ in Thailand), Thailand
Rev. Jeanne Audrey Powers (Methodist), USA
Mr. Rakotondrainy (Reformed), Madagascar
Mr. Ilari Rantakari (Lutheran), Finland
Dr. Sharon H. Ringe (United Church of Christ), USA
Rev. Hugh A. A. Rose (United Church of Canada), Canada
Dr. Letty M. Russell (Presbyterian), USA
Ms. Dorinda Sampath (Presbyterian), Trinidad
Ms. Gisela M. Ott Sandri (Lutheran), Brazil
Ms. Annekee Schilthuis-Stokvis (Reformed), Netherlands
Ms. Eva Schirmer (Ev. Uniert und Herrnhuter Brudergemeinde), Federal Republic of Germany

Rev. Eva Renate Schmidt (Lutheran), Federal Republic of Germany
Ms. Helen Schmidt (Lutheran), Federal Republic of Germany
Ms. Suad Shehadi (Presbyterian), Lebanon
Ms. Thelma A. Smart (Baptist), Canada
Ms. Mary Soon (Lutheran), Singapore
Ms. Marjorie Spence (Uniting Church), Australia
Rev. Esther Suter (Reformed), Switzerland
Ms. Eugenia Sykacz (Orthodox), Poland
Ms. Veronica Swai (Lutheran), Tanzania
Ms. Elisabeth A. Streefland (Reformed), Netherlands
Bishop Frederick H. Talbot (African Methodist Episcopal), USA
Rev. Elizabeth S. Tapia (Methodist), Philippines
Ms. Myriam Tétaz-Gramegna (Reformed), Switzerland
Ms. Lucy Tijerina (Presbyterian), Mexico
Ms. Dora E. Morales Valentin (Presbyterian), Cuba
Ms. Litia V. Veisa (Methodist), Fiji
Rev. Manfred Wendler (Lutheran), German Democratic Republic
Ms. Janet Wesonga (Anglican), Uganda
Rev. Manfred Wester (Lutheran), Federal Republic of Germany
Prof. Marthe Westphal (Reformed), France
Rev. Friedrich Emanuel Wieser (Baptist), Switzerland
Ms. Amy Chi Fong Wong (Anglican), Hong Kong
Ms. Houda Zacca (Orthodox), Lebanon
Ms. Rose Zoé-Obianga (Presbyterian), Cameroon

Consultants

Father Ambrosius (Orthodox), Finland

Dr. Madeleine Barot (Reformed), France

Ms. Angelica Brun (Reformed), France

Ms. Fernanda Comba (Waldensian), Italy

Dr. Anezka Ebertova (Reformed), USSR

Ms. Padmasini J. Gallup (Church of South India), India

Rev. Jacquelyn Grant (African Methodist Episcopal), USA

Rev. Gordon Gray (Presbyterian), North Ireland

Ms. Seni Happimaa (Orthodox), Finland

Ms. Christian Howard (Anglican), England

Ms. Sang Wha Lee (Presbyterian), Korea

Dr. Martti Lindqvist (Lutheran), Finland

Ms. Marie-Thérèse van Lunen-Chenu (Roman Catholic), France

Dr. Jean Baker Miller, Wellesley College, USA

Dr. Elisabeth Moltmann-Wendel (Reformed), Federal Republic of Germany

Prof. Jürgen Moltmann (Reformed), Federal Republic of Germany

Ms. Gloria Perez, Mexico

Ms. Yousriya Loza-Sawiris (Orthodox), Egypt

Rev. Eginhard Schmiechen (Lutheran), German Democratic Republic

Ms. Margaret Sonnenday (Methodist), USA

Rev. Christa Springe (Lutheran), Federal Republic of Germany

Dr. Juan Stam (Evangelical), Costa Rica

Ms. Minako Suzuki (United Church of Christ), Japan

Ms. Mary Tanner (Anglican), England

Dr. Phyllis Trible, Union Theological Seminary, USA

Ms. Hildegard Zumach (United), Federal Republic of Germany

Observers

Ms. Erica Brodie, Secretary General—World YWCA (Geneva)

Ms. Ursula Ebert, Evangelisches Missionswerk (Federal Republic of Germany)

Ms. Valerie Ford, Disciples of Christ (USA)

Ms. Kiyoko Kasai Fujiu, Commission on Status & Role of Women—United Methodist Church (USA)

Ms. Eva von Hertzberg, Lutheran World Federation (Geneva)

Rev. General Mcoteli, The Reformed Presbyterian Church of South Africa (Transkei)

Mr. Kevin Muir, Secretary of Laity Commission of Roman Catholic Church in England and Wales (England)

Dr. Margarethe von Müller, Union of Catholic Women's Organizations (Federal Republic of Germany)

Ms. Libbie Patterson, Dir., Women's Concerns—Fuller Theological Seminary (USA)

Ms. Maria Teresa Porcile Santiso, Representing Vatican Secretariat for Promoting Christian Unity (Uruguay)

Sister Teresa, Diakonia, International Deaconness Federation (England)

Stewards

Mr. Hans-Michael Bach, Federal Republic of Germany
Ms. Alison Ruth Baxter, Scotland
Ms. Rosalind Agnes Bell, England
Ms. Ellen Maria Doolke, Sweden
Mr. Herman Ekenhorst, Netherlands
Ms. Cath Fluter, Canada
Ms. Jaana Inkeri Hallamaa, Finland
Mr. Richard Hughes, England

Mr. Alan James, England
Mr. Peter M. F. Kaan, England
Ms. Eszter Karsay, Hungary
Ms. Hildegund Niebch, Federal Republic of Germany
Mr. Burkhard Schmidt, Switzerland
Ms. Paula Lynne Short, USA
Ms. Annette Waffenschmidt, Federal Republic of Germany

Press

Ms. Jo-Ann Price Baehr, National Catholic News Service, USA
Ms. Beverly Boche, Minnesota United Methodist, USA
Ms. Leoni Caldercott, England
Ms. Sarah Cunningham, *A.D. Magazine*, USA
Ms. Heather Formini, Australian Broadcasting Commission, England
Ms. Betty Gray, Church Women United, USA
Ms. Frances Gumley, *Catholic Herald*, England
Mr. Martyn Halsall, *The Guardian*, England
Ms. Rosemary Hartill, BBC/Religious Affairs, England
Mr. Görel Bystrom Janaru, UAS, Sweden
Mr. Arthur Jones, *National Catholic Reporter*, England/USA
Ms. Marianne Katoppo, Indonesia
Mr. Friedrich König, Lutheran World Federation Press Service, Geneva
Rev. Christine Lässig, Federation of Ev. Churches in the GDR, German Democratic Republic
Ms. Kirsty Lehnert, Wales

Ms. Carolyn Lewis, *The Lutheran*, USA
Mr. Matthieu van Lunen, Femmes et Hommes dans l'Eglise, France
Ms. Wendy Ryan, American Baptist Churches, USA
Mr. Carlos Reyes, photographer, England
Ms. Faith A. Sand, *Missiology*, USA
Ms. Ammu Joseph Saran, *Eve's Weekly*, India
Ms. Angelika Schmidt-Biesalski, Deutschlandfunk, Federal Republic of Germany
Ms. Josie Smith, Radio Sheffield, England
Ms. Marlies Spiekermann, Federal Republic of Germany
Ms. Betty Thompson, Board of Global Ministries, USA
Ms. Marie Unger, Nordelbisches Missionswerk, Federal Republic of Germany
Ms. Pauline Webb, BBC, England
Ms. Judy Weidman, Board of Higher Education and Ministry—The United Methodist Church, USA
Mr. Stephen Whittle, New Broadcasting House, England

WCC Staff

Rev. S. Wesley Ariarajah, Dialogue with People of Living Faiths and Ideologies

Ms. Margaret Beguin, Personnel Office

Mr. John Bluck, Department of Communication

Ms. Gwendoline Cashmore, World Mission and Evangelism

Ms. Eileen Chapman, Family Ministries

Rev. Janet E. Crawford, Community of Women and Men in the Church study

Mr. Samuel M. Isaac, Interchurch Aid (CICARWS)

Ms. Yvonne Itin, Community of Women and Men in the Church study

Rev. Dr. Michael Kinnamon, Faith and Order

Dr. William H. Lazareth, Faith and Order

Ms. Kathy Lowe, News and Information (One World)

Dr. Ma Mpolo Masamba, Family Ministries

Ms. Monique McClellan, News and Information (Radio)

Ms. Midge Austin Meinertz, Income Coordination and Development

Rev. Dr. Constance F. Parvey, Community of Women and Men in the Church study

Dr. Philip A. Potter, General Secretary

Ms. Heather Stunt, Publications

Rev. Bärbel von Wartenberg, Women in Church and Society

Ms. Anne Williamson, Faith and Order

British Council of Churches Staff

Ms. Jo Graham

Ms. Anne Lewis

Ms. Joanne Smith

Local Organization

Ms. Jean Mayland

Technician

Mr. Jean-Michel Laubli

Volunteer Staff

Ms. Liv Sovik

Interpreters

Ms. Elisa Eklund-Benbassat

Ms. Donata Coleman

Mr. Martin Conway

Ms. Ulrike Duchrow

Ms. Tomoko Evdokimoff

Mr. Robert Faerber

Ms. Karin Lebbe

Ms. Christine Mear

Ms. Renate Sbeghen

Ms. Bärbel Simons

189

B

Documentation: Steps in the Process 1974–1982

Background

The Community of Women and Men in the Church study is a special program emphasis of the WCC, lifted up at the Nairobi Fifth Assembly: *Breaking Barriers,* Nairobi 1975, pp. 62, 107–9, 309–10. 7 pp., English.

The program has its origins in the 1974 Berlin consultation of "Sexism in Church and Society," and the Accra Meeting of the Commission on Faith and Order: *Sexism in Church and Society—Discrimination Against Women:* A Report of a WCC consultation, West Berlin 1974. WCC, Geneva 1975, 150 pp., English.
Uniting in Hope; reports and documents from the Commission on Faith and Order, Accra, 1974. WCC, Geneva, 144 pp., English.

The first broad outlines of the program were established by the Faith and Order Core Group: *For the Years Ahead;* a program of the Commission on Faith and Order. WCC, Geneva, 1976, 37 pp., English. These outlines were later affirmed and detailed by the Standing Commission Meetings at Loccum, Taizé, and Annecy.

The Study Book

The direct preparation of the Sheffield consulation started with the designing of a study book appropriate to the participatory, reflection/action nature of the project. It was translated at local initiative into thirteen languages, republished several times in English and German, mimeographed and adopted to community situations in every continental area.

Introduction: Vision for a new community/What is the Community of Women and Men in the Church study?/The past: Berlin, Accra, Nairobi/The present:

A study desk and study groups/The future: church involvement/The aims of the study/Practical suggestions for study groups/Learning through the study/What do we hope to gain from the study?/Registration form. Available through the WCC in English, French, German, Spanish.

Local Reports

Toward a fuller community of women and men in the church. This document contains two working papers:

1. *Towards an account of hope from women* (17 pp.), a collection of statements and reflections from women in various parts of the world about their hopes for the church, written for the plenary of the WCC Commission on Faith and Order, Bangalore, August 1978.
2. *The response of the Faith and Order Working Group* (16 pp.). CWMC, WCC, Geneva, 1978; English, French, German.

Sharing in one hope; Reports and documents from the meeting of the Commission on Faith and Order, Bangalore, 1978. WCC, Geneva, 1978, 290 pp., English.

Answers to the CWMC study. Quantitative analysis of 147 local group reports received from Africa, Asia, Latin America, North America, Europe, the Middle East, the Pacific, and the Caribbean. WCC Documentation Service, 147 pp., English, French, Spanish, German.

Statistics, based on a quantitative analysis of 147 local group reports. WCC Documentation Service, 6 pp., English.

The CWMC—Newsletter. Excerpts of local group reports providing a survey of opinions in various parts of the world, in preparation for the Sheffield consultation. WCC, 12 pp., English, French, German.

Women in a changing world—Newsletter. Excerpts from local group reports dealing with main themes emerging from the study. WCC, June 1981, 20 pp., English

Working resources in dialogue form. Selected responses from community study groups in Europe, prepared for the European consultation in Bad Segeberg, FRG. WCC, June 1980, 18 pp., English, French, German.

Regional Reports

Report of the Asian Consultation, held at the United Theological College, Bangalore, August 1978. Report of proceedings and program/The journey of an idea/The impact of the Scriptures, of culture and tradition, and of the class system on the roles of men and women in the churches/Suggestions for changing the church structures/Reports of workshops/Plenary report adopted by the consultation/List of participants. Bangalore, 1978, 106 pp., English.

A space to grow in, report of the European regional CWMC consultation, held in Bad Segeberg, FGR, June 20-24, 1980. A message from the conference/Working groups/Bible study/Tensions and dreams/The road ahead/List of participants. 32 pp., English; 31 pp., French.

The African Regional Consultation, held in Ibadan, Nigeria, September 5-19, 1980. Sharing is not what we would like it to be/Identity: social and cultural questions/Scripture and tradition/Church structures/Evaluation and recommendations/Appendix: in pursuit of community life, a spiritual journey. 27 pp., English.

Middle East Council of Churches Consultation, Beirut, Lebanon, January 22-26, 1980. Who is woman? A variety of approaches/Scripture and tradition: woman as equal to man/Resources for further study and dialogue/Bibliography/List of participants. 86 pp., English.

Latin American Consultation, March 15-19, 1981. Final document: women and Latin American society/Women in the Christian community/Theses and proposals for circulation among churches and theological schools in order to stimulate discussion. WCC, Spanish; 18 pp., English.

Authority and Community in Christian Tradition—USA Consultation, March 25-28, 1981. A study document of the Commission on Faith and Order, National Council of Churches of Christ in the United States, prepared as a contribution to the Sheffield consultation. Questions of authority and power/God, Christ, and Community/New creation. 23 pp., English.

A Gathering to Share Our Hope. Final report on the U.S. participation in the community study. Includes a chapter on "The Ups and Downs" of the community study, an introduction to the U.S. section report, the report itself, and an evaluation of points of convergence and difference.

Women and Unity: Problem or Possibility? Sees the "problem" of the community study as a hope for Christian unity in the shift from working models of dominance and subordination to models of cooperation and sharing.

Specialized Consultations

Ordination of women in ecumenical perspective. Workbook for the church's future. Klingenthal Consultation, September, 1979. Purpose of the workbook: to aid the churches in their dialogue on the ordination of women issue; to help the women and men in the churches that do and do not ordain women to appreciate its ecumenical context and its challenge; to help those engaged in the debate to further their understanding of each other and to be mutually corrected and enriched; to make a contribution to the background materials on ministry for the ongoing Faith and Order work on "one baptism, one Eucharist, and a mutually recognized ministry," and to the Community of Women and Men in the Church study. WCC, Geneva, 1980. 96 pp., English.

Towards a theology of human wholeness. Theological anthropology; Consultation at the Niederaltaich Benedictine abbey, FRG, September 1980. Report in five sections: I. Methodology; II. The state of brokenness and the struggle for transformation, the image of God; III. Created in God's image, relationships between women and men; IV. Towards a theology of human wholeness in African tradition, *imago Dei;* V. Recommendations for future work, list of participants. WCC, 1980. 53 pp., English.

The authority of Scripture in light of new experiences of women, Amsterdam Consultation, December 1980. The purposes of the consultation are: to explore the basic character of scriptural authority in different contexts and to consider its relationship to the new experiences of women; to describe the issues experientially rather than purely analytically, exposing the interlace of Scripture and culture; to examine the role that Scripture has played and plays in supporting and vindicating male dominance; to provide a forum for an exchange of experiences and perspectives that has the model of a subject/subject dialogue rather than "objectified" presentations of the issues; to illustrate the use and misuse of Scripture, past and present, within the context of the relationship between the authority of the Bible and the authority of experience; to prepare a working document to aid in clarifying the issues. WCC, 1980, 32 pp., English.

Preparation for Sheffield

Section Working Papers, for discussion at the Sheffield consultation, with an introduction and questions to aid reflection. Consists of seven sections: I. Scripture in new community; II. Identity and relationships in new community; III. Ministry and worship in new community; IV. Marriage, family, and life styles in new community; V. Authority and church structures in new community; VI. Justice and freedom in new community; VII. Tradition in new community. WCC, 1981. 45 pp., English.

Preparation for WCC Central Committee at Dresden, August 1981

The Journey from Sheffield to Dresden, report on the Sheffield international consultation of the Community of Women and Men in the Church study, including: I. Voices of broken community; II. Presentation of the process; III. How the community study dealt with selected issues; IV. The presentation of the recommendations (Doc. 1.3.1.); V. Discussion of the study; VI. The Letter from Sheffield to the Churches. WCC, English (III, IV available in French and German; VI available in French, German, and Spanish).

Final Report for the Commission on Faith and Order, Lima, Peru, January 1982

Plenary Presentation (January 9). I. The issues of Scripture in the community study–Mary Tanner; II. "Unity and the Human Community"–Letty M. Russell; III. Ministry–Nicholas Lossky; IV. Responses–Robert J. Wright, Raymond E. Brown, and Mercy Amba Oduyoye.

Plenary Actions—I. Contributions of community study to assembly preparations; II. Contributions of community study to baptism, Eucharist, and ministry and one apostolic faith; III. Contributions to study on the unity of the church and the renewal of human community; IV. Minutes–Commission on Faith and Order, Lima, 1982.

APPENDIX
C

Bibliography: For Further Reading

This bibliography is from the many English books that have been recommended during the process of the community study. In making a selection, there is always the risk that some of the best books are overlooked. The English titles of the bibliography are arranged according to main issues that have emerged during the study process. Some of these books can move from one category to another, but in each case, they make a contribution to the section of which they are a part. Where possible multiconfessional and multicultural considerations are taken into account along with the historical and ecumenical dimensions of the subject under consideration.

A more complete bibliography on ministry is available in *Ordination of Women in Ecumenical Perspective*. Also, additional resources on Scripture are found in "Authority of Scripture in Light of the New Experiences of Women," and on tradition in "Toward a Theology of Human Wholeness." The usefulness of the bibliography is to see one's own questions from the perspective of other churches and global partners. Preference is given to books published since 1974. Of special importance is a popular summary of the Sheffield conference by Betty Thompson entitled *A Chance to Change: Women and Men in the Church* (Philadelphia: Fortress Press, 1982).

1. Scripture

Balch, David L. *Let Wives Be Submissive: The Domestic Code in 1 Peter*. Chico, Calif.: Scholars Press, 1981.

Brown, Raymond E., et al., eds. *Mary in the New Testament: Collaborative Assessments by Protestant and Catholic Scholars*. Philadelphia: Fortess Press, 1978.

Chatterji, Jyotsna. *Good News for Women*. Delhi: ISPCK, 1979.

Davies, Steven L. *The Revolt of the Widows: The Social World of the Apocryphal Acts*. Carbondale, Ill.: Southern Illinois University Press, 1980.

Flesseman-Van Leer, Ellen. *The Bible: Its Authority and Interpretation in the Ecumenical Movement*. Geneva: WCC, 1980

Mollenkott, Virgina R. *Women, Men and the Bible*. Nashville: Abingdon Press, 1977.

Otwell, John H. *And Sarah Laughed: The Status of Women in the Old Testament.* Philadelphia: Westminster Press, 1977.

Ruether, Rosemary, ed. *Religion and Sexism: Images of Women in the Jewish and Christian Traditions.* New York: Simon & Schuster, 1974.

Russell, Letty M. *The Liberating Word: A Guide to Non-Sexist Interpretation of the Bible.* Philadelphia: Westminster Press, 1974.

Scanzoni, L. and Hardesty, N. *All We're Meant to Be: A Biblical Approach to Women's Liberation.* Waco, Tex.: Word, 1975.

Stagg, Evelyn, and Stagg, Frank. *Women in the World of Jesus.* Philadelphia: Westminster Press, 1978.

Stendahl, Krister. *The Bible and the Role of Women: A Case Study in Hermeneutics.* Philadelphia: Fortress Press, 1966.

Stone, Merlin. *When God Was a Woman.* New York: Dial Press, 1976.

Swidler, L. *Biblical Affirmations of Women.* Philadelphia: Westminster Press, 1979.

Trible, Phyllis. *God and the Rhetoric of Sexuality.* Philadelphia: Fortress Press, 1978.

Wahlberg, Rachel Conrad. *Jesus According to a Woman.* Ramsey, N.J.: Paulist Press, 1975.

———. *Jesus and the Freed Woman,* Ramsey, N.J.: Paulist Press, 1979.

2. Tradition

Bainton, R. H. *Women of the Reformation: From Spain to Scandinavia.* Minneapolis: Augsburg, 1977.

———. *Women of the Reformation: In France and England.* Minneapolis: Augsburg, 1973.

———. *Women of the Reformation: In Germany and Italy.* Minneapolis: Augsburg, 1971.

Bakan, David. *And They Took Themselves Wives: The Emergence of Patriarchy in Western Civilization.* New York: Harper & Row, 1979.

Børresen, K. E. *Subordination and Equivalence.* Washington, D.C.: University Press of America, 1981.

Clark, E., and Richardson, H. W., eds. *Women and Religion: Readings in the Western Tradition from Aeschylus to Mary Dale.* New York: Harper Forum Books, 1977.

Clark, Elizabeth. *Jerome, Chrysostom and Friends.* Lewiston, N.Y.: Edwin Mellen Press, 1979.

Confessing our Faith Around the World. Faith and Order Paper No. 104. Geneva: WCC, 1980.

Daly, Mary. *Beyond God the Father: Toward a Philosophy of Women's Liberation.* Boston: Beacon Press, 1973.

Daniel, Kiran, and Jin, Lee Soo. *Asian Women.* Singapore: Christian Conference of Asia, 1977.

Dowell, Susan, and Hurcombe, Linda. *Dispossessed Daughters of Eve: Faith and Feminism.* London: SCM, 1981.

Engelsman, Joan Chamberlin. *The Feminine Dimension of the Divine.* Philadelphia: Westminster Press, 1979.

Jewett, Paul K. *Man as Male and Female*. Grand Rapids: Wm. B. Eerdmans, 1979.

Kastner-Wilson, Patricia, ed. *A Lost Tradition: Women Writers in the Early Church*. Washington, D.C.: University Press of America, 1981.

Katoppo, Marianne. *Compassionate and Free: An Asian Women's Theology*. Geneva: WCC, 1979.

Koyama, Kosuke. *Three Mile an Hour God*. Maryknoll, N.Y.: Orbis Books; London: SCM; 1980.

Mbiti, John S. *Concepts of God in Africa.* London: SPCK, 1970.

Moltmann, Jürgen. *The Trinity and the Kingdom of God: The Doctrine of God*. London: SCM Press, 1981.

O'Faolain, J., and Martines, L., eds. *Not in God's Image*. New York: Harper & Row, 1973.

Plaskow, Judith. *Sex, Sin and Grace: Women's Experience and the Theologies of Reinhold Niebuhr and Paul Tillich*. Washington, D.C.: University Press of America, 1980.

————, and Christ, Carol. *Womanspirit Rising: A Feminist Reader in Religion*. New York: Harper and Row, 1979.

Pobee, John S. *Toward an African Theology*. Nashville: Abingdon Press, 1979.

Rayan, Samuel.*The Holy Spirit*. Maryknoll, N.Y.: Orbis Books, 1978.

Ruether, Rosemary. *Mary—the Feminine Face of the Church*. Philadelphia: Westminster Press, 1977.

————. *To Change the World: Christology and Cultural Criticism*. New York: Crossroad, 1981.

Russell, Letty M. *The Future of Partnership*. Philadelphia: Westminster Press, 1979.

————. *Growth in Partnership*. Philadelphia: Westminster Press, 1981.

————. *Becoming Human*. Philadelphia: Westminster Press, 1982.

Ware, Father Kallistos. *The Orthodox Way*. London: A. R. Mowbray, 1979.

Women and Men in Asia. WSCF Asia Book No. 5. Hong Kong: World Student Christian Federation, 1978.

3. Authority and Church Structures

Bria, Ion, ed. *Martyria/Mission: The Witness of the Orthodox Churches Today*. Geneva: WCC, 1980.

Daly, Mary. *The Church and the Second Sex with a New Postchristian Introduction*. New York: Harper & Row, 1975.

Elizando, Virgil, and Greinacher, Norbert, eds. *Women in a Men's Church*. New York: Seabury Press, 1980.

Episkope and Episcopate in Ecumenical Perspective. Faith and Order Paper No. 102. Geneva: WCC, 1980.

Erdozain, Placido. *Archbishop Romero: Martyr of Salvador*. Translated by John McFadden and Ruth Warner. Maryknoll, N.Y.: Orbis Books, 1981.

Gage, Matilda J. *Women, Church and State*. New York: Arno Press, 1980.

Hageman, Alice. *Sexist Religion and Women in the Church: No More Silence*. New York: Association Press, 1974.

How Does the Church Teach Authoritatively Today? Faith and Order Paper No. 91. Geneva: WCC, 1979.

Humez, Jean M. *Gifts of Power: The Writings of Rebecca Jackson, Black Visionary, Shaker Eldress.* Amherst, Mass.: University of Massachusetts Press, 1981.

Lange, Ernst. *And Yet it Moves . . . Dream and Reality of the Ecumenical Movement.* Translated by E. Richardson. Geneva: WCC; Grand Rapids: Wm B. Eerdmans; Belfast: Christian Journals Ltd.; 1979.

Patelos, Constantin, ed. *The Orthodox Church in the Ecumenical Movement: Documents and Statements 1902–1975.* Geneva: WCC, 1978.

Ruether, Rosemary, and McLaughlin, E. *Women of Spirit.* New York: Simon & Schuster, 1979.

Ruether, Rosemary, and Keller, Rosemary. *Women and Religion in America: Volume 1, the Nineteenth Century.* New York: Harper & Row, 1981.

Thomas, Hilah, and Keller, Rosemary. *Women in New Worlds: Historical Perspectives on the Wesleyan Tradition.* Nashville: Abingdon Press, 1981.

Webb, Pauline. *Where are the Women?* London: Epworth Press, 1979.

4. Ministry and Worship

Clark, Linda; Ronan, Marian; and Walker, Eleanor. *Image Breaking, Image Making: A Handbook for Creative Worship with Women of Christian Tradition.* New York: Pilgrim Press, 1981.

Cornwall Collective. *Your Daughters Shall Prophesy: Feminist Alternatives in Theological Education.* New York: Pilgrim Press, 1980.

Crotwell, Helen Gray, ed. *Women and the Word: Sermons.* Philadelphia: Fortress Press, 1978.

Emswiler, Sharon Neufer, and Neufer, Thomas. *Women and Worship: A Guide to Non-Sexist Hymns, Prayers and Liturgies.* New York: Harper & Row, 1974.

———. *Wholeness in Worship: Creative Models for Sunday, Family and Special Services.* New York: Harper & Row, 1980.

Goetemoeller, D., and Hofbauer, R. eds. *Women and Ministry: Present Experience and Future Hopes.* Washington, D.C.: Leadership Conference of Women Religious, 1981.

Grollenberg, L., et al. *Minister? Pastor? Prophet? Grassroots Leadership in the Churches.* New York: Crossroad; London: SCM; 1979.

Hoch-Smith, V., and Spring, A. *Women in Ritual and Symbolic Roles.* New York: Plenum Press, 1978.

Jewett, Paul K. *The Ordination of Women.* Grand Rapids: Wm. B. Eerdmans, 1980.

Miller, Casey, and Swift, Kate. *Words and Women.* New York: Doubleday Anchor Books, 1977.

New Women, New Church, New Priestly Ministry. Proceedings of the Second Conference on the Ordination of Roman Catholic Women. Rochester, N.Y.: Women's Ordination Conference, 1980.

An Orthodox Approach to Diaconia. Consultation on Church and Service. Geneva: WCC, 1980.

Parvey, Constance. *Ordination of Women in Ecumenical Perspective.* Faith and Order Paper No. 105. Geneva: WCC, 1980.

Raming, Ida. *The Exclusion of Women from the Priesthood: Divine Law or Sex Discrimination?* Translated by Norman R. Adams. Metuchen, N.J.: Scarecrow, 1976.

Sawicki, Marianne. *Faith and Sexism: Guidelines for Religious Educators.* New York: Seabury Press, 1979.

Schillebeeckx, Edward. *Ministry.* New York: Crossroad; London: SCM; 1981.

Spender, Dale. *Man Made Language.* Boston and London: Routledge and Kegan Paul, 1980.

Swidler, Arlene. *Sistercelebrations: Nine Worship Experiences.* Philadelphia: Fortress Press, 1974.

————, and Swidler, Leonard. *Women Priests: A Catholic Commentary on the Vatican Declaration.* Ramsey, N.J.: Paulist Press, 1977.

Tavard, George H. *Women in Christian Tradition.* Notre Dame, Ind.: University of Notre Dame, 1973.

Tetlow, Elizabeth. *Women and Ministry in the New Testament.* Ramsey, N.J.: Paulist Press, 1980.

Thiering, Barbara. *Deliver Us from Eve.* Sydney: Australian Council of Churches, 1977.

Ware, Father Kallistos. *Man, Woman and Priesthood.* London: SPCK, 1978.

Watkins, Keith. *Faithful and Fair: Transcending Sexist Language in Worship.* Nashville: Abingdon Press, 1981.

Weidman, Judith L. *Women Ministers: How Women are Redefining Traditional Roles.* New York: Harper & Row, 1981.

5. Justice and Freedom

Anderson, Gerald H., and Stransky, Thomas F. *Mission Trends: Liberation Theologies in North America and Europe, No. 4.* Ramsey, N.J.: Paulist Press; Grand Rapids: Wm. B. Eerdmans; 1979.

Barrios de Chungara, Domitila, and Viezzer, M. *Let Me Speak! Testimony of Domitila, A Woman of the Bolivian Mines.* New York: Monthly Review Press, 1978.

Burke, Mary P. *Reaching for Justice: The Women's Movement.* Washington, D.C.: Center for Concern, 1980.

Christian Obedience and the Search for Liberation: An Orthodox Perspectice. Geneva: World Student Christian Federation, 1979.

Collins, Sheila D. *A Different Heaven and Earth.* Valley Forge, Pa.: Judson Press, 1977.

Daly, M. *Gyn-Ecology: The Metaethics of Radical Feminism.* Boston: Beacon Press, 1979.

Fabella, V., ed. *Asia's Struggle for Full Humanity: Towards a Relevant Theology.* Maryknoll, N.Y.: Orbis Books, 1980.

Gray, E. Dodson. *Green Paradise Lost.* Wellesley, Mass.: Round Table Press, 1981.

Huston, Perdita. *Third World Women Speak Out: Interviews in Six Countries on

Change, Development, and Basic Needs. New York: Praeger, 1979.

Joseph, Gloria, and Lewis, Jill. *Common Differences: Conflicts in Black and White Feminism.* New York: Doubleday Anchor Books, 1981.

Migrant Women Speak. Geneva: WCC; London: Search Press; 1978.

Neal, Marie A. *A Socio-Theology of Letting Go: The Role of a First World Church Facing Third World Peoples.* Ramsey, N.J.: Paulist Press, 1977.

Osthathios, Geevarghese Mar. *Theology of a Classless Society.* Maryknoll, N.Y.: Orbis Books; London: Lutterworth Press, 1980.

Richesin, Dale, and Mahan, Brian, eds. *The Challenge of Liberation Theology: A First World Response.* New York: Orbis Books, 1981.

Rogers, Barbara. *The Domestification of Women: Discrimination in Developing Societies.* London: Tavistock Publications, 1980.

Ruether, Rosemary. *New Women/New Earth: Sexist Ideologies and Human Liberation.* New York: Seabury Press, 1975.

Russell, Letty M. *Human Liberation in a Feminist Perspective.* Philadelphia: Westminster Press, 1974.

Sintado, C., ed. *Voices of Solidarity.* Geneva: WCC, 1981.

Soelle, Dorothee. *Suffering.* Philadelphia: Fortress Press, 1978.

Struggling to Survive: Women Workers in Asia. Hong Kong: CCIA/URM, 57 Peking Rd., 5/F, Kowloon, Hong Kong, 1981.

Thomas, T. K. *Testimony and Asian Suffering.* Singapore: Christian Conference in Asia, 1977.

6. Identity, Relationship, Marriage, and Family Life Styles

Barnhouse, Ruth T., and Holmes, Urban T. *Male and Female: Christian Approaches to Sexuality.* New York: Seabury Press, 1976.

Burghardt, Walter, S. J. *Women: New Dimensions.* Ramsey, N.J.: Paulist Press, 1975.

Carmody, Denise Lardner. *Women and World Religions.* Nashville: Abingdon Press, 1979.

Christ, Carol P. *Diving Deep and Surfacing.* Boston: Beacon Press, 1980.

Clinebell, Charlotte. *Meet Me in the Middle.* New York: Harper & Row, 1973.

Devados, T. S. *Hindu Family and Marriage.* Madras, India: University of Madras, 1979.

Katz, Naomi, and Milton, Nancy. *Fragment from a Lost Diary and Other Stories: Women of Asia, Africa and Latin America.* Boston: Beacon Press, 1975.

Kroll, Una. *Flesh of My Flesh.* London: Darton, Longman & Todd, 1975.

Kuo, Eddie, C. Y., and Wons, Aline K., eds. *The Contemporary Family in Singapore.* Singapore: University of Singapore, 1979.

Mbiti, John S. *Love and Marriage in Africa.* London: Longman Group, 1973.

Miller, Jean B. *Toward a New Psychology of Women.* Boston: Beacon Press, 1977.

Moss, B. and Moss, R. *God's Yes to Sexuality.* London: British Council of Churches, 1980.

Nelson, James B. *Embodiment: An Approach to Sexuality and Christian Theology.* Minneapolis: Augsburg, 1978.

Oduyoye, Mercy. *The Asante Woman: Socialization Through Proverbs.* Ibadan, Nigeria: Institute of African Studies, University of Ibadan, 1978.

O'Grady, Alison. *Voices of Women: An Asian Anthology.* Singapore: Asian Christian Women's Conference, 1978.

Orthodox Women, Their Role and Participation in the Orthodox Church, report of the WCC consultation in Ayapia, Romania, 1976.

Other World Council of Churches Publications Related to the Study According to the Scriptures: The Image of Women as Portrayed in the Sacred Writings of the World's Major Religions. Geneva: World YWCA and WCC, 1975.

Sexism in the 1970s, report of the WCC West Berlin consultation, 1974.

Sharing in One Hope, report from Bangalore, Faith and Order Commission, 1978.

The United Church of Christ. *Human Sexuality: A Preliminary Study.* New York: United Church Press, 1977.

Washbourn, Penelope. *Becoming Woman: The Quest for Wholeness in Female Experience.* New York: Harper & Row, 1976.

Wold, Margaret. *The Shalom Women.* Minneapolis: Augsburg, 1975.